Jeanne Guyon's Apocalyptic Universe

Jeanne Guyon's Apocalyptic Universe

Her Biblical Commentary on Revelation
with Reflections on the Interior Life

BY Jeanne de la Mothe Guyon

INTRODUCTION AND TRANSLATION
FROM THE ORIGINAL FRENCH BY

Nancy Carol James

FOREWORD BY
William Bradley Roberts

PICKWICK *Publications* · Eugene, Oregon

JEANNE GUYON'S APOCALYPTIC UNIVERSE
Her Biblical Commentary on Revelation with Reflections on the Interior Life

Pickwick Publications
An Imprint of Wipf and Stock Publishers
199 W. 8th Ave., Suite 3
Eugene, OR 97401

www.wipfandstock.com

PAPERBACK ISBN: 978-1-5326-6282-9
HARDCOVER ISBN: 978-1-5326-6283-6
EBOOK ISBN: 978-1-5326-6284-3

Cataloguing-in-Publication data:

Names: Guyon, Jeanne, author. | James, Nancy Carol, translator. | Roberts, William Bradley, foreword.

Title: Jeanne Guyon's apocalyptic universe : her biblical commentary on Revelation with reflections on the interior life / by Jeanne Guyon ; translated by Nancy Carol James.

Description: Eugene, OR: Pickwick Publications, 2019 | Includes bibliographical references.

Identifiers: ISBN 978-1-5326-6282-9 (paperback) | ISBN 978-1-5326-6283-6 (hardcover) | ISBN 978-1-5326-6284-3 (ebook)

Subjects: LCSH: Guyon, Jeanne Marie Bouvier de La Motte,—1648–1717 | Bible—Revelation—Meditations | Bible—Revelation—Criticism, interpretation, etc. | Bible—Revelation—Devotional literature | Spiritual life—Catholic Church | Quietism

Classification: BX4705.G8 A25 2019 (print) | BX4705.G8 (ebook)

Manufactured in the U.S.A.   04/05/19

Dedicated to Hannah and Melora

Contents

Permissions

Foreword

S OME YEARS AGO, WHEN I was in my early twenties, I happened into two simultaneous studies of the book of Revelation. I didn't intentionally seek a study of Revelation. Indeed, because of the ubiquitous appearance in those days of Hal Lindsey's best-seller, *The Late, Great Planet Earth*, I found myself avoiding the material of the book of Revelation, not wanting to associate with the latest craze. It was fashionable to take sides in passionate, and often divisive, discussions of this elusive material. Lines were drawn, categories were discovered (or fabricated!), and people seemed to be quite enjoying themselves in what became a kind of internecine warfare among believers. Perhaps because of this unpleasant sport, I found myself avoiding Revelation.

How then did I happen into two studies at once? The parish I belonged to in Houston, Texas (River Oaks Baptist Church) had as its pastor a scholar of impressive skills. This man, the Rev. Dr. Bill G. West, was an extraordinary, theologically progressive preacher. In those days, Baptist parishes, whether conservative or progressive, had a tradition of preaching sermons that lasted thirty to forty-five minutes, easily claiming most of the time allotted for worship. It is a testimony to this pastor, then, that most of his parishioners did not dread, but indeed eagerly anticipated, his sermons. To this day, decades later, I can still recall the content of specific sermons—carefully researched, intelligently prepared, passionately articulated. In my current denomination (Episcopal) hardly anyone would tolerate a forty-five minute sermon, even one of superb quality, so these long speeches impress me all the more in retrospect. Since I was the Minister of Music at this parish, I heard a lion's share of sermons from this man, often engaging him in conversation about them later. At one point he asked that I take notes on the quality of his content and presentation, which I did.

During the same period I was a member of a nascent Christian theater company, then called the After Dinner Players (now the A.D. Players), that has gone on to become a respectable arts institution in the city of Houston, complete with a fine, permanent theatre that showcases a full season of plays, sacred and secular, and touring companies that perform to audiences far and wide. The founding director Jeannette Clift George had already enjoyed an impressive career as an actress—primarily with Houston's storied Alley Theater—before she turned to directing and playwrighting. The company was borne of Mrs. George's zeal for Bible study and her belief that lives (including her own) were transformed by the study of scripture. Though nominated for a Golden Globe ("The Hiding Place") and highly regarded by theatergoers and critics, she ultimately turned her primary attention from acting to developing the theater troupe, who performed Mrs. George's own biblically based plays. The performances in those days were in diverse venues: parish halls, church basements, the nave or sanctuary of churches, school auditoriums. Mrs. George began writing her own material out of necessity. She discovered she had the ability to expand stories from scripture that made the characters alive, engaging, and, perhaps most disarming, comical. These characters were interesting, flawed, creative creatures of God, whose humorous foibles made them approachable for audiences. As part of the actors' weekly training, Mrs. George required regular Bible study. We could attend her own popular, long-established weekly sessions, or else find another class on our own.

So it happened that I was the recipient of two simultaneous studies of the book of Revelation, one taught by my pastor, the other by my director, both of them serious and passionate, but, at the same time, remarkably different. To some extent the two studies touch upon the extremes of Revelation interpretation.

From my pastor I learned a contemporary, theologically progressive handling of the book. This interpretation assumes that most of the events described in Revelation have already occurred. This viewpoint posits that specific, historic events occurred in the first centuries of the Common Era, described by John's narrative. The reason that much of the language seems vague and confusing today is that we don't know the details of the events described by John as well as did his contemporary audience, nor do we comprehend imagery commonly understood in the era. Indeed, this perspective claimed that the readers (or hearers) of John's message would largely have understood. The metaphors, the allusions, the dramatic incidents were not intentionally bizarre or confounding, but would have been relatively clear to people who understood their own environment and context.

From my director I learned a version of Revelation that assumes that the vivid, sometimes frightening, sometimes assuring, words of John describe events that are yet to come. Eschatological and apocalyptic, this version is the more popular interpretation of Revelation. The bizarre creatures and events of Revelation are considered mysteries—that is, the meaning is hidden. Perhaps the most common question is, "When will the events of the last days occur?" The only dependable teaching is found in scripture, "But about that day and hour no one knows, neither the angels of heaven, nor the Son, but only the Father" (Matt 24:36). This passage is remarkable in that Jesus states that even he, the Son, did not know the timing of the latter-day events.

Studying with these two teachers simultaneously was a gift. Though as young adults we are often far more dogmatic than our elders, who are old and wise enough to see truth as complex and nuanced, nevertheless, I put my critical faculties on hold and listened attentively to each teacher, attempting to maintain an open mind. I am grateful for this opportunity to study Revelation from two disparate views.

Madame Guyon felt strongly that the Book of Revelation was important for the individual, the church, and the universe. She certainly took a rather literal interpretation of the writings of John, more akin to my director than my pastor. There is a sense in which people who take such a position are likely to be more serious and passionate about Revelation than those who believe the metaphorical language pertains to events already accomplished. After all, if we are convinced that monsters and fire and judgment are headed in our direction, we are inclined to pay attention.

Madame Guyon was a deeply pious woman, and her piety is woven into her writing on Revelation, as is true in her works previously studied by Nancy James. By now Dr. James is thoroughly steeped in the life and theology of Jeanne Guyon, this being her twelfth book on the scholar and mystic. What the reader may expect from Guyon is a book of ardent devotion. Guyon had the fervor of a modern evangelical (though with a broader theological spectrum) in both her reading of scripture and her practice of the Christian life.

Whatever school of thought the reader adopts regarding interpretation of the book of Revelation, she will encounter in James' translation of Guyon a rich, deep text, full of dynamic movement. Guyon allows the graphic portrayals and dramatic language of Revelation to capture her mind, heart, and imagination. If her personal spirituality sometimes makes twenty-first-century Christians ill at ease, perhaps it is because Guyon spoke of her faith in unapologetic, passionate language not characteristic of our age. Ever the faithful translator, James does not soft-pedal Guyon's syntax, but allows her to speak as authentically in English as she did the French of her day.

As with her previous translations of Guyon, James writes with such clarity, precision, and natural grace that she makes English sound like the mystic's first language. Indeed, what the reader most wants in a translator is invisibility—that is, we want to see straight through the translator to the original author. We want the translator to be a lens that allows us to see the object clearly. And the object here is never in question: Madame Jeanne Guyon's explication of the Revelation of John, told from the perspective of a person of faith.

Did James gravitate naturally to Guyon scholarship because of their shared traits, or is James so saturated in Guyon that her speech and behavior have begun to reflect those of Guyon? Either way, the reader is in the hands of two women with mutual simpatico. They both handle biblical material with respect, with care, and with a believer's devotion.

William Bradley Roberts
Virginia Theological Seminary
Alexandria, Virginia

Preface

I HAVE LONG YEARNED TO understand the book of Revelation and the mystery of the second coming of Jesus Christ. I have wanted to know what the experience of the apocalypse will be like with its endless strife, suffering, and tribulations, yet blessed with the glorious promise of the coming new heaven and new earth. In Jeanne Guyon's *Commentary on Revelation* I found the faithful understanding of the second coming that I desired. I now present this commentary in its first full English translation. Guyon's *Commentary on Revelation* describes the new and spiritual universe that is coming into being through the mediation of the crucifixion, resurrection, and glorification of our savior Jesus Christ.

Even as a child, I was curious about the second coming and wanted to have an interior understanding of this, our ultimate fulfillment in heaven. The passion for understanding the second coming came at least partially from my experience in Fairbanks, Alaska. I loved my years of living on the isolated Eielson Air Force Base in Alaska's interior because of the spectacular astronomical events involved with the mysterious Northern Lights and the glorious Midnight Sun. I also loved reading the book of Revelation because it had all these elements of the natural world that I loved so deeply with its mention of the blood moon, powerful sun, and the spiritual rainbows, so like the universe in our northern globe. In my Alaskan years I saw the white snow glistening in the moon creating designs of light splashing with innate passion. I then read about Jesus Christ with eyes of fire, hair as white as snow, surrounded by living seas of crystal. The foundation of the New Jerusalem will shine with splendid colors of precious gems, not unlike the Northern Lights shining in the midnight black skies.

These Northern astronomical events are incredible and overwhelming and beautiful. The huge moon hung low on the horizon, providing the only light that we had in weeks of darkness. The Northern Lights in the winter danced as if the Holy Spirit made a secret and unannounced appearance, revealing beauty and grandeur and kindness. The compelling events in the skies showed me the truth of Psalm 19.

The heavens are telling the glory of God;
and the firmament proclaims his handiwork.
² Day to day pours forth speech,
and night to night declares knowledge.
³ There is no speech, nor are there words;
their voice is not heard.
⁴ yet their voice goes out through all the earth,
and their words to the end of the world. (Psalm 19:1–4)

I received the beauty of Alaska's astronomy as signs of the goodness of God's created universe. They helped create within me a yearning for the new and spiritual universe that will come into being through the mediation of Jesus Christ.

The Bible interprets these signs in our skies as showing the ultimate and trustworthy faithfulness of our God. Peter said, "But the day of the Lord will come like a thief, and then the heavens will pass away with a loud noise, and the elements will be dissolved with fire, and the earth and everything that is done on it will be disclosed" (2 Pet 3:10). I had fully received that strong and secure message. The stars could be rolled up and disappear, the sun will not rise, and the moon will drip with blood, yet Jesus Christ will still be there, loving, merciful, and kind.

As I traversed the mystery we call reading the book of Revelation, I still find myself looking forward in the scriptures to the next astronomical event. Jesus Christ sends angels as messengers to say that the universe is changing and that everything will pass away. John of Patmos describes the face of Jesus Christ shining like a sun in full force, shows us an angel wrapped in a rainbow, and reveals the woman with the moon under her feet. I find these spiritual images comforting and hope that others will also understand that the coming universal changes are times of suffering, yes, but they are only birth pangs that precede the full revelation of Jesus Christ as the beginning and the end, the Alpha and the Omega.

I present this first full English translation with prayers of thanksgiving that our Lord shows us what must come before we enjoy eternity lived in the presence of Jesus Christ.

Acknowledgements

M ANY PEOPLE HAVE CONTRIBUTED to this volume. I am grateful for the support of Dr. Carlos Eire during my dissertation work on Jeanne Guyon. I thank the Rev. William Roberts for his understanding of Jeanne Guyon's theology and his foreword, which makes a substantial contribution to this book.

I want to thank the parishioners of St. John's, Lafayette Square, Washington DC for their dialogue about Jeanne Guyon and her rich theology.

Many thanks go to my family who shares my passion for the work of Jeanne Guyon. Roger, Hannah, and Melora have read, explored and researched Jeanne Guyon along with me. I am grateful that we share this love.

Above all, I think my readers who share a love for Jeanne Guyon and her ideas about interior faith. Guyon's books have been kept alive by those who continue to seek a profound interior life where Jesus Christ lives and moves and has his being. I hope that Guyon's Christian interior faith lives for centuries yet to come.

Introduction

I N GUYON'S COMMENTARY ON Revelation we see the magnificent grace of
Jesus Christ in action. Guyon creates rich and interwoven meanings of an
entirely new understanding of the spiritual foundations of the universe. In
the suffering of the apocalypse, the faithful know the fire of God revealing
the meaning and purpose of human the history. Guyon builds on the scripture that says, "You shall be holy, for I am holy" (Lev 20:7 and 1 Pet 1:16).
The faithful are called into living holiness, but this path includes suffering,
war, and tribulation as the believer seeks the strong revelation of God. As
she says, the plagues must come first to purify and prepare us. When we
remain in living holiness, the faithful person rests in God's goodness, while
God recreates the living image of God within the interior life of the believer.
This necessarily requires an annihilation of the sins of Adam and a disengagement of idols from our lives. This life of living holiness prepares us for
the greatest of all blessings: union with Jesus Christ.

As Guyon knew from her own unjust incarcerations, the fight for this
living holiness comes with intense attacks from evil. During the apocalypse,
the abyss of evil sends out the beast, the dragon, the false prophet and others
who lead humanity astray to fight against the truth of Jesus Christ. With the
second coming of Jesus Christ, the source of evil is ultimately destroyed and
the universe itself remade as a new heaven and earth. After these wars between good and evil, Guyon say there is victory for the persecuted church.

Guyon writes that Jesus Christ's messages tell the church to express the
faith with integrity. However, churches frequently have interior corruption
that causes them to join with the world to persecute the faithful and bring
untold suffering. John of Patmos testifies that there will be a century in the
future when Jesus Christ comes to rule his kingdom and the universe. Those
who have suffered for their faith will have a judgement given for them and
they will reign with Jesus Christ.

The suffering of the believer though results in eternal fruit. Guyon says
that God allows evil to attack people, but that the evil itself will destroy evil
within the victim. She says that God "uses evil to fight evil." For example,
a person will know the pain of the scorpion bites but as this is endured

with faith, the person's heart becomes less filled with propriety and becomes more dependent on God (Rev 9:3–4). Guyon says that the point of the evil is to annihilate the faithful, yet as the believer prays during the persecution, the person's soul becomes filled with the living Word of God. In brief, God uses the evil of persecution in combat against the evil within the faithful person, causing an increased sanctification. With a completed annihilation, the interior and mystical death brings the death of self-centeredness, and propriety. The soul then knows the joy of a restored state of innocence where nothing resists God. Annihilation and mystical death lead to a state of fulfilling consummation and union with God. Souls of this degree experience the mystical incarnation, when Jesus Christ wants them to bear his own state. In calling out to Jesus Christ, these souls are already consummated and removed from the world that is unworthy of these people. Guyon writes, "We must *keep what we have* for this time."

Guyon understands Jesus Christ's actions as full of meaning with layer upon layer of meaning and purpose that comes from God's will. The Lord has multiple purposes in each action. Guyon shows the great harmony and unity of these purposes when we live in and act on the will of God. As we experience and live the states of being of Jesus Christ, we grow naturally into union with him. This transformation of the interior life becomes a good fruit out of human suffering.

Guyon's commentary on Revelation shows the complexity and beauty of her symbolic interpretation. She combines many of the symbols to show the meaning Jesus Christ gives us in three specific arenas: the consummation of historical events, the role of the church, and the growth of the individual soul.

One of Guyon's distinctive interpretations shows the meaning in these arenas for the four-winged creatures who each call out a different colored horse. Guyon compares the character of the four living creatures with the four horsemen of the apocalypse and interprets these as a unified message describing both the historical events of the apocalypse and the consecutive states of the growing soul. The living creature of a lion calls forth the first white horse of easy victories. The living creature of an ox calls forth the second red horse of being hurt and proclaiming truth. The living creature of a human being calls forth the third black horse as the living judgment of the living God. Fourth, the living creature of an eagle calls forth the fourth pale horse of death, which brings consummation.

According to Guyon, in history we are moving toward or are in the final stage of the eagle. Guyon believed that in the seventeenth century, she was living in the third stage and history was moving toward the time of interior spiritual animation called the eagle. Could we be in the fourth stage now when we will be animated by the Spirit like the Eagle?

In Guyon's second distinctive interpretation, she states that the woman giving birth to the son in the sky is the church giving birth to those of interior prayer, as well as a reflection on Mary giving birth to Jesus. The dragon wishes to destroy this interior life of prayer and yet God intervenes to stop this ultimate destruction of faith.

In Guyon's third distinctive interpretation, the seven seals show truthful historic events through which the world must pass. They also show seven states through which the individual soul must pass to find perfection and fullness of truth.

Every symbolic event has multiple interpretations. In her basic structure, she says every symbol has a meaning for the soul, the church, and the universe. All of these symbols can be interpreted for the faithful and nonfaithful, for the spiritually mature and the immature. Guyon contrasts these distinctions between those living in the simplicity and truth of the New Jerusalem or living in the multiplicity and lies of Babylon.

Guyon believes that the goal of Revelation is to show Jesus Christ's ultimate victory for human beings and the persecuted church. She states that the time of apocalypse spans from the beginning of the church until the end of time. Her understanding of the many centuries needed to fulfill the apocalypse does provide a dignity and meaning to the history of human suffering. The intense suffering that many have suffered for generations will have an answer in the judgment given by God in the apocalypse. In Guyon's perspective, the events of the apocalypse are indeed already happening, but we do not know when the final consummation will happen. During our lives, God sends rays of understanding that interpret the suffering circumstances described in the apocalypse to prepare us for the universal joy of the second coming of Jesus Christ.

Guyon's profound thinking about the apocalypse, the marriage of the Lamb, and the second coming needs a longer exposition in future publications. This book is already underway and should be published soon.

The Apocalypse of the Apostle John

> The Revelation of Jesus Christ, which God gave him to show his servants what must soon take place; he made it known by sending his angel to his servant John. (Rev 1:1)

J ESUS CHRIST EXPRESSES MANY hidden and profound mysteries in *The Revelation of Jesus Christ*. Jesus Christ reserves the right *to show to his servants* his mysteries. He gives his servants a gift to understand and a taste for this sweet and clear intelligence in Revelation. The book uses ordinary terms to write about things that are distant from ordinary reality However, Jesus Christ will make the message heard in the hearts of believers who read it.

John says that this book will describe *what must soon take place*. First, we understand that centuries for God are only moments. Also, this begins the revelation of what was to come from the birth of the church until the end of the world, but particularly what must happen at the end time. O strong and prodigious time that begins a new era which consummates all other times with mystery and rigor. God finds pleasure in revealing the mystery of all ages to the eyes of his servants and showing the effects of his power, so contrary to the thought and knowledge of human beings! O God eternal, Word of God, immolated Lamb, here is the day of your glory and triumph. Here is the time when the dragon will be chained for all time. Here also the time of the most horrible war and the strangest tempest of oppression on your servants. The dragon makes his last attacks, but you will defeat, O Lord Jesus, you defeat. Amen!

John says that these mysteries are made *known by sending his angel*. God uses two ways of revealing himself to his servants. First, God reveals himself in them and for them, so they reveal this to others. This profound revelation comes immediately and without mediation within the advanced soul. The soul discovers that she possesses a treasure, but she does not know how God communicated this to her.

The kiss of the mouth (Song of Solomon 1:1) reveals these secrets. John received the ineffable wedding kiss in the eternal generation of the Word from the bosom of the Father and his incarnation. Through the kiss of Jesus with his flock, the Word makes an indissoluble marriage with humanity. Jesus Christ paid for this painful kiss with his life, but it produced and gave birth and salvation to all Christians. John also revealed the eternal wedding of the Lamb in heaven with the ineffable and continual kiss of the Word to human beings. God revealed this kiss in heaven where the slain and immolated Lamb enjoys the glory of his immolation.

Secondly, through his *angels* God sends demonstrated knowledge regarding his kingdom and church in distinct and exterior actions for all of the centuries. This manifestation reveals exterior matters of the actions and reign of Jesus Christ and the destruction of the devil's empire.

These two forms of revelation, God gives to souls of high degree, as he also gave to the patriarch Joseph in his dreams with power to interpret exterior events. Many people have mediated revelations, without having unmediated revelation. Unmediated revelation with the direct communication of God to the soul are much more perfect. Some have both types of revelation and this is the consummation of all revelations.

> Who testified to the word of God and to the testimony of Jesus
> Christ, even to all that he saw. (Rev 1:2)

John speaks of himself in this scripture and gives testimony both to the Word and actions of Jesus Christ. We also must give testimony in believing, confessing, and obeying the Word as we imitate the actions of Jesus Christ.

> Blessed is the one who reads aloud the words of the prophecy,
> and blessed are those who hear and who keep what is written in
> it; for the time is near. (Rev 1:3)

Those who *read and hear* these words of Jesus Christ are very *blessed*. They *read* in Jesus Christ his virtues. Having this benefit, they *keep* them his words in their heart and practice them in their actions. *For the time* for fulfillment of these words *is very near*, both in the church in general and in the very soul which has the happiness and blessing of this.

> John to the seven churches that are in Asia: Grace to you and
> peace from him who is and who was and who is to come, and
> from the seven spirits who are before his throne. (Rev 1:4)

John sends these messages both to the churches and to all the faithful. He wishes us the *grace, peace*, and tranquility of Jesus Christ, the eternal Word, *who was* at the beginning and *who is* in the present. He *is to come* without end and without interruption in eternity.

The *seven premier angels stand in the glorious presence of the Lord, ready to serve him* with the grandeur and elevation of God. As soon as Jesus Christ reigns absolutely in the soul and establishes his throne there, the soul also has the blessing of seven spiritual gifts. The seven spiritual gifts include the Spirit of the Lord, wisdom, understanding, counsel, might, knowledge, and fear of the Lord (Isaiah 11:1–2).

You, Jesus Christ, are the *first* who found birth in the bosom of death and found immortality in the tomb. The sepulcher has become a cradle for eternal life. You communicate this new birth with life and immortality to all who are happy enough to follow you! You, the first of the predestined and first to rise from the dead, alone can justify. You are the King of kings, *the Prince of the kings of the earth*. All power is contained in you and only through you can we reign. You are the One *who loves us*, O Jesus, with an excessive love, and with this love you surrendered yourself to death in order to raise the dead and deliver us from a second death. As the spiritually dead were full of the filth and corruption of *their sins*, you *have washed* them with your *blood*. And not only to wash them, but to cleanse their sins but those of a thousand worlds.

> And from Jesus Christ, the faithful witness, the firstborn of the dead, and the ruler of the kings of the earth. To him who loves us and freed us from our sins by his blood, ⁶ and made us to be a kingdom, priests serving his God and Father, to him be glory and dominion forever and ever. Amen. (Rev 1:5–6)

To all these infinite graces, you have added new ones: you have been made our *King* and we are part of your kingdom. You exercise on us your sweet kingdom and we are subject to it. You make us reign as kings ourselves and of all other creatures. It is in reigning, O Love, we are perfectly subject to you.

You made us *priests* and we sacrifice ourselves and all creatures to your supreme power. You have made us priests in the most transcendent way, giving us the power to sacrifice to you incessantly, and to benefit from your immolation. These priests are *priests of God the Father*, since they offer the same sacrifice of his Son, that his Son himself offered, who as the great Priest of the order of Melchizedek, has sanctified all sacrifices.

To him be glory and dominion in all things, because he is the author of all things, a sovereign *kingdom* over all people as well as other creatures! We voluntarily submit to your kingdom so that he reigns in us and over us, *Amen!*

Look! He is coming with the clouds;
every eye will see him,
even those who pierced him;
and on his account all the tribes of the earth will wail.

So it is to be. Amen. (Rev 1:7)

O Love, you are always ready to come, and the scripture says well, *Behold for his presence comes. He comes*, O human, to knock on our heart but we do not receive him! But happy times, very fortunate century, century closer than one thinks, you come, and you will come, the Bridegroom of our souls comes. Yes, he comes, and *nothing is more assured.* And how do you come, O God? *With clouds*, in the sacred darkness of faith. *Every eye*, that is to say, all understanding will discover and *see* in the naked darkness which he chooses for his hiding place. The times are coming when all people will become interior and embrace the light of faith. All will convert and believe in him; all will adore in spirit and in truth. *Those who pierced him* are those sinners who have lost their baptismal grace and yet after the greatest crimes will convert. Every *eye shall see.* Yet Satan will stir up the Antichrist to destroy all living people on the earth, but the slain Lamb will be their defense. The time for vengeance on the demon will arrive and he will lose the power to harm people. Then *all tribes of the earth*, without any exception, *shall shout* from joy when the Lamb's strength appears. He will be admired with joy and astonishment by all people who experience this happiness. *There is nothing truer or more assured.* O happy and blessed time, you are closer than we can imagine! But before this time, O God, be assured, that there will be persecutions and reversals. You know this, Lord Jesus. Amen!

"I am the Alpha and the Omega," says the Lord God, who is and who was and who is to come, the Almighty." (Rev 1:8)

The Word is *the beginning and the end.* When the people asked Jesus, *Who are you?* Jesus spoke of being there from the beginning (John 8:25). He is the principle of all things because all was made by him. When he is our interior principle, we will be moved, led, and animated by him.

Jesus said to him, *I am the way, and the truth, and the life* (John 14:6). He describes three historical eras in this scripture. In the first age of the church, Jesus Christ is the *Way* with believers following in his footsteps. This was the century of the martyrs, as Jesus said to Peter, the first apostle of the church, *Follow me!* (John 21:22). Peter died on the cross, like his good master. They followed Jesus Christ as the Way.

The second age of the church is the one with Jesus Christ as the *Truth*. This is the age of confessors when they supported the truth with all their might through their writing and publishing.

The third age will come and is coming soon with Jesus Christ as the *Life*. He comes to enliven and make people interior. This age must last until the end of the world, until the time of the Antichrist. Jesus Christ desires to be present and to be the *beginning* and *end* of all his creatures. The universe, the church, and the soul will be consummated in heaven in the bosom of Divinity. This is the Lord *who is and who will be* always, and who lives within us in a very special manner. He is the *Almighty* because all power is given to him on heaven and on earth. He will show his power and his conduct will be elevated beyond human comprehension.

> I, John, your brother who share with you in Jesus the persecu-
> tion and the kingdom and the patient endurance, was on the
> island called Patmos because of the word of God and the testi-
> mony of Jesus. (Rev 1:9)

Writing this apocalypse to all the faithful and all the church, John is our *brother*, since he is the first to be entrusted by our shared Father with his ineffable secrets. In his profound interior John has more access than any other to Jesus. He experienced in his interior what is then manifested to others. He *participated* with pain *in the afflictions* of Jesus Christ by accompanying him with faith to Calvary and then participated in Jesus Christ's *reign*. John also participated *in his patience* by suffering all the persecutions from sinners with love and kindness. This great apostle was full of charity, because he had drunk in deeply the heart of his Master. Charity opened John's heart (and not the spear of human beings). O heart of Jesus Christ opened before the eyes of John, what fires and flames did you throw into the heart of this great saint! John was persecuted, according to his own testimony, *because of the word of God* and for have confessed Jesus. He was not surprised that the same thing happened to him, and, to the contrary, he held this as blessedness.

> I was in the spirit on the Lord's day, and I heard behind me a
> loud voice like a trumpet [11] saying, "Write in a book what you
> see and send it to the seven churches, to Ephesus, to Smyrna, to
> Pergamum, to Thyatira, to Sardis, to Philadelphia, and to Laodi-
> cea." [12] Then I turned to see whose voice it was that spoke to me,
> and on turning I saw seven golden lampstands. (Rev 1:10–12)

The Spirit transported John, so he could be attentive to the great things that it pleased God to show him for the usefulness of the church.

John describes all the circumstances. It was, he said, *on the Lord's Day,* a day destined for repose and tranquility, of calm and peace. *I heard behind me a great voice* like a trumpet, so strong and loud that I could not ignore it. This strong voice was the voice of the Son of God who would be heard to the ends of the earth.

John must *write what he sees* to tell future generations as an infallible sign what must happen in the coming centuries, and in all the ages of the church, and within the individual soul. *Asia* is one of the largest parts of the world, a place of conquest for Jesus Christ, where *the book* must be *taken* into the seven cities of this part of the world.

Then I turned to see whose voice spoke to me, which shows that this vision was representative and outside of him. *And being turned, I saw seven golden candlesticks.* These seven golden candlesticks are the seven spirits of heaven and the seven gifts of the Spirit for the church.

> And in the midst of the lampstands I saw one like the Son of Man, clothed with a long robe and with a golden sash across his chest. (Rev 1:13)

Jesus Christ is always in the midst of the *seven* gifts of the Holy Spirit, and where he lives, the seven gifts are found. *The long robe* represents his purity and innocence and the *golden sash* signifies his love.

> His head and his hair were white as white wool, white as snow; his eyes were like a flame of fire. (Rev 1:14)

His head represents his superior part; therefore, the *whiteness* signifies his integrity. *His hair* was also very *white,* to signify his simplicity and purity of thought, as well as his antiquity. He is as eternal as God, although he came into time as a man incarnate by taking on a mortal body. *His eyes were like a flame of fire* because the Word is the knowledge of the Father. He is the *eye* and strong as the Word. But love made him change his figure and take a human soul and body with eyes and organs like ours, whose knowledge has rapport with ours, although it is under his hypostatic union. As his love made him take this form, his eyes appear like *fire,* for us to understand that he is light and heat. He does not only enlighten us but warms us with his love. His eyes also represent Divinity. The mutual and reciprocal gaze of the Father and the Son produces a love as great and infinite as this gaze. God gazes upon us with love.

> His feet were like burnished bronze, refined as in a furnace, and his voice was like the sound of many waters. (Rev 1:15)

The Son of Man's feet of polished bronze represent his humanity. When hit, the sound of bronze is the cry of all the sins of the world. On him fall the blows of our sins. The *furnace* of his Divinity composed of fire and flames made his feet of *fire* as he walks to us out of love to save us. *His voice is like the sounds of many waters*, strong and full, because by his Word strong and profound graces are given to us. He is like a river that sprinkles and floods the whole soul, making it fertile.

> In his right hand he held seven stars, and from his mouth came a sharp, two-edged sword, and his face was like the sun shining with full force. (Rev 1:16)

The seven stars are the gifts of the Holy Spirit that he distributes with grace to humans. He gives us knowledge about himself according to the different capacity of souls. In his hand he holds all the graces that save humanity. *The sword* of his Word *has two sides* to cut off sin and everything that is opposed to his work. The sword cuts away all that is in us of Adam that has insinuated itself into the soul. *His face* represents the glory of his beautiful soul in his hypostatic union.

> When I saw him, I fell at his feet as though dead. But he placed his right hand on me, saying, "Do not be afraid; I am the first and the last." (Rev 1:17)

As soon as you appear to us, O my divine Savior, humans *fall as though dead* because all that is within us of Adam dies. We need to die so that we give place to the new Adam and let the new Adam do his work. But we are *not to be afraid* because he *places his right hand* on us and supports our soul. When it seems that all is going to die and end in disaster, we find a greater salvation, a stronger life, and more assured support. *Do not be afraid*, he says to the soul, *because I am the first and the last*. "It is I," he says, "that you find when you enter into the Way. You also find in me the last consummation. I said that it was good that I go away, and that is the beginning (John 16:7). The soul must lose sight of my first coming and that she must lose the light and feeling of me for a long time. So this new revelation appears entirely extraordinary and frightens her all the more, because she has lost the sight of me for a long time and also because my second advent is very different from the first, because now she has rapport with me. I am therefore the beginning and the end of all things. Whoever is the first among the saints is also the last, because all their holiness is found contained in me. Everything is reunited."

> And the living one. I was dead, and see, I am alive forever and
> ever; and I have the keys of Death and of Hades. (Rev 1:18)

O Word of God! You are the One who is. You are the Principle of all beings.
There is no being who does not emanate from you. *You have life* in you, and
nothing has life that does not participate in your life. However, even though
you are the essential life who came into the world only to give life to humans, you had to suffer *death*. As you were immortal by nature, you wanted
because of your generous love and charity to take a mortal body so that you
could destroy death in us by submitting to death. Therefore, you *were dead*,
O Essential Life, you submitted to a voluntary death to deliver all humanity
from a necessary death. You have been among the dead, but you are now
living to die no more, and you have entered into all your rights. You have
destroyed death by your same death that appeared to leave you destroyed.
Instead, you destroyed death and received essential life in your womb. You
were given death and rested in full life. My Savior holds in his hands *the keys
of Death and Hades*. O Love, if you close a door, who can open? If you open,
who can close? Opening and closing are done according to your will. But I
say that the soul trusts you has a singular advantage because no one is put
into hell without you opening the door. You close this door for those who
trust in their own merit and you open your breast to those who recognize
themselves as unworthy.

> Now write what you have seen, what is, and what is to take place
> after this. [20] As for the mystery of the seven stars that you saw in
> my right hand, and the seven golden lampstands: the seven stars
> are the angels of the seven churches, and the seven lampstands
> are the seven churches. (Rev 1:19–20)

Jesus Christ again called to John to *write* all *that he has seen*. Revelation
shows what Jesus Christ has said and done since his resurrection. John is not
only writing *what is to take place* but what Jesus Christ is speaking.

These words of Revelation are admirable. We see well the dignity of
the pastors since Jesus Christ himself compares them to *angels* who *are in
his hand* like *stars* to enlighten and guide people. What virtue and wisdom
do we see in them? We have to watch them as brilliant stars, like distinguished lights in the sky of the church? If pastors are like stars, the faithful
who compose the *church*, must be in a perfect union, as they are like a
golden lampstand that it to say in love, burning like fire and illuminated
with the same light.

> "To the angel of the church in Ephesus write: These are the words
> of him who holds the seven stars in his right hand, who walks

among the seven golden lampstands: "I know your works, your toil and your patient endurance. I know that you cannot tolerate evildoers; you have tested those who claim to be apostles but are not and have found them to be false. ³ I also know that you are enduring patiently and bearing up for the sake of my name, and that you have not grown weary. ⁴ But I have this against you, that you have abandoned the love you had at first." (Rev 2:1–4)

Revelation tell of the faithfulness of God towards us and the faithfulness that he requires from us. We see the contrast between the purity of God and the impurity of the creature. The pastors can see the greatness of their obligations to their ministry. God will ask an accounting of their virtues, such as love toward their flock and their pastoral zeal. The faithfulness of God is admirable in how he gives his servants knowledge of the defects of souls and his exactitude in accounting all the good that they do. But also, what faithfulness does he require in the soul, what purity does he ask, since his divine light would find obscurity and impurity even in the Sun?

For finally, there is nothing, it seems, more virtuous than this pastor and church, according to the description that the Savior himself makes. However, he reproaches him that *he has abandoned the love he had at first.* O Love, it seems to me, there are no followers to whom you should not make this reproach! Where are those who have conserved their first ardor? Alas! Where do you find them? They are very rare! In the beginning, it is only service and love; after that, it is only money and misery. We need to have ardor at the beginning, so we can love and serve, yet frequently this is imperfect. We must never tire of doing the will of God or leave God's way because of pains, dangers, fears, uncertainties, and persecutions.

> Remember then from what you have fallen; repent, and do the works you did at first. If not, I will come to you and remove your lampstand from its place, unless you repent. ⁶ Yet this is to your credit: you hate the works of the Nicolaitans, which I also hate. (Rev 2:5–6)

Remember *the state* from which *you have fallen.* Who of us has the pure faith of our early belief? We need to repent and gain the faith we have lost.

Jesus Christ loves those who do not do actions of heresy, yet do not hate the people involved. Indeed, the more we experience trouble because of their false faith and deregulated morals, and yet have love for their person, we have zeal to pull them out of their mistakes by gentleness more than disputes.

> Let anyone who has an ear listen to what the Spirit is saying to the churches. To everyone who conquers, I will give permission to eat from the tree of life that is in the paradise of God. (Rev 2:7)

O God, you are the victorious victor and only through you can we conquer. You are, O Jesus, the Lamb victorious over the demon and nature. No one can conquer except in you and through you. But *whoever will be victorious through the loss of herself will eat from the tree of life that is in the paradise of God*. But what is the fruit from the tree of life? O Jesus, you give yourself to eat in communion, and the annihilated soul eats in her interior. She receives you as life. To the measure that we are lost in you, you become our life, food, and support. You are the *tree of life in the paradise of my God*, because you have life within you and all the saints live only in your life. You make all the blessed alive in your life and they live only the life that you communicate as you live only the life that your Father communicates. But it is for *those who have an ear to listen* and to hear God.

> "And to the angel of the church in Smyrna write: These are the words of the first and the last, who was dead and came to life. ⁹ I know your affliction and your poverty, even though you are rich. I know the slander on the part of those who say that they are Jews and are not but are a synagogue of Satan. ¹⁰ Do not fear what you are about to suffer. Beware, the devil is about to throw some of you into prison so that you may be tested, and for ten days you will have affliction. Be faithful until death, and I will give you the crown of life." (Rev 2:8–10)

God says many times that he is *the first and the last*, so that we understand that he is our animating principle and end. The same faith which tells us that he created us tells us that we desire to return to him. We use our strength to return to him as our end and the consummation of all perfection through unity. However, in this century, all who place on God all their hopes and desires, are called heretics and fools. O God, your judgments are different than those of people, as your ways are different from ours!

Jesus Christ is the first and the last, God and man, who being *the first* in the bosom of the Father is the last for humanity, as it says in the prophets, *But I am a worm, and not human; scorned by others, and despised by the people* (Psalm 22:6). He was dead, but now he is alive. We who share in his death, have hope to share in his life. O humans, who are in desolation and in death, think that he died for you and you live in him.

Is there anything more comforting for a poor afflicted soul? *I know*, says God, *your affliction.* I know you. Isn't this the greatest consolation for you? I know *your poverty, even though you are rich*. What does that mean? It means that the greatest of riches is found in the greatest of poverty. A human who is deprived of all good, desires nothing and finds in her deprivation contentment, even though abandoned from all help and support. She consecrates herself all the more to God even with the estrangement that she feels and because of this possesses a treasure and immense wealth. Because the rich can desire something, they are neither contented or satisfied. But the poor of this type are perfectly content and full and have no care about anything. Without cares, they are perfectly rich.

But these people so peaceful and happy are not known to others because God hides them in his sanctuary from the eyes of others. Their holiness will only be known in eternity. They are *slandered* and condemned by all the world. They pass for the most miserable in the earth. But who persecutes and slanders them? *Those who say that they are Jews and are not*, that is to say, those who pass for devoted but place all their devotion in certain exterior ceremonies and persecute the humble and spiritual. But, O dear abandoned ones, O interior souls, O children of Abraham and the faith, *do not fear what you are about to suffer*. It will be for you an advantage. You will be persecuted like saints, who rendered to God a great service by their suffering with faith the slander against them. They fear nothing because they know that *Satan* knows well that his empire is never more destroyed than when souls work to let God reign inside them and to assist others to do the same. Satan arouses the strangest persecutions against them and will throw some of the God's dearest children and most faithful servants *into prison*. Satan blinds the judges and the ministers of justice. He has the guilty pass as the most innocent. He makes those most attached to the church appear as enemies of the church, but we must fear nothing, but all of this will only be a test.

For ten days you will have affliction. These ten days signify the years in which you endure persecution, which will be designed for different souls. O poor interior souls, what you will suffer! The time will come when it will be a shame and confusion to be with God. Your afflictions are extreme but have courage! *Be faithful until death* and support your faith unto death for the interests of God for you will suffer. Do not lose your faith and trust. Your death *will give you the crown of life*.

> Let anyone who has an ear listen to what the Spirit is saying to the churches. Whoever conquers will not be harmed by the second death. (Rev 2:11)

There are two deaths through which we pass, the mystical death and the natural death. The mystical death gives Jesus Christ a place to conquer in us and through us. Whoever is happy enough to conquer by the first death, will not know the sadness of being *harmed by the second death*. The second death for them is both a pleasure and refreshment. It does not say that those do not die but only that they *will not be harmed by the second death* because this death will be for them a passage from death to life. But it takes a particular intelligence to hear this.

> "And to the angel of the church in Pergamum write: These are the words of him who has the sharp two-edged sword: [13] I know where you are living, where Satan's throne is. Yet you are holding fast to my name, and you did not deny your faith in me even in the days of Antipas my witness, my faithful one, who was killed among you, where Satan lives. [14] But I have a few things against you: you have some there who hold to the teaching of Balaam, who taught Balak to put a stumbling block before the people of Israel, so that they would eat food sacrificed to idols and practice fornication. [15] So you also have some who hold to the teaching of the Nicolaitans. (Rev 2:12–15)

Jesus Christ offers his name according to the state of the people to whom he speaks. To those who are in affliction and in death, he shows them that he has died and he lives, so that they may hope that they will have a most blessed life after they suffer a cruel death. But to this who tolerate heresy, O, he speaks only of his sword because it is the sword of his Word that destroys heresy. *I know*, he tells us, that you have kept your faith, even in a state of apprehension because one of the faithful was killed among you. However, this cannot please me because you suffer that Satan shares the age of the church, tolerating a mixture that is offensive to me. O God, your rigor is extreme!

> Repent then. If not, I will come to you soon and make war against them with the sword of my mouth. [17] Let anyone who has an ear listen to what the Spirit is saying to the churches. To everyone who conquers I will give some of the hidden manna, and I will give a white stone, and on the white stone is written a new name that no one knows except the one who receives it. (Rev 2:16–17)

O God, you *give some of the hidden manna*. What is this hidden manna but you? Your holy communion on the altar is the hidden manna. This secret and intimate manna lives within us. This manna is *hidden* in the darkness of faith. O all mysterious but very real Word!

You give us a *white stone*, which is no other than divine immobility where you confirm the soul in a most exquisite grace with purity and an inconceivable candor. There the soul is *given a new name* which is engraved on the white stone which shows a new life in God. The *stone* signifies permanence and the *whiteness* purity. In the Old Testament, new names were given to Abraham, father of all believers and souls of faith, to Sarah, and to Israel. In the New Testament, Peter and Paul received new names. This name only God himself can give because no other can put a person in this state. O grand and wonderful state! Who will understand this unless you experience it?

> "And to the angel of the church in Thyatira write: These are the words of the Son of God, who has eyes like a flame of fire, and whose feet are like burnished bronze: I know your works—your love, faith, service, and patient endurance. I know that your last works are greater than the first." (Rev 2:18–19)

O God, the admirable expressions in this book! The *fire coming out of his eyes* shows knowledge and love of God the Father. The *feet of brass* show his humanity united with divinity, making such great fires capable of engulfing a thousand worlds. However, where are those who let themselves be ignited with fire? Alas! We are all ice even with such a great conflagration.

Conformity with the qualities of which Jesus Christ speaks about is admirable. He speaks here with a pastor of high perfection and ardent love, encouraging him to persevere in the imitation of God's extraordinary love. But for what does Jesus Christ praise this great pastor? For his *faith*, because the measure of his faith is the measure of all graces, and exterior and interior advancement. *As you have believed, so let it be done for you*, says Jesus Christ (Matthew 8:13). Next, he praises him for his *love*. Faith and love are companions. Where there is much faith, there is much love, and where there is a much love, there is a much faith. But also, where there is little faith, there is little love, and where there is little love, there is a little faith. We measure our love by faith.

But how do we know this faith? By a general, continual, and persevering abandonment in both the interior and the exterior, which even the most distressing states do not cause us to turn back. Confident faith and a full trust remain even in its apparent loss. We never change our way, even with the biggest disasters. It is then that we know the solidity of our faith and the truth of our love.

This angel praises his *patience* in suffering his injuries while in *service* and his faithfulness to serve as a true pastor. But mainly the angel praises that his *last works are* much *greater than the first*, and that his vigilance is much stronger at the end than at the beginning. O, where do we find such pastors? They are very rare!

"Yet I hold this against you, that you tolerate the woman Jezebel, who calls herself a prophetess, who teaches and misleads my servants to play the harlot and to eat food sacrificed to idols. [21] I have given her time to repent, but she refuses to repent of her harlotry. [22] So I will cast her on a sickbed and plunge those who commit adultery with her into intense suffering unless they repent of her works. [23] I will also put her children to death. Thus, shall all the churches come to know that I am the searcher of hearts and mind and that I will give each of you what your works deserve." (Rev 2:20–23)

But, O Pure Love, O Divine Exactor, from whom nothing may be hidden, what reproaches do you give to your pastor, to which you have given such great praises? O God, with your purity, all other purity is impure! O pastors, governors of the flock of Jesus Christ, your call is strong, and what an accounting you will have to render. It is not enough for you to be holy yourself, but for others to also be holy. And God is not content that you banish these types of sins from your heart, but that you banish them from your church and from the middle of your flock. Sins such as fornication and adultery rob God of the honor we give him.

We must give God honor because otherwise we have a fornication of the heart and an adultery of the spirit. This is a thousand times more dangerous and evil than that of the body because it removes our heart and spirit from God to whom they belong uniquely. Once removed, they prostitute themselves to idols or to infamous creatures.

This miserable *Jezebel* signifies the corrupt nature taking the spirit away from the attachment to God to engage in disorderly and brutal desires. God invites us to *repentance*. But in his desire to save humanity, and seeing that his invitation is nothing to them, what does he do? He *stops them and puts them in a sickbed* with infirmities and diseases. This is the ordinary way of God to bring people back through their mistakes, diseases, and afflictions. This brings the person back to his duties and obliges him to necessary repentance when he did not embrace God's will voluntarily.

God assures us that he is *the searcher of hearts and minds*. O Lord, you are the judge of all! Ah, we are blind about ourselves! We hide our true heart under another heart. We cover ourselves with worldly excuses and hide our wrong intentions. We act out of self-love and yet persuade ourselves and others that we are working for God. However, God *gives each of us what our works deserve*. Those who have a great multitude of works and hope for a great reward will be astonished to see that God, who searches the hearts and minds, will find these works empty. Our works are not counted by their number but by their goodness. That is why they are weighed on the scale and not by numbers. O how the world will be surprised! Those who have a great number of works and have worked well will be found without works. Others that have seemed very useless will have a heavy weight of good works. O God, it is very good that you have a reason to reserve for yourself justice in all things!

> "But to the rest of you in Thyatira, who do not hold this teaching, who have not learned what some call 'the deep things of Satan,' to you I say, I do not lay on you any other burden; 25 only hold fast to what you have until I come." (Rev 2:24–25)

God is wonderful, for though he seems to reproach this good pastor for what is done in the church, God promises him that he will not carry the burden of the iniquities of others. Since God is exact and pure, he is full of goodness and compassion for the weakness of creatures.

He adds, *Only hold fast to what you have,* that is to say, hold on to my grace so that you persevere in faith, love, patience, and service to the flock. My God, you are admirable! You beautifully soften the wounds that you seem to make.

> "To everyone who conquers and continues to do my works to the end, I will give authority over the nations; 27 to rule them with an iron rod, as when clay pots are shattered—28 even as I also received authority from my Father. To the one who conquers I will also give the morning star. 29 Let anyone who has an ear listen to what the Spirit is saying to the churches." (Rev 2:26–29)

God reserves a wonderful advantage for those who conquer by the interior death, in which all is destroyed, because the believer does not rest in propriety. In this soul, Jesus reigns solely. The souls faithful to Jesus give him all the glory of the victory, without attributing anything to themselves. This is good justice, because he only has the victory in us. This shows that nothing in this world, either exterior or interior, has been able to prevent this victory in those emptied and annihilated souls. These people who do not oppose Jesus in anything are quite rare! *I will give them authority over the nations.*

They have authority over the nations in many ways. First, they have very great authority over both souls and bodies. Secondly, they have authority over themselves, because they no longer find resistance to Jesus within themselves. Thirdly, because they are annihilated, God frequently uses them for the governance of his church. God makes these people pastors, when the church seems at the height of destruction.

We must see all the circumstances. God wants souls to faithfully *keep* his will *to the end,* that is to say, they become united at their end and he gives them power among the nations. As he has said, *To rule them with an iron rod,* with authority so strong that nothing can resist it. Because these souls are annihilated, they have not a rigorous authority, but they have divine power. They dispose of things as it pleases them and reveal even things that are most interior and hidden. This makes it clear that divine power is communicated to them. As Jesus Christ says, *I received authority from my Father.* The same power is communicated is to them. The same power I have received from my Father works in them.

Jesus Christ adds, *I will also give them the morning star.* The star of the morning precedes the dawn. The morning light brings pink light and this rosy light falls almost as soon as it is lifted. These people have a right and advantage that God gives them, that is, when they instruct docile souls in the interior way, the true spirit of Jesus Christ. Like a beautiful dawn, Jesus Christ does not fail to shine in them the beautiful day of his grace. Like a beautiful rose, he sends at the same time into hearts a very abundant consolation and divine unction. It is the same *star of the morning,* which announces the day to the travelers who want to walk in the way of perfection.

> "And to the angel of the church in Sardis write: These are the words of him who has the seven spirits of God and the seven stars: I know your works; you have a name of being alive, but you are dead. [2] Wake up, and strengthen what remains and is on the point of death, for I have not found your works perfect in the sight of my God." (Rev 3:1–2)

How many of these pastors are *dead* but *appear to be alive?* They are dead lacking the vigor and life to keep their flocks. Also, they are not animated by the interior Spirit and pure love. Through their actions they seek the vain illusion of reputation.

Whoever has the Spirits of God, the seven gifts of the Holy Spirit and *the seven stars* of divine lights, discovers what is most hidden. They find the One who reveals that *you were dead,* although you appear alive to all others. *Wake up* to get out of this death. *Strengthen what remains* and let those escape the debris that your lack of vigilance has caused. Strengthen them, so they do not perish like the others because they are on the point of dying through your fault. How many negligent pastors are there, from whose hands the wolf takes away the sheep? It is quite a horror to eat the butter and milk of the flock, and to be clothed with their wool, but not to keep, defend, and support the flock.

Remember then what you received and heard; obey it, and repent. If you do not wake up, I will come like a thief, and you will
not know at what hour I will come to you. (Rev 3:3)

As the evil of this pastor is personal, he must repent. A true repentance is to
do the contrary action changing what was done before. The pastor should
now watch for the source of the evil and fill the fold with good dogs who
take away the power of vice. God asks for specific remedies, but they cause
pain while healing. This is what the *repentance* of God asks for with justice.
O negligent pastors, who should be attending! The Master *will come like a
thief, and you will not know at what hour I will come to you*. But who do you
think he will take away? It will not only be your flock exposed to danger for
a lack of a vigilant pastor, but it will be yourself. He will ask you for your soul
and the soul of your brother.

> "Yet you have still a few persons in Sardis who have not soiled
> their clothes; they will walk with me, dressed in white, for they
> are worthy. ⁵ If you conquer, you will be clothed like them in
> white robes, and I will not blot your name out of the book of
> life; I will confess your name before my Father and before his
> angels." (Rev 3:4–5)

All towns have some holy people. Frequently the most corrupt places have
the greatest saints. *Have not soiled their clothes* is to have not lost the grace of
their baptism, which is a great advantage. Those who are *walking with Jesus
Christ in white clothes* include those who have not been unfaithful since
their conversion.

Those who conquer have been entirely destroyed, died, and annihilated, where the new Adam has conquered and destroyed the first Adam.
They are restored to the first grace more perfect than the state of innocence.
According to Paul, our *redemption is abundant and superabundant*, and
restores human beings to its first state with all the advantages this has. Otherwise, redemption would not be equal to the grace of creation, so it would
not be abundant. The soul in whom the grace of redemption has expanded
receives the state of innocence more perfect than the first. Those who have
conquered in him and through him participate in his happiness. This is why
their robes are white because they are dressed in vestments of innocence,
their name will never more *be blotted out of the book of life* and they will
never have mortal faults anymore. Jesus Christ has *confessed them*, he has
recognized them before God the Father as his own. He receives them as
adoptive children, heirs of God, and coinheritors of Jesus Christ.

"Let anyone who has an ear listen to what the Spirit is saying to
the churches." (Rev 3:6)

We need to have divine intelligence to understand these things and not
be scandalized by them. O God! In this century the greatest truth passes
for errors and blasphemies! Those who speak these truths are hated and
contradicted by creatures. Instead, crimes, folly, and garbage pass for gal-
lantries. And your servants, O Lord, become infamous! They are esteemed
as rubbish of the world because they support your name (1 Cor 4:13). O, the
derangement, perversity, and corruption of this century! We are ashamed
to be with God. Those who in the past centuries were saints now pass for
infamous. They are regarded with indignation. It seems, my God, that you
are blind, or that you do not know all things. You see them and conceal
them to test the patience of your servants.

> "And to the angel of the church in Philadelphia write: These
> are the words of the holy one, the true one, who has the key of
> David, who opens and no one will shut, who shuts and no one
> opens: [8] I know your works. Look, I have set before you an open
> door, which no one is able to shut. I know that you have but little
> power, and yet you have kept my word and have not denied my
> name. [9] I will make those of the synagogue of Satan who say that
> they are Jews and are not, but are lying—I will make them come
> and bow down before your feet, and they will learn that I have
> loved you." (Rev 3:7–9)

This is the only pastor for whom he has no words of reproach. The pastor *has but little power,* but God has made the pastor strong. Because he
has no strength in himself, he finds all his strength in God. What qualities
does Jesus regard well? Holy and true qualities. Because the good pastor
was perfectly annihilated, all his holiness was in God. Jesus is holy for him.
He praises him primarily because of the two qualities for which Jesus has
regard: holiness and truth. Jesus promises him souls, this being the highest reward that a pastor like this can claim in this life. Because he has no
propriety, his only interest is God's interests and only desires to win hearts
for Jesus Christ's kingdom. *They will bow to your feet,* says God, *acknowledge*
their fault, and discover by experience that they will receive graces through
you, and know *how much I love you.* The greatest sign of the love of God is
to want to serve him to win hearts.

The holy and true God says to his servant that *he has the key of David.*
This *key* is his incarnation, by which he is born of David according to the
flesh to open to all the predestined. It is Jesus Christ *who opens and no one
will shut, who shuts and no one opens.* What is this opening? Jesus Christ

through his incarnation has the key of David and opens the heart of God the Father. If he does not open God's heart, no one can ever enter there. But when he has once opened it, nothing in the world can close it. He *opens the door* to his servants, so they can enter and hide with him. So then the pastor without being pulled from his union with Jesus Christ acts entirely for his neighbor and make thousands of converts.

> Because you have kept my word of patient endurance, I will keep you from the hour of trial that is coming on the whole world to test the inhabitants of the earth. (Rev 3:10)

Kept my word of patient endurance is to suffer because of the will of God. When we suffer like this, we still have a way *to keep the word of patience.* God talks to the soul, filling it with well-being. David says, *Do not keep silence toward me* (Psalm 28:1). For as God waited a long time for the soul, she waits for God. Persevering in her patience, she keeps the word, doing all God's will. And God as the author rewards her faithfulness and *keeps this soul* himself at the time of *trial.* O, a soul kept in this way is well-guarded! When the whole world succumbs to the temptation, she is well-guarded.

In some centuries, men are so full of corruption that they try to corrupt the saints. The time of the martyrs was one type of *temptation* and strong persecution. The history of saints has many examples of trials of this sort. In our century a *trial* happens when the servants of God are persecuted and afflicted continually, despised of people. The world treats them as the manure of the ground. The martyrs were all the more esteemed because they resisted more strongly. Yet in our time, the closer they are to God, the more they are despised.

Some saints though resisted pain but could not resist the temptations of pleasure. God permits this to *test* us. In temptations of pleasure, physical nature and demons are joined together, which makes this more difficult to conquer. We recognize them as demonic.

But alas! Where do we find this who are faithful to bear this trial? Out of ambition, everyone wants to please others and gain credit. They work to establish himself on the ruins of his brother. We do not bother to please God or to be esteemed by him, as long as we please humans, and they return esteem. We want only the world's values. We do not look at the virtues of Jesus Christ, because the world condemns him. However, the true servants of God suffer outrages without complaining and calumny without justifying themselves. These are those that God *keeps* with a particular protection in the *hour of trial.*

"I am coming soon. Hold on to what you have, so that no one will take your crown. [12] The one who is victorious I will make a pillar in the temple of my God. Never again will they leave it. I will write on them the name of my God and the name of the city of my God, the new Jerusalem, which is coming down out of heaven from my God; and I will also write on them my new name." (Rev 3:11–12)

My God, what a wonderful mystery! Jesus Christ assures the angel that he *is coming soon*. We must *keep what we have* for this time.

Jesus Christ also comes soon to souls of high degree by the mystical incarnation, when he wants them to bear his own state. In calling out to Jesus Christ, these souls are already consummated and removed from the world that is unworthy of these people. We can understand this in two ways. First, God raises us by his goodness into this state, so we do not fail by our own fault. The second sense is that the soul is being reduced by annihilation. The most harmful temptation is under the pretext of duty or perfection, we leave our state. Instead, we must rest in this state. Otherwise, *the crown will be given to another*. The crown of crowns is that which is reserved for the state of annihilation. The annihilation of Mary was so great that the Word became her very crown.

Whoever *will be victorious* will have the *advantage* of being *a column in the church* unshakeable by its firmness. These people are the support of the church, although they are not always known for such. O God, you will that one day your servant will be this strong. Make your servant a firm column that will resist the shaking of the building. My God, support your church. Make the Spirit strong. Support your church and revive it in all its members. Join and unite all the lackluster members and give us all vigor and life. Support us, Lord. The demon opposes your kingdom with all his might.

This scripture says again here that God places the soul in divine immobility in himself and confirms that she *will never leave*. O happy state for this soul that she will never lose her God anymore! *The name of God will be written on her*, on her heart and arm, as was given to the spouse in the Canticles, when the Lord says, *Set me as a seal on your heart, as a seal upon your arm* (Song of Solomon 8:6). The name that is engraved on this person is an entire consecration both exterior and interior. There is only God both inside and outside of this person. Jesus Christ also writes on her *the name of the city of my* God. He does this in two ways. First, Jesus Christ associates her with the number of saints and gives her all the characteristics of holiness which writes the name of the holy city of God on her. Secondly, he places in this soul all the traits and characteristics of the purity of the church. This soul is a small church but a church so pure and completed that all interior and exterior traits of Jesus Christ are expressed in this person. Then every facility is rendered for these external practices. Also, at the end of their days, these people after having been annihilated, will be the lights of the church. Because of this favor, all the nations will come to know the Lord.

Jesus Christ adds that he will write the *name of the New Jerusalem, which is coming down out of heaven.* What is this *New Jerusalem*? It is the church already formed that the Holy Spirit comes to fill. This Spirit is going to be spread on the church soon, soon, as it is written, You will *all be taught of the Lord* (John 6:45). How can there be signs of the Lord if they do not listen to the Lord, and pay attention to his voice? But if they listen, as David says, *Let me hear what the God the Lord will speak* inside of me (Psalm 85:8). When they listen, they will not fail to be taught by him. Because of this, the demon fights with all his might against prayer and loving attention paid to God. The demon inspires even shameful crimes done by those who call themselves people of prayer (like *the Jews who called themselves Jews and were not*) to persecute the people of God and to make the innocents look guilty. But after this tempest comes the lull, after the combat comes the victory. The Holy Spirit *comes from God* to fill all the creatures. This accomplishes the Word of the prophet Joel who says, *I will pour out my spirit on all flesh* (Joel 2:28). In the early church, the Holy Spirit came on the apostles and the general assembly. This Spirit though was not spread *on all flesh*, although it was spread on every soul there. There will come a time when the prophecy is fully accomplished with the Spirit spread on all flesh.

In another place, Jesus Christ says that he will give the victorious a new name. And in this scripture, he says he will write on them *his new name.* These two scriptures reveal two different experiences. In the first, the new name is given only when the soul has lost her self–centeredness through annihilation and she has passed into God. But here Jesus gives *his name again,* which is the name of Christ and Savior to use this person to save many souls. His name brings pure suffering that crucifies her with him. And these graces are reserved for very few.

> "Let anyone who has an ear listen to what the Spirit is saying to
> the churches." (Rev 3:13)

It takes a profound intelligence to understand this. If there was only a natural sense hidden under these words, it would not be so often repeated. *Who has ears, hear.* But this has a high and profound mystical sense. Do not be surprised that this is so frequently repeated. O profound words, who will understand you!

"And to the angel of the church in Laodicea write: The words of the Amen, the faithful and true witness, the origin of God's creation: [15] I know your works; you are neither cold nor hot. I wish that you were either cold or hot. [16] So, because you are lukewarm, and neither cold nor hot, I am about to spit you out of my mouth." (Rev 3:14–16)

No matter how poor a pastor, he is the *angel of his church* and it his title. But sometimes instead of being a guardian angel, the pastor is a seductive angel who makes people fall into the abyss. Jesus Christ states here his character. "I am," he says, "*the Amen*, the true being. There is nothing outside of me. It is I who am the essence. All other beings only subsist in me or by me. I am. And everything that is not me is nothing." Why the *Amen*? He has nothing to add here because when Jesus Christ says, "I am the One who is," this is all that may be said of him affirmatively.

Jesus Christ repeats that he is the *faithful and true witness*. He also testifies to reveal the bad. This is why, being as exact as God is, it is a terrible thing to fall into the hands of the living God (Hebrews 10:31). So that it is not terrible for us, we must put all our conduct into his hands and act only by his motions and follow his Spirit. Then all our works will be done in assurance. He will be the faithful and true witness and he will not reject any of our works that he has made. I say he will have made them, since, he adds, he is the *Principle of God's creatures*. All creatures are created by the Word and all life emanates from God and so all works may be looked upon as God's works. We see Jesus Christ as the agent in these works. We only operate by dependence on Jesus Christ's Spirit. Jesus Christ only is the power.

The reproach that Jesus Christ makes through John to this pastor is appalling. These lukewarm *people* are opposed to receiving the true Spirit of God, the interior Spirit. Their nonchalance toward God is so strong that they have no heat left, yet it seems to them like a conflagration. They do not comprehend the magnitude of this situation. The love that they have for themselves makes them believe that they are good and they do not doubt this. Everything said to pull them out of this state offends them. They look with blindness at others. They do not want to know Jesus Christ or to confess him. It is an evil almost irremediable because it is nurtured and sustained by their self-love. They prefer themselves and look upon sinners with disdain and contempt. In order to raise themselves, they condemn other who are burning hot and cold. Certainly these people are more opposed to receiving the Spirit of God than the worst of sinners. Jesus Christ says concerning them, *I wish that they were cold* because they would be easier to convert and would receive with humility what he gives. *Or if they were hot*, they would do what he desires. But because *You are lukewarm, and neither cold nor hot, I am about to spit you out of my mouth.* Ah, these are the most frightening words in the world! If you are vomited out, there is no hope, because we never take back what we vomited. A thing thrown out can be taken back, but a thing vomited can never be restored. O this is terrible! These words should cause us to tremble and fear for those living in this nonchalance. Even good souls can at times feel this tepid, but God only allows this for their purification. This is only an outside feeling while the heart still burns inside. Yet these lukewarm people think they are filled with heat, but instead are tepid.

> "For you say, 'I am rich, I have prospered, and I need nothing.'
> You do not realize that you are wretched, pitiable, poor, blind,
> and naked." (Rev 3:17)

This is very strange that tepid people believe that they are richer in graces than others and believe they *have prospered* spiritually. They do not seem to *need* anyone, and they believe that everyone needs them. They would even force everyone to take their advice. The other good pastor mentioned before this one was poor in appearance, but infinitely rich. Yet this latter pastor thought himself rich and yet was *poor* in God and his graces. He is *wretched* because he only loves himself and can never be truly happy. The most essential elements of pure love, which include abandon to God, perfect surrender, submission to the will of God, and possession by God are missing. He is *miserable* because although he appears happy in his exterior, he is under cruel tyranny in his interior by the love of glory and the desire to be esteemed by others, although he is nothing. This is true that when people such as this pastor are shown the slightest contempt or have the slightest affliction, they are absolutely overwhelmed. They are *poor* and *naked*, entirely corrupted because not being clothed by Jesus Christ or animated by his Spirit, they are very poor and naked. They are *blind*, because being in the most wretched state possible, they believe they are doing well.

> "Therefore I counsel you to buy from me gold refined by fire
> so that you may be rich; and white robes to clothe you and to
> keep the shame of your nakedness from being seen; and salve to
> anoint your eyes so that you may see." (Rev 3:18)

O Love, only you can communicate perfect love, which is the *gold refined by the fire*. Only you can put into our soul the spirit of faith, which is a very pure gold. Only you can place in us God's principle for his creatures, which produces perfect works of love, which no fire can damage. Therefore, it is to you that we go to *buy this gold*. But what do you want us to give you for the price, since we are as poor and naked as this pastor? *Come, he* says, *to me with or without money and without any price* (Isaiah 55:1). He only asks that we give ourselves to him, that we abandon to him without reserving anything, so that he makes works full of value. It is he who gives us *white robes* of innocence and simplicity. He reveals this to the souls of his servants when he leads them to adoption as children. This dress of innocence repairs us and covers the shameful nudity of human nature, stripped of the original justice. Before the fall reduced the human being to this shameful nudity, people were clothed in the habit of innocence. With the fall, they knew they were naked. Therefore, we must go to Jesus Christ to be healed, so that he clothes us with himself. Without doubt, he repairs our simplicity and innocence which gives us advantages over even the first state before the fall. The grace of redemption surpasses the grace of creation, and repaired innocence must be more abundant than original innocence. If it were not, the church would not sing, *Felix Culpa O happy sin!* More can be read about this in Romans 5.

Furthermore, Jesus Christ invites us to go to him, so to speak, under the signs of *wine* and *milk*, of love and innocence. For love, he communicates advantages to us that Adam never had. We have complete innocence having washed our robe in his blood. We have been given the first whiteness with a new luster, as in Isaiah he had promised, *Though your sins are like scarlet, they shall be as white as snow* (Isaiah 1:18). Love is now incomparably more abundant. According to the thinking of the church, the apostles in receiving the Holy Spirit were confirmed in grace. This is not the same as Adam's innocent state since he was sinning. Jesus Christ invites everyone to love and innocence.

He adds that he will put *a salve for our eyes* so we see clearly. This salve is no other than the Spirit of faith, which will infallibly deliver us from the blindness of our own reasoning and self-concern. We know then that we are poor when we had thought we were rich. We know then that we are nude when we thought we were clothed.

> "I reprove and discipline those whom I love. Be earnest, there-
> fore, and repent. [20] Listen! I am standing at the door, knocking; if
> you hear my voice and open the door, I will come in to you and
> eat with you, and you with me." (Rev 3:19–20)

The greatest sign of God's love for us is that God warns us of our faults. God *reproves* and *disciplines* us. As for those whom God does not love, he keeps their punishment for the day of his wrath. But *for those whom he loves,* he notes their slightest mistakes and *reproves* them. This is the advantage of prayer. An interior person has within herself a director who relates incessantly, a Master who reproves and chastises continually. It seems that God has no other point in situations than to correct the soul. This is the greatest sign of his love. We must then be *earnest* toward ourselves, to let God punish us with his strength. We remain with him while he punishes us.

> "Listen! I am standing at the door, knocking; if you hear my voice and open the door, I will come in to you and eat with you, and you with me." (Rev 3:20)

So if we hear him approach the door of our heart, we open to him and give ourselves to him without reserve. We consecrate ourselves to him. Jesus Christ *enters* us. But what is the way to *hear his voice* if we do not listen to him? O Love, you speak to the heart and you hear us because you are attentive to the voice of your creatures. Yet creatures are not attentive to you and do not discern your voice. They do not listen to you. But if creatures energetically remain attentive and listen to your voice, they will hear infallibly. The creature will hear that you will come to her which will surprise her because she did not expect such a singular grace.

But what do you say? Jesus Christ is not satisfied with only this. He admits those who listen to his banquet. He shares his feast and his caresses with her. She will be nourished and taste a food forever delicious. O Christians, who are born for such a great good, it is up to you to have this. Will you not be rigorously punished with justice, if you deprive yourself of this by your fault? We falsely believe that this is a grace reserved for very few people and that is it almost impossible to obtain. Yet eternal truth assures us that nothing is easier. What could be easier than to *open* to a person who stands incessantly at your door and knocks continually? To hear and listen to the One who always speaks? There is nothing easier. He asks nothing of us except to open and listen to him, so that he *come in us*, to be forever present and admit us to his feast, to *eat with us*, that is to say, to share our sorrows. We also *eat with him* that is to say, he shares his divine will with us. O the blindness of creatures is immense, that we may have such a great good and yet we refuse and use as an excuse that this is difficult! O, all we must do is reach out our hand! The blindness is great today. What has been the joy, praise, and glory of past centuries and will be in the future, is the shame, confusion, and ignominy of this century.

> "To the one who conquers I will give a place with me on my throne, just as I myself conquered and sat down with my Father on his throne. [22] Let anyone who has an ear listen to what the Spirit is saying to the churches." (Revelation 3:21–22)

The throne of Jesus Christ is the heart of his Father, who has already given him the Word and will give this to him throughout eternity. Through Jesus

Christ's death and victory over hell and nature, humanity has been given the privilege of his Divinity. *Whoever conquers* over nature and demons through Jesus Christ will be received into God and will share his *throne. Whoever has ears,* listen to these things, and understand the goodness and mercy of God for his poor creatures and yet the ingratitude of his creatures who do not want to participate in his goodness and take the trouble to do this.

> After this I looked, and there in heaven a door stood open! And the first voice, which I had heard speaking to me like a trumpet, said, "Come up here, and I will show you what must take place after this." (Rev 4:1)

After Jesus showed us the door of our heart, *he opened* at the same time *the door to heaven,* to show that he will open heaven to those who open their heart. This will come at a time in the future, where the person's heart will be opened and *God's voice will be heard.* O God, as much as you are misunderstood in this century, so much will you be esteemed and followed in future centuries!

> At once I was in the spirit, and there in heaven stood a throne, with one seated on the throne! ³ And the one seated there looks like jasper and carnelian, and around the throne is a rainbow that looks like an emerald. (Rev 4:2–3)

Jesus Christ shows John the *throne* of God and the light of God's majesty so to show the glory he prepares for his elect and to give us a sense of God's holy grandeur. God is *seated* on this throne because his repose is never interrupted. This is One, but we cannot say more but because God has no form or figure and looks like the color of *jasper and carnelian,* which shows his immobility and immutability, the firmness and duration of his glory. The *rainbow that looks like emerald* signifies peace and reconciliation only found in Jesus Christ, as the rainbow signifies. These saved will have the advantage of this reconciliation through hope in the Divine Savior. This rainbow surrounds God as the mark of the humanity of Jesus Christ which covers his Divinity.

> Around the throne are twenty-four thrones, and seated on the thrones are twenty-four elders, dressed in white robes, with golden crowns on their heads. ⁵ Coming from the throne are flashes of lightning, and rumblings and peals of thunder, and in front of the throne burn seven flaming torches, which are the seven spirits of God. (Rev 4:4–5)

The *twenty-four elders* are the holy patriarchs and prophets, the most faithful and cherished by God. From antiquity they are the foundation of the other saints. God showed them to John to let him know the magnificence and the glory that he reserves for those admitted to his feast. The prophet-king David knew something similar when in his transport he exclaimed, *O how great is the multitude of thy sweetness, O Lord, which thou hast hidden for them that fear thee!* (Psalm 30:20). On these magnificent thrones the Son of Man will seat those who have conquered in him and through him. These thrones are reserved for those who leave everything to follow him, as Jesus promised to his apostles when he said, *Truly I tell you, at the renewal of all things, when the Son of Man is seated on the throne of his glory, you who have followed me will also sit on twelve thrones, judging the twelve tribes of Israel* (Matt 19:28). These elders also *dressed in white robes* show that they had been preserved or restored in their innocence by the future grace of Jesus Christ, whose fullness and fulfillment that had not had until after the death of the same Jesus Christ. They had *crowns* of perfect love. O God, what is a human, that you honor him with so many graces and so much glory! Eternal and immortal glory! But, O foolish human, who loses the divine and eternal will for a moment of pleasure which does not even merit the name of pleasure! O ambitious ones who want to be kings in this world, why do you not want to be kings in heaven? O great saints, you are the closest to God, because you look like to no other but the Son of God. You have been the most annihilated. This is why you surround the throne of the one who was annihilated himself, taking the form of a servant and slave. The measure of annihilation is the measure of glory. O David, you occupy one of the highest thrones. We must not doubt it, since it is said of Jesus, that *he will possess the throne of David his father* (Luke 1:32). Jesus Christ did not possess your temporal throne, though he came from your lineage. As David had been on earth the faithful imitation of Jesus Christ, David also imitates him more in glory than any other. The reign Jesus Christ has in David and that David possesses in him will have no end. We cannot comprehend the high degree of glory to which David has been raised through his profound abasement to which he was reduced. Those who are happy enough to participate in the annihilation of these great saints will share in their glory.

There are heretics who recognize many saints in the old law but do not want to recognize them in the new. Yet some believe there were no great saints in the ancient law, because Jesus Christ had not died and resurrected yet. Yet there were saints equally in the ancient law and in the new, all sanctified by the sight of Jesus Christ and the blood that he spread. Others say that we are no longer in the time of the saints, as if the hand of God were shortened. They condemn in the current saints what they admire in those who preceded them under the pretext that we are not in the century of saints. This is a horrible abuse. Let them learn that, although in this century malice is at its height, yet it will be the century where there will be the greatest saints which will continue into future centuries. God takes pleasure in making a multitude of innumerable saints in all times and places of the world. If there were no more saints, the world would perish because God only suffers the unjust because of the righteous. They support God in his works, even when they seem close to ruin. We will see this in heaven.

There are *seven angels*, superior to all the others, who are all light and flames, and are incessantly before the throne of God as *lamps* always *burning* to give homage to the sovereign grandeur. These *Spirits* are the closest to God who has coming out of the *throne voices, light, and thunders*. This marks the supreme majesty of God, his grandeur and his magnificence. O God, as Moses said who had seen the majesty of God, you are *admirable, terrible, merciful, and compassionate* (Exodus 34:6).

> And in front of the throne there is something like a sea of glass, like crystal. Around the throne, and on each side of the throne, are four living creatures, full of eyes in front and behind: [7] the first living creature like a lion, the second living creature like an ox, the third living creature with a face like a human face, and the fourth living creature like a flying eagle. (Rev 4:6–7)

This *sea in front of the throne* signifies the extreme purity needed to reach the throne and unite with the saints and the church. Just like a few drops of water composes part of the sea, all are mixed, joined, and united into one. We no longer distinguish them individually, unless we separate them out drop by drop. This shows the unity of souls who arrive in God. They are all consummated in their unity, although each has its only small droplet. It is necessary that the soul be annihilated in God to reach his throne. The crystal sea shows the unity and purity of their souls.

The *four living creatures, full of eyes* are not only the four Evangelists, who have been filled with the knowledge of Jesus Christ, what he has said and done, so that they can announce it to all. They also signify the four states of the church and of his saints. The *first, the lion* is the state of saints who defended the church and the reign of Jesus Christ with force and vigor and with an invincible courage. These had been elevated and nourished by the lion of the tribe of Judah, Jesus Christ, who gave them an invincible strength. It was the time of the martyrs. *The second creature is like an ox.* This is the Spirit of the time of the confessing saints who made their voices heard to defend the church. The *third represented a man.* This is the time when the saints were employed only to imitate the exterior of Jesus Christ.

These were the lives of solitary and anchorite saints who worked in exterior exercises of piety. And the *fourth* is the one to come which is that of the eagle, that flies over all the others. This is those to whom the interior spirit of Jesus Christ, is communicated. Everything will become interior. It is not that the martyrs did not have the interior, and all the four advantages, noted here. The confessors, the anchorites, and the interiors also participate in the strength and virtues of the interior. But it is because, although these qualities are peculiar to all, they have each excelled in the quality which is particular to them. They are *full of eyes* because they are full of light and knowledge. They have surrounded the *throne* of God.

Each creature symbolizes one of these well-known living creatures. We give John the *eagle* because he is flying higher than anyone else (Ezekiel 17:3). The eagle was in the bosom of divinity and drew marrow from Jesus by discovering through Christ's humanity the benefits of divinity. The eagle has the overview of everything and takes the highest branch to plant it in fertile ground with abundant waters. He searched for what was most profound in Jesus Christ, his eternal generation. It is certain that the time will come that the purest lights will be discovered in the church. The earthly and animal will be gone, and all will be spiritual and divine. People will need the sun, like the eagle, for the pure lights that will be given to them. All animals have eyes but eyes proportionate to what they are. But the eagle has eyes that see without the dazzling lights of the sun. It is here that the special qualities of man are changed into those of an eagle.

These creatures mark the different states through which souls pass before arriving at the throne. The first stage is all fire, vigor, and courage, like the lion. In Psalm 34:10, David seems to compare himself to a lion, *The young lions suffer want and hunger, but those who seek the Lord lack no good thing.* The second animal of ox was like David, when he said, *I am become as a beast before thee: and I am always with thee* (Psalm 72:23). Following this, we lose this quality of beast, and we become, it seems, all human. We have nothing, neither courage nor stupidity, and we lose this animal life and become entirely human. This is more painful than the others because the human is subject to evil and misery. This is the time of the desolation of the cross. But following this, we become an eagle. As much as we had been attached to the earth, now we become just as detached from the earth. It was this light that made David say, *Who satisfies you with good as long as you live so that your youth is renewed like the eagles* (Psalm 103:5). He also says, *O that I had wings like a dove!* (Psalm 55:6). This state removes the soul from the other three states because the first three hold something from the previous state. But this last state of great purity is entirely different and will come soon.

> And the four living creatures, each of them with six wings, are
> full of eyes all around and inside. Day and night without ceasing
> they sing, "Holy, holy, holy, the Lord God the Almighty, who
> was and is and is to come." (Rev 4:8)

The six wings of these animals are the means by which they ascended and
fled to God. Two wings are understanding and faith, two wings are memory
and hope, and two wings are will and love. With these gifts of knowledge and
faith, remembering and hope, will and love, we are brought before the throne
of God. Faith changes into certain knowledge, hope changes into joyful sight,
and the will changes into pure love. The *eyes all around and inside* mark their
exterior and interior illumination. Discovered and penetrated entirely by
light, they are at home. *They sing day and night without ceasing*, which means
they sing equally in the day of pleasure and the night of affliction, both in
the state of interior light and darkness. They sing, *Holy, holy, holy* because in
all time God is equally holy. They surround the throne to give the glory due
because of his holiness. It seems that they say: "You only are holy. We know
no other holiness but yours. Nothing is holy except you. We only desire your
holiness. Because God only is holy, everything else is impure." But where
does singing of this type come from? Only from God's holiness, and the desire that everyone recognize him as such. Jesus Christ is a lion, Prince above
all others, and the martyrs show his courage. The martyrs give all their glory
to the holiness of God. Among the confessors, he is a famous ox whose voice
roared above all the others. Jesus Christ is also a human being among the
solitaries and anchorites, or those who have a rank in the world. Also, Jesus
Christ is the first among the interiors who held the first rank of eagle that will
surpass all others in the elevation of their flight.

These four animals cry incessantly *God is holy* and God is also *the Almighty*. Because he is only holy, he *alone* can make saints. *God was and is
and is to come*. Nothing has been, is, and will be except by God. O God, who
is infinite glory, what can we give you, you who are infinite? As creatures
that you support, we give you all the glory.

> And whenever the living creatures give glory and honor and
> thanks to the one who is seated on the throne, who lives forever
> and ever, [10] the twenty-four elders fall before the one who is
> seated on the throne and worship the one who lives forever and
> ever; they cast their crowns before the throne, singing, [11] "You
> are worthy, our Lord and God, to receive glory and honor and
> power, for you created all things, and by your will they existed
> and were created." (Rev 4:9–11)

These four creatures *give glory and thanksgiving* continually *to the One who is seated on the throne, who lives forever and forever* because the Word has always been and will always be. All the saints will always owe the One much glory and gratitude because to the One is due all the glory of their holiness and sanctification. The Word gave himself for them and sanctified them with his blood. They recognize fully his superabundant and generous mercy.

The twenty-four elders who represent the most annihilated saints closest to God *fall before him.* This abasement of the body shows their entire being is annihilated before God who is everything for them. They give knowledge of God to all future centuries and show that the way to honor God is through their annihilation. They want to do in heaven what they did in earth. *They cast their crowns* again *before the throne* at his feet, to show that he is their king who reigns in them and on them, to continually govern and lead them. They have given him all the rights that they had in themselves and he reigns perfectly in them. And as King, they live in his kingdom. In this way, they glorify God as he wants to be glorified through annihilation and by giving him all their rights that they had in themselves.

They say to God, *"You are worthy, our Lord and God,* to receive glory and honor and power. No one is worthy of you. You are infinitely glorified in yourself and you must be in all your creatures. We owe you honor and homage as our only Sovereign, with all the kingdom and power." They recognize that you are the only power and that you can do everything in them, for them, and by them. All the rest is only weakness.

For you created all things. You have created them anew, giving them a new being and life. All of this is done *by your will* and not by any merit that is in them to attract such a great grace. Created by your power, you renew them in your will. Everything happens in the divine will. When a soul abandons her own will, whatever that may be, she begins to enter a new state and into a new creation.

> Then I saw in the right hand of the one seated on the throne a scroll written on the inside and on the back, sealed with seven seals. (Rev 5:1)

This scroll is no other than Jesus Christ, the man-God. He is *written on the inside and outside* with the truth of God, which he came to bring to the world. Without him this truth would not be known. *On the inside,* as Word, he is the truth of God. *On the outside,* he is the scroll that all humanity must read. The truth has always been hidden in God. O God, you are the only truth, and humanity is full of lies. God creates this truth by generating his Word, because the Word is the faithful expression of himself. Only the Son can represent the Father. The demon is jealous that this truth is communicated to human beings and slipped into the world at the beginning in the lie. Because God is all truth and God only can produce truth in human beings, the demon is all lies and can only produce in human beings lies and vanity, contrary to the truth. So all truth is of God, and all lies and deception are of the demon.

The scroll was *in the right hand of God because the Word is also all the power of God.* As Matthew 28:18 says, *All authority in heaven and on earth has been given to the Word.* In heaven, he is given power to express all the truth of God. On earth, he is given power to manifest this truth to human beings. As John assures us in John 1:14, they *saw the fullness of his grace and his truth.* But as human beings had lost the truth and substituted lies for it, Jesus Christ came to report truth to the world like a *scroll written* on the *inside* with all the interior fullness of God and all the truth of God. Written *on the outside,* the character of divinity is to be imitated by human beings. Then the truth was reestablished in the world, and the lie was chased away. The oracles of the devil, the father of lies, no longer stopped the truth from being revealed. And as Jesus Christ did not remain forever on the earth, after ascending into heaven, he sent the Spirit of his truth in our hearts in order to banish the lie.

This truth has permanently remained since that time on the earth. And where does this remain? In the church. But even though the truth remains in the church, individual people have often diverted and separated from this truth. The truth holds its seat in the three powers of the soul: in the understanding, memory, and will. Very frequently, faith is the only place where the truth lies. But we also need love and hope where Jesus Christ communicates his truth. There are in us, spirit and heart: the spirit is for the common and general belief, while the heart is to receive the anointing and the Spirit of truth, which is the *interior Spirit.* This is why Paul says in his writing, "*The Spirit* of truth *has been poured into our hearts.*" This is the interior Spirit given and received because as Jesus Christ is a scroll written inside and outside in truth, the church is a scroll written inside and outside in truth, and we too must be the same. We are to embrace the *exterior* of the church with its practices, services, and commandments with our faith. We are to let ourselves be led, moved, and governed through divine motion by the truth of the *interior.* We must be written *inside* with the truth and dive motion of the Spirit of Jesus Christ. And *outside* we must be written with Jesus Christ's life, his example, actions, and maxims of all that he practiced externally. By doing this, we will be put in truth.

The scroll is sealed with seven seals because before being in the perfection and fullness of truth, we must pass through seven degrees or states and be filled with seven gifts of the spirit. Also, the world will also pass through them before the consummation of truth in the world. It is an admirable thing that the human being is like a little world in which God delights in drawing in miniature what he has done in the vast expanse of the universe. As God composed his body of natural things and elements, he also created the world and composed it of his Spirit and his interior in a like way that all is in the world, be it political or moral and spiritual, also happens in him.

> And I saw a mighty angel proclaiming with a loud voice, "Who is worthy to open the scroll and break its seals?" ³ And no one in heaven or on earth or under the earth was able to open the scroll or to look into it. (Rev 5:2)

O God, there is no person *in heaven*, not even an angel or the greatest saint, who can *open the scroll*, and was worthy to do this. To open the scroll is no other than to open your bosom. Who can do that, O God, in heaven, on earth, or under the earth? Who is worthy to look into you? For though you show your heart to your servants, no one is worthy to look into it, and they cannot do it by themselves. Who can consider and discover Jesus Christ and his truth? O God, you alone can do this because by looking at your Word, you produce it. But who can look at you? Who can open your bosom and discover your truth? Who can *break* your *seals*, without which you remain always hidden and sealed, and never be manifested to human beings?

We also have in us seven failings that prevent the truth from being manifested in us. No living man or creature may break the seal, as no creature, not even the most perfect angel, can open the bosom of God and manifest his truth.

> And I began to weep bitterly because no one was found worthy to open the scroll or to look into it. ⁵ Then one of the elders said to me, "Do not weep. See, the Lion of the tribe of Judah, the Root of David, has conquered, so that he can open the scroll and its seven seals." (Rev 5:4–5)

O John, are you weeping? What caused your tears will be your greatest joy. The joy of a heart that loves comes from the knowledge that all power is in God. Your tears come from your ignorance for when the mystery is disclosed, you will be filled with joy. One of the elders consoled you, and *said, Do not weep* because the strong and invincible *Lion of the tribe of Judah* of the immortal *Root of David has conquered*. He conquered the lie by his death *to open the scroll* in favor for humanity and to manifest his truth. O God, it seems that in our time the truth is once again banished from the earth and returned to heaven, with so little truth in this world! But the time will come by your strength and power alone, O strong and bold Lion, you will break the seal and open the scroll, and open the new. In breaking the last seal, you show your truth to humanity in a new way. O human beings, who are presently in the lie, the time is coming when truth will have all your glory and your light of day. In his own time, Paul complained that creatures *suppress the truth* (Romans 1:18). Truth is also held captive in the present time. But you, Lord, will free the truth, soon, soon. Before this happens, truth will be tied down by iron. People will believe that they have destroyed truth but suddenly the chains will be broken, the door of the prison opened, and truth will show itself to the people with more brilliance and will fill them with joy and pleasure. The redemption of Jesus Christ will reach all over the earth.

> Then I saw between the throne and the four living creatures and among the elders a Lamb standing as if it had been slaughtered, having seven horns and seven eyes, which are the seven spirits of God sent out into all the earth. (Rev 5:6)

Between the throne and the four living creatures was a *Lamb slaughtered* for the sins of the world. This Lamb without stain has erased all of our iniquities. He let himself be immolated as an innocent victim to send the truth to human beings and let it be manifested to destroy error and lies. The immolated Lamb washed the robe of human beings in his blood, covered them with his wool, and nourished them with his flesh. This holy victim without stain still lives in his immolation *between the creatures and the elders* because it is he who makes the happiness of all the saints and the consummation of all the states. O Lamb who was immolated and died for love, how do all people not die of love for you!

The Lamb has *seven eyes and seven horns*: the seven eyes are the lights of his Spirit and his truth. The seven horns are the abundance of his graces that he distributes to human beings. So it is said, that he was *full of grace and truth* (John 1:14). The graces are *the horns* and the truth *the eyes*. These truths are spread by the *seven* gifts of the *Holy Spirit* and *these spirits* and these graces *are sent out into all the earth* and one day will be received throughout the earth everywhere. There will be *one flock, one shepherd*, one spirit, as Paul says, there is only *One Spirit through all and in all* (Ephesians 4:4–6).

> He went and took the scroll from the right hand of the one who was seated on the throne. [8] When he had taken the scroll, the four living creatures and the twenty-four elders fell before the Lamb, each holding a harp and golden bowls full of incense, which are the prayers of the saints. (Rev 5:7–8)

O Lamb, *you took the scroll from the right hand of the One who sits upon the throne* since you receive the truth from him in his eternal generation. You receive this truth for yourself from the One who begets you. But here, after your temporal birth, and after having been immolated, you receive from your Father the power to communicate this truth to human beings.

The living creatures and the elders fell before the Lamb to show their respect, joy, and recognition that the Lamb will manifest his truth on the earth. The Lamb will remove the chains that holds humanity captive. The *harps* they hold show their praise and the agreement of their will with God's will, to which they have not the least opposition, difference, or contrariety. *The golden bowls are the prayers of the saints.* This shows well how the saints intercede for our brothers and sisters and present their prayers to have God's answer. These prayers are in *bowls of gold* to show that these prayers come from the purest love. These prayers are well described as *a perfume* because the true prayer is that of annihilation. Just as the perfume comes only out of the destruction of the gum sap, our prayers come out of the fire of annihilation which devours us.

> They sing a new song: "You are worthy to take the scroll and
> to open its seals, for you were slaughtered and by your blood
> you ransomed for God saints from every tribe and language and
> people and nation." (Rev 5:9)

The soul in her consummation is placed in a state to *sing a new song* known only to God of deliverance and joy, of happiness and contentment. The soul did not sing before its perfect renewal. She did not even know she was to sing a song that looks at God only as now all the interests of the creature are perfectly annihilated. We can say nothing about this song except it is inexplicable.

They rejoiced that Jesus Christ is *worthy to take the scroll* of truth and *open its seals* that had been hold captive and to manifest it to all the earth. They praise him that he *ransomed* them and all humanity by the price *of his blood* because he ransomed them *for God*, so that they belong to God, removing them from the captivity of the demon and putting them in freedom of the truth. *You ransomed them*, O Lord, to manifest your truth to them, *to all tribes*, that is to say, all Christians and *all people and nations.* There will be no exceptions to this, all religions and all people, including the Jewish and Islamic faiths, and even the most barbarous, will be associated with the sequel to the kingdom of Jesus Christ. They will all receive the Spirit of truth, which will be spread all over the earth. We will see in eternity the wonderful inventions of providence to save all people.

"You have made them to be a kingdom and priests serving our
God, and they will reign on earth." (Rev 5:10)

The annihilated souls are *kings* because they reign over all creatures. They
are in perfect contentment without subjection. They are *priests* who sacrifice
incessantly to God a host of praises. They reign not only in heaven but also
on the earth. Their reign as king begins in this life. O that the ambitious
should have this noble ambition to rule in this way! Their reign would be
full of peace, exempt from all trouble, chagrin, and worry.

> Then I looked, and I heard the voice of many angels surround-
> ing the throne and the living creatures and the elders; they
> numbered myriads of myriads and thousands of thousands,
> [12] singing with full voice, "Worthy is the Lamb that was slaugh-
> tered to receive power and wealth and wisdom and might and
> honor and glory and blessing!" (Rev 5:11–12)

The angels surrounded the throne of God and the living creatures and the elders.
This shows two things. First, there are saints in the rank of angels and even
higher than the angels. Except for the seven spirits, which are the seven lamps
that are always in front of the throne of God, there is no hierarchy where there
are not saints. These blessed spirits have an inexhaustible love for human beings. These innumerable holy spirits continually praise God before the throne
according to the magnificence of the majesty of God. O God, your goodness
is infinite! You are happy throughout eternity. However, as if you had not
been fully satisfied with enjoying yourself, you wanted to create creatures
who could participate in this happiness. You caused an increase in acciden-
tal glory, but not an increase in essential glory. You wanted not only to love
yourself but to make yourself loving. This is the design of creation, to make
creatures capable of loving you and enjoying you, and that you love and enjoy
yourself. You wanted to extend outside what you do inside of yourself. In
contemplation, you engender your Word. In loving, you produce your Holy
Spirit. You have made everyone capable of contemplating and loving which is
the ability that both angels and saints in heaven and human beings on earth
have. You create your own Word in them. You love them and produce your
Holy Spirit in them. Therefore, the end of creation is to make human beings
who love and contemplate. However, some humans believe that loving and
contemplating is an impossible thing for humans and so they condemn this.
Actually, human beings love and contemplate naturally.

They sang in a full voice to be heard in all the earth, that the Lamb
without a stain, *who was killed,* who was immolated for love, *was worthy
to receive sovereign* power, which was due to him through his eternal birth

as God. He is also due sovereign power as conqueror and victor through his death. *The* wealth of *Divinity*, that is to say the glory of God, is on Jesus Christ because his humanity is united with the glory of God. He is due *wisdom* because he is wisdom incarnate and full *power*. He is due *honor, glory, and blessing* for all and in all things.

> Then I heard every creature in heaven and on earth and under the earth and in the sea, and all that is in them, singing, "To the one seated on the throne and to the Lamb be blessing and honor and glory and might forever and ever!" ¹⁴ And the four living creatures said, "Amen!" And the elders fell down and worshiped. (Rev 5:13–14)

This passage helps us see two things, the reunion and harmony of *all creatures* who will one day give God glory due to him with a common voice. It is said, *every creature in heaven and on earth and under the earth and in the sea* sings, that is to say, everybody without exception.

All creatures praise God in their own way. There is not one from whom God does not derive singular glory. All God's creatures recognize that *honor, glory, and power* are in him. All their praises are made in common accord with the angels and saints, all animated and inanimate creatures, on the earth and under the earth where the souls in purgatory are. The children of the furnace, Shadrach, Meshach and Abednego invite all creatures to praise God (Dan 3:52). In Psalm 148, David invites all creatures to praise God. They understand that all creatures can give God a glory and praise that only God knows.

> Then I saw the Lamb open one of the seven seals, and I heard one of the four living creatures call out, as with a voice of thunder, "Come!" ² I looked, and there was a white horse! Its rider had a bow; a crown was given to him, and he came out conquering and to conquer. (Rev 6:1–2)

The *Lamb* begins *to open the seven seals* that close the scroll and prevent the truth from being manifested to human beings. And *one of the four living creatures*, who proclaims the truth and reveals Jesus Christ who confesses and manifests truth, exhorts John to *come* and *look*. It is necessary to *go* to Jesus Christ to discover his wonderful truth. However, we do the opposite. We look for truth in reasoning which is why we do not discover it. We must seek truth in Jesus Christ and abandon ourselves to him for this. Before Jesus Christ came, there were philosophers who made efforts to discover the wisdom and truth. They even called themselves wise, until one more enlightened than all the others made them understand that there was only one God of wisdom. This philosopher Plato said that all wisdom is enclosed in God. But since then we have only had amateurs of wisdom who could not discover either wisdom or truth, until Jesus Christ became incarnate. He who is Incarnate Wisdom reveals wisdom to human beings by becoming a human being. He also brought truth to the earth, which had been banished since the sin of Adam. As Jesus Christ assured Pilate, *For this I was born, and for this I came into the world, to testify to the truth. Everyone who belongs to the truth listens to my* voice (John 18:37). We must go to Jesus Christ for the truth.

Saint Augustine, whose spiritual light was unequaled, sought for truth a long time without finding it, because, as he said himself, he looked for truth in the lie where it was not. But when he looked for truth in Jesus Christ, he found it. This is why David asked God to send his mercy and his truth, that is to say, to send Jesus Christ who brought salvation and truth to the world. This is what makes the living creatures who surround the throne of God like heroes of the truth. They invite him to *come, look,* and discover the truth in Jesus Christ.

Then the Lamb *opens one of the seven seals* to show *a white horse and its rider had a bow.* This is the first state of the soul who is led by Jesus Christ, to whom he wants to show his truth. This is also the first age of the church. This is a state of combat and victory. You conquer and fight with advantage. The *crown* is given for *victory.* You win continually victory after victory, one victory brings another. All the combats have rewards and crowns. The soul sees the work of his hands and has a pile of trophies. Then comes large combats, wars, and repentance. This was the first animal, the lion, who called for the combat.

The first *horse* is *white* because the soul receives here the whiteness of repentance. This first state of combat is very full of sweetness. This is more a victory than a fight because the soul feels so great a facility for everything that it seems that the enemies fall at her approach. Also, the soul is given a bow so it seems that she fights from a distance. She hurts without receiving any injury. We fight the most distant enemies and the enemies of God are stopped, so they do not attack. These were the first fights of the Israelites, where their enemies fell at their feet before they touched them.

> When he opened the second seal, I heard the second living creature call out, "Come!" [4] And out came another horse, bright red; its rider was permitted to take peace from the earth, so that people would slaughter one another; and he was given a great sword. (Rev 6:3–4)

The state of the believer changes with the removal of this *second seal* which prevents the truth from being manifested. This *red horse* does not have the whiteness of the first horse with its peaceful and easy combats. After the opening of the second seal, the soul begins to turn brown, which is more beautiful.

Its rider was permitted to take peace. This is the first test of the soul, which makes her suffer a lot. She loses this sweet peace, this tranquility that caused a favorable presence of God. She is now placed in troubles, fears, and agitations. There is neither crown nor victory for it does not appear to the soul that she triumphs, nor does she fight, but she only feels that they are hurting her. She *was given a great sword,* but this sword works for defense only. She is not allowed to destroy or kill. Everything is hidden from her. This is a mutual war, very different from the first. We attack and are attacked but the wounds we receive are much more painful than the harm we do to the enemy. This is the beginning of the persecution from creatures when we lose peace within and without. And where does God come from? God wants *to take peace from the earth.* God wants the soul to lose peace that she had in herself, so that she leaves herself. This is the ox that calls because the fight is more violent.

> When he opened the third seal, I heard the third living creature call out, "Come!" I looked, and there was a black horse! Its rider held a pair of scales in his hand, ⁶ and I heard what seemed to be a voice in the midst of the four living creatures saying, "A quart of wheat for a day's pay, and three quarts of barley for a day's pay, but do not damage the olive oil and the wine!" (Rev 6:5–6)

The third horse was black. Then the state of the soul becomes even more terrible. No longer brown, this soul is now black as in *I am black and beautiful* (Song of Songs 1:5). There is no more combat. O humanity, *come and look.* The soul no longer fights, and neither is she fought by foreign enemies. It is her own weight that wins. She has in her own hands *a pair of scales.* This signifies that she is not attacked by enemies and no longer has a fight. She does not win anymore and is no longer wounded. She neither attacks nor defends but her own weight wins over everything. She does nothing, but everything is examined by the weight of God. She feels an emptiness and a profound deprivation. If she is given a little passing consolation, which is very rare, it is sold to her so dearly that nothing more can be done. However, it is still forbidden to touch *wine and oil.* That is to say, the soul is again sustained and fortified by a secret unction, by a strong wine and oil, however she does not know this.

When he opened the fourth seal, I heard the voice of the fourth
living creature call out, "Come!" [8] I looked and there was a pale
green horse! Its rider's name was Death, and Hades followed
with him; they were given authority over a fourth of the earth, to
kill with sword, famine, and pestilence, and by the wild animals
of the earth. (Rev 6:7–8)

The *fourth living creature* is the eagle whose name is *Death*. It seems to me
that there is something different about this, which is, that this bird next to
the sun, to whom truth is revealed more than any other, is called however to
see Death. What do you mean? Death alone can give the benefit of receiving
truth and life. Death was seated on *a pale horse* to show that this has terrors
and fears. Hell follows Death because Death would be nothing in itself if it
did not have such a fatal consequence. It seems that the soul who is in this
state has an infallible loss, and that the moment of her death will precipitate
her into hell. She is not deceived about this because she often experiences a
purgatory so terrible that it is an entire living hell. Yet this Death has only
the power to attack *a fourth of the earth*, that is to say, the principal and last
part. Or it might be, it begins with the fourth part, or the inferior part. This
is the one who tests all these things.

But what sorts of inventions does Death use to kill? Four types of inventions. The first is *the sword* that are blows, spikes, and pains most sensitive.
Following this is another type of torture, whose pain is less alive and less
sensitive, but it is more cruel, profound, and extended. This is the *famine* for it
is necessary to know that if God did not mix these four together, there would
always be some part in the human being who would take life. Simultaneously God pierces and penetrates on all sides by swords and double blows; he
deprives the soul of any support, consolation, or force. Finally, the soul falls
into deprivation and the failure of famine. This languor deprives the soul of
all support and life. When these blows and the famine are joined together,
we have the *contagious disease*, that fills us with misery and weakness and
sometimes sins appear. O poor creature, what will you be in this state? You are
continually beaten, wounded, and deprived of support. Furthermore, you are
sent diseases, which cause the greatest weakness. Everything goes by degrees
until death consumes the great quartet of parts of the earth, *a fourth of the
human being* in the exterior, the interior senses, the powers, and the foundation (Vulgate translation). First, there are the exterior and sensitive blows.
Secondly, there is a deprivation of strength and support. But not content just
to withdraw strength and support, next a contagious disease is sent who completely destroys all the forces and consumes those who were saved from the
sword and famine. But if this were only a little, there remains a man's figure,

and some hope for help and hope, when suddenly the *wild beasts*, the beasts of the earth come to devour and engulf this poor soul, so that nothing remains. There is then a strange persecution from the beasts, which are joined to these three states that carry the soul, which makes her more sensitive, increases the pain, and finally devours her. Besides this, she feels this strangely. Often nature, like a ferocious beast, devours itself. All these evils united together cause *death*. O God, you have the strangest inventions to destroy creatures who are yours without reservation.

Those weak spirits who believe that these three states are imaginary are wrong. You have to actually pass through them. That is why it is not wise to let these souls read these things, unless that they are very advanced and have a proven strong spirit.

> When he opened the fifth seal, I saw under the altar the souls of
> those who had been slaughtered for the word of God and for the
> testimony they had given. (Rev 6:9)

My God, how beautiful is this passage! When the soul is annihilated by a complete, continual, and total sacrifice, the corrupt human nature and sins are destroyed, *the souls of those who had been slaughtered for the word of God are under the altar*. This does not mean only the martyrs who suffered in the body, but those who suffer for the interior—those who are killed in their honor by the denouncement and calumnies of others. Others strangely persecute interior people and feel that this is just to do so. And why do they do this to them? *For the word of God* because they announce the truth. *The testimony they had given* is founded on the truth they feel in their depth. The Spirit bears witness to our being God's children, the interior Spirit. That is what causes all the persecutions that happen to them.

> They cried out with a loud voice, "Sovereign Lord, holy and true,
> how long will it be before you judge and avenge our blood on
> the inhabitants of the earth?" (Rev 6:10)

God hides for a long time the persecution that is done to his servants because he uses these persecutions to destroy and annihilate his children. It seems that God is putting himself for a time in the party of their persecutors. But then comes another time when these unencumbered souls cry for vengeance: The Spirit asks this for them.

But in what way do they ask for this vengeance? You, *Lord*, they say, *holy and true*, you know all the evil that we have suffered, we have honored your holiness with a supreme worship. We have done this in you alone, and we have let ourselves be destroyed for you.

We have confessed your truth; we have the task of making it known to people. This is what has caused the evil. We are the martyrs of your holiness and the truth, and the truth you have in yourself is manifested in our souls. Just as in the primitive church there were martyrs of the faith, now in the last times we are martyrs of your truth and your holiness.

God has suffered as sacrificial victim on his *altar* and if these souls are *underneath*, it is not only to cry vengeance. But, O God, what vengeance do you make for those who have treated them this way? For a while it seems you hide the evil that they have suffered, and that you take the part of this outrage. But the time will come, the time comes, that God will ask again for the last drop of this blood from the *inhabitants of the earth*, that is to say, those motivated by self-love who have spread the martyr's blood.

> They were each given a white robe and told to rest a little longer, until the number would be complete both of their fellow servants and of their brothers and sisters, who were soon to be killed as they themselves had been killed. (Rev 6:11)

These servants of God have suffered much from strange persecutions. After these things, I say, *they will be given* a new life and the *white robe* of innocence. They are delivered from all evils, I mean for those who stay alive, and none of the creatures can cause them pain. They take no vengeance on others. *They are told to rest a little longer* in a profound peace that they feel inside despite the persecutions, *until their brothers and sisters,* those who are united in a particular manner, *suffer the same persecutions as they themselves had been persecuted* because these people too must pass through the same states.

Vengeance will not be done until all those who must suffer these things will have suffered them. They will however be clothed with glory and immortality. In the right time, there will be just punishment and truth will be manifested in the world. The souls are given a white robe and begin entering into truth.

> When he opened the sixth seal, I looked, and there came a great earthquake; the sun became black as sackcloth, the full moon became like blood, [13] and the stars of the sky fell to the earth as the fig tree drops its winter fruit when shaken by a gale. (Rev 6:12–13)

Here God makes known to us through John the way he conducts his servants and also shows us the punishment for the wicked who persecute his servants. This passage communicates many things simultaneously. First, he shows us some of what will happen at the end of the world and describes this. We see clearly here what the events will be.

Secondly, we see the vengeance that God will take on those who persecute his holy servants in their lives or by martyring them. It is certain that God will put those people who have persecuted his servants in a strange fright. They will see the harm that they have done. The truth will be shown to them as well as their crimes, and the wrong they have done by persecuting the servants of God. *The sun* of their spirit *will become black* and the *moon* which is like their memory will only depict *bloody*, tragic, and disastrous things to them. *The blood* of Abel which they have spread will be represented to their spirit because Abel was from the beginning of the world the figure for interior souls who love purely. On the other hand, Cain was the figure for self-love and proprietary persons who persecute pure love. Because Abel made a pure sacrifice what he did was precious and he was received with pleasure whereas Cain would not serve others. Cain persecuted Abel and became Abel's executioner. This happens also in our day, but the blood of Abel cries out incessantly. It seems that people like Cain become all brutal and earthy. *The stars in the sky fall to the earth*, that is to say, the light of humans becomes darkness, and they take the qualities of a brute.

Thirdly, he describes certain states in which God tests some souls through his grace and mercy to show the rigors of his justice. This last meaning is for those souls in whom God is pleased to exercise both mercy and the rigors of justice. First, all their inferior part is placed in trouble and combustion with strange frights. They feel God's justice in all its rigors. The *sun* of justice which illuminated them so wonderfully is hidden and obscured. In the place of sweet lights and favorable influences, there is only darkness. *The moon* turns into blood. There are only thoughts of carnage and images of death. The graces seem to fall to the ground.

> The sky vanished like a scroll rolling itself up, and every mountain and island was removed from its place. [15] Then the kings of the earth and the magnates and the generals and the rich and the powerful, and everyone, slave and free, hid in the caves and among the rocks of the mountains, [16] calling to the mountains and rocks, "Fall on us and hide us from the face of the one seated on the throne and from the wrath of the Lamb; [17] for the great day of their wrath has come, and who is able to stand?" (Rev 6:14–17)

Following the two explanations that have begun to be made, we can say the following. First, as for those who have persecuted the saints, *the sky will vanish*, all help from heaven and hope from heaven will vanish. *Like a scroll rolling itself up*, hope seems to be withdrawing from them, because there is a point of sin without mercy. Often persecuted people get the conversion of their persecutors who enter into knowledge of the appalling pain they caused. They ask *the mountains* to *hide them* as they seek everywhere a place of refuge.

Those who through an excess of God's mercy also feel the strong rigor of God's justice, experience also the same thing, but in a different way. The *sky vanishes like a scroll rolling itself up*. There is no more sky for them. All hope is removed from them. But when the sky rolls in this way, it will unfold, they will find it all the more favorable, since it seemed to them more rigorous. Until then they will be in an inconceivable desolation without refuge. It even seems that their spirit is *shaken*. If they think they can hide in some mountain, that is to say, to find some consolation in people who are like *mountains* because of the eminence of their graces, and like *rocks* by their immobility, everything has been changed into pain and crosses. The pains become very bad and violent, so that they say, O let the mountains fall on me! The slightest relief given to them torments them because they continually see God's anger toward them. This anger of God who pursues them everywhere is an intolerable torment. Jesus Christ appears only as a lamb whose sweetness is changed into fury. Whatever way these people turn, they see the impression of the anger of God who pursues them without mercy.

O God, what a strange torment for such a soul! If hell even opened, the soul would throw herself into it. Hell is preferred to this anger of God. She would tear herself apart if she were allowed but it is not given her to do. Far from appeasing, all she can do seems to anger God. She initially makes some attempt, but seeing the futility of her efforts, she is forced to cease and rest and to suffer the terrible torment only to satisfy God. There is no such horrible state in all life. It is a state for very strong souls. This is the state of Jesus Christ in the Garden of Gethsemane, when he bore the sins of all humanity. He carried the anger of his Father in an excessive manner proportionate to be God, a state that could have consumed a million creatures. It was this terrible state that made him sweat blood. Ah, *who will survive* in such a terrible state? It is necessary that God raises the soul with a superhuman force to carry this in the way I have just described. It is necessary that the mystical incarnation be made after the resurrection. The souls must be in a state not only to bear the states of Jesus Christ but to carry Jesus Christ himself in his states.

> And after these things I saw four angels standing on the four
> corners of the earth, holding the four winds of the earth, that
> the wind should not blow on the earth, nor on the sea, nor on

any tree. ² And I saw another angel ascending from the east,
having the seal of the living God: and he cried with a loud voice
to the four angels, to whom it was given to hurt the earth and
the sea, ³ Saying, Hurt not the earth, neither the sea, nor the
trees, till we have sealed the servants of our God in their fore-
heads. (Rev 7:1–3)

When God wants to punish the persecutors of his servants, or he wants to
exercise justice for those souls who are entirely devoted to him, God stops
all the sweet and consoling influences from wherever they come, either interior or exterior, from God, creatures, or one's self. When God wants to
punish the malicious persecutor, he stops all inspirations and graces. And
why? It is not that God does this to prevent the sinner from converting but
lest the sinner misuses these graces.

But before the fury of God is exercised on the guilty, so that the saints
are not included in the punishment of the guilty and so that the demon has
no power over the saints, God *marks them with his seal.* The saints now
have almost no temptations because after the soul has suffered many combats by the power of God, the powers of the demon are weakened. God
protects, guards, and marks them with his seal. The demon and sins no longer approach them, because they have been renewed and their robes have
been washed in the blood of the Lamb. They *will not harm them* and in the
general punishment on the universal Day of Judgement, in the day for his
vengeance, the faithful will not be part of this.

And I heard the number of those who were sealed, one hundred
forty-four thousand, sealed out of every tribe of the people of
Israel. (Rev 7:4)

The Spirit of God gives the soul the *mark* of the *seals* and the character of the
divine, which are the signs of all interior people. In the judgment, they will
not be found guilty or punished. The more depravity and malice there are in
the century, the servants of God are more raised in holiness and numbers.
God takes pleasure to make by a pure effect of his mercy this counterbalance
to the rigor of his justice.

God takes pleasure in showing mercy to the whole world and to the
individual soul. When the lower part of the soul experienced a terrible baseness, humiliating and unsettling, the senses and passions revolt. Then God
marks the center, the supreme part of the soul, with his seal so that it is not
damaged. So great is the separation of the two parts of the soul, that one is
never quieter than when the other is the most agitated.

There are no countries or nations where there are no servants of God, interior people who worship the Father in spirit and in truth. These interior people are marked with the seal and the character of divinity, which is simplicity and unity. O Love, we will know only in eternity the number of interior souls that you have sealed and marked. They are the *children of Israel*, who have been released from the ruin of Egypt.

> After this I looked, and there was a great multitude that no one could count, from every nation, from all tribes and peoples and languages, standing before the throne and before the Lamb, robed in white, with palm branches in their hands. [10] They cried out in a loud voice, saying, "Salvation belongs to our God who is seated on the throne, and to the Lamb!" (Rev 7:9–10)

The saints marked by the character of God in their interior are a *great multitude that no one could count*. O God, there will be no places, no country, no nations, in which you do not exercise your mercy. We will only see in eternity the grandeur and the extent of your mercy that surpasses all that we may say. All the saints *are standing* which shows their firmness, consistency, and the state of their immobility. They are *robed in white*, because they have been renewed and dressed in the robe of innocence. They are all enlightened by the truth because all these states that have been described, all these seals that were opened, were opened only for the sake of truth. And what is this truth so sealed, hidden, and unknown? It is that *salvation belongs to our God* only. God alone makes salvation and operates in the soul. It is God, say these saints, *who saved us* by his goodness. To God only belongs the glory. The theme of the saints in heaven will be God's eternal gracious actions. They sing forever, "Salvation belongs to our God!" O God, how is it possible that the truth of heaven, which is the happiness and joy of the saints, passes for falsity and chimeras on the earth!

> And all the angels stood around the throne and around the elders and the four living creatures, and they fell on their faces before the throne and worshiped God, [12] singing, "Amen! Blessing and glory and wisdom and thanksgiving and honor and power and might be to our God forever and ever! Amen." (Rev 7:11–12)

The human beings' advantage over the angels is the humans' ability to suffer for God. But the angels have an advantage over human beings which is not to sin in their continual annihilation. If a human arrives in the state of continual annihilation, she participates in the happiness of an angel. This is what John means when he writes, *They fell on their faces*, that is to say, they remain in a continual annihilation, *before the throne* of God. The angels *stood before the throne*, which is their state of impeccability. *They fell down* which is their state of annihilation.

In annihilation, human beings stand in the singular grace of the happiness of angels. They *fall* because they are annihilated. Impeccability by grace only comes from annihilation. Some angels in heaven at the beginning of the world were strengthened in their annihilation to rise against God. That is what made them sin and precipitated them into hell. If an angel or a saint in heaven weakens in annihilation, they leave their impeccability. If a human being leaves her state of annihilation for even a moment, she will be in sin and fault. If she is promptly re-established, her sins are light. Even though the release from annihilation would have made her commit sin, her re-establishment in the state of annihilation puts her in grace and erases her sins. If the loss of her annihilation is long, her sins become longer and more grievous. If a soul, who was annihilated, never returns to her annihilation, she could no longer come out of her sin, and would fall from abyss to abyss and precipice to precipice.

There are four figures in scriptures that show the sin of leaving annihilation. These are the sin of angels, the second Adam, the third David, and the fourth Saul. First, the angel Satan came out of his annihilation and sinned but as he was established by this moment forever in the state which he had deliberately embraced, he left annihilation forever, without means of ever returning to it. Satan never left his sin.

Second, the man Adam first left and then returned to his annihilation. As it says, *You are dust, and to dust you shall return* (Genesis 3:19).

Third, David left his annihilation. What happened to David, this just man who lived according to the heart of God but left his annihilation? Scripture says, David *was walking about on the roof of the king's house*, there he *walked* out and withdrew from annihilation. What happened to him? He became complacent and sinned. It seems that this release from annihilation gives immediate life to the senses and passions. But when David was restored to grace, what does he say about himself? That he was greatly reduced as well as humbled and humiliated. When we are annihilated, we enter into God. When we leave our annihilation, we leave God. David said, *I am become as a beast before you but I am always attached to* you. And in another place, *For you bless the righteous, O Lord; you cover them with favor as with a shield* (Psalm 5:12).

Fourth, Saul left his obedience to the Lord and his annihilation. He remained in his rebellion and sin and never returned to his annihilation.

The annihilated person does not sin if she remains in her annihilation. As it is written, *My substance is as nothing before thee. And indeed all things are vanity* (Psalm 38:6 Douay-Rheims 1899 translation). This is to say that the human who lives within herself and consequently is not annihilated is an abyss of vanity and sin. But the annihilated person does nothing that displeases God because she resists nothing in the will of God. If someone resists the will of God, she is either not annihilated or she goes out of her annihilation.

Excluding sin absolutely, annihilation makes the greatest glory for God. Truly no one can worship God except through annihilation because this surrenders our being in homage to the sovereign being of God. That is why we use external prostration in our body to worship and show the prostration and annihilation of the Spirit. Is it not said of the three Magi, *They knelt down and paid him homage* (Matthew 2:11)? This was the grace of annihilation given to them at the nativity. All the way it took for them to get to Jesus Christ shows the spiritual way it takes to get to Jesus Christ. But when they arrived at him, Jesus Christ communicated to them the grace of annihilation, which is that of true worship and adoration. Jesus Christ, who was the model for all prayer, habitually prostrated himself on the earth to worship. The point is not so much to teach us an external posture to pray as it is to mark the state of our soul must be in when we pray and worship. In this state of annihilation, we give God all the glory that a creature can give to her Creator.

This is why the angels say, *All Blessing and glory and wisdom and thanksgiving and honor and power and might be to our God*. Only annihilation can do this with purity. First, annihilation gives God *blessing* because it recognizes God beyond all praise. Secondly, it gives him *glory*, the grandest that we can give, which is the glory due to the one and only sovereign being. God alone *is*. Therefore, God's character is that he is very jealous and makes many *actions of grace*. Because she remains in her annihilation, she recognizes that all is in God and all comes from God. From annihilation, she gives to God all the acts of grace which she can possibly do. She returns to him sovereign *honor* and the worship of God by honoring God. Also, when Jesus Christ wanted to teach us to honor God in God, what did he do? *He annihilated himself, taking the form of a slave* (Philippians 2:7). From annihilation, he has rendered to God so great a homage that even with all God is, he cannot receive a greater homage. We give him back the power since by the annihilation we are all in God's will and we do not resist this. Then God's will makes us as happy as those in heaven. God who created all things from nothing uses this same nothing to do the greatest things. Until the person comes to this state of nothing, God cannot use her, because the person is always in a position to rob God of his glory.

Finally, we need to see that all *power* is in God. In annihilation, there is no being, life, or subsistence. O God, I desire all creatures always to honor you by annihilation.

> Then one of the elders addressed me, saying, "Who are these, robed in white, and where have they come from?" [14] I said to him, "Sir, you are the one that knows." Then he said to me, "These are they who have come out of the great ordeal; they have washed their robes and made them white in the blood of the Lamb." (Rev 7:13–14)

When the soul is annihilated, then she is dressed in the robe of innocence. To be made a new creature in Jesus Christ, she must enter into annihilation, without which she still holds on to the old nature, conserving her impurities and imperfections. But when God sends the Spirit to annihilate this soul gradually, she is created anew. When this dust of a human being, which by its sin had taken a form other than that which God had given it, is returned to her dust in annihilation, then God creates her again and makes her into a new creature in Jesus Christ clothed in the *white robe* of innocence. But alas! We only reach a state so happy only by the most profound annihilation and we are only annihilated by the most extreme afflictions. The martyrs who gave their lives had to be annihilated. Life's quickly raised cruel torments are short in comparison to that which must be suffered in annihilation. God spares nothing, either interior or exterior. O God, what inventions you make to destroy and annihilate a soul that abandons herself to you without reserve? Yet the soul after annihilation reenters in a state of the first innocence. Jesus calls us and returns us to the bosom of annihilation, which we had left.

Therefore, the souls that are *robed in white* are the annihilated souls but *where have they come from?* They have come out of themselves. After having passed through annihilation and total destruction, they finally arrive here. Their robe was dirtied with sin and covered with the dust of combat. They were red through *afflictions*, ignominy, poverty, and miseries through which they had passed. Through their loss of themselves and entering the state of annihilation, *their robe* has been made *white in the blood of the Lamb*. O fortunate souls, having such a wonderful good! Your sins that were scarlet are now as white as snow. God converts the evil into good and makes his grace abound where the sins abounded. O blood of the divine Lamb without stain, you save by reestablishing the soul in a wonderful purity! Those who are whitened in this way are happy, no longer bearing and feeling their miseries because you have given them a light-filled state that only you can give. Those who no longer find strength, purity, or holiness in themselves are forced to leave themselves and become annihilated by total abandonment in the sea of the blood of the Lamb, which strengthens them with an inconceivable purity. O whoever finds this salvation is happy! Ah purity that surpasses even that of innocent Adam! This is the effect of the superabundant redemption of Jesus Christ. O brothers and sisters, if you want to be cleansed, throw yourself into his purity, and you will lose your dirt, and be given divine purity.

> For this reason they are before the throne of God, and worship him day and night within his temple, and the one who is seated on the throne will shelter them. [16] They will hunger no more, and thirst no more; the sun will not strike them, nor any scorching heat. (Rev 7:15–16)

The annihilated soul is in an intimate and permanent union with God. She is always *before the throne of God* and she is herself God's throne. She serves God *day and night* as God wants this soul to serve him by doing all his will. God does not need any creature and with God's perfect independence, what service can she give him? And where does she serve God? In her interior, which is the *temple of God* because we must not believe that it is an exterior service that God wants. She does what God asks from her which is to remain in a continual union of will with God, the greatest service that she may render God. This was the service that Jesus Christ rendered God while he was on earth.

But these souls are perfectly recompensed for their work! Where do they arrive? The same *One who is seated on the throne* makes a throne of their heart. *He lives* and remains with them in a permanent manner *inside them*, as he has promised in the gospel. Jesus says, *Those who love me will keep my word, and my Father will love them, and we will come to them and make our home with them* (John 14:23).

They will hunger no more and thirst no more and have full satisfaction. As they no longer have their own wills, they have no desires, tendencies, and inclinations. They are no longer *scorched by the heat* of passions, which bothers those who are not well annihilated. They are not harmed by the heat of sin or concupiscence. They are in refreshment and joy. O state, which none can comprehend except those who experience it! The soul who arrives here is placed in truth because truth and annihilation are the same thing.[1] Truth is the expression, and annihilation is the operation. She remains with

---

1. Guyon's footnote says, "Truth is the expression of reality, and annihilation is the one that produces it by its operation. Truth is the exhibition of reality and annihilation is what operates it, produces it, and what makes truth come."

the all of God and stays in her nothingness. No one will ever be in the truth, except by annihilation.

> For the Lamb at the center of the throne will be their shepherd;
> "he will lead them to springs of living water." "And God will
> wipe away every tear from their eyes." (Rev 7:17)

The *Lamb* without stain, Jesus Christ, to whom they are surrendered with any reservation, *who leads them* and places these souls in such a happy and sublime state. He serves as their Pastor having led them through the frightful deserts and the dry aridity of pure faith. They have endured all these afflictions which he has suffered with them. He led them with his cross through dreadful and terrible places, where they saw nothing by abysses and precipices, where they found little water or herbs for food. He led them by annihilation into the breast of God, who is *the spring of living water.* There he gives them water to drink because as his Father is the source, he is himself the spiritual torrent flowing from this source. He becomes their living and life-giving bread and nourishes them with his flesh and the water of his blood. It is there that God *wipes every tear from their eyes,* which ends their afflictions and evils. There is only peace and joy in the Holy Spirit.

> When he opened the seventh seal, there was silence in heaven
> for about half an hour. ² And I saw the seven angels who stand
> before God, and seven trumpets were given to them. ³ Another
> angel, who had a golden censer, came and stood at the altar. He
> was given much incense to offer, with the prayers of all God's
> people, on the golden altar in front of the throne. ⁴ The smoke of
> the incense, together with the prayers of God's people, went up
> before God from the angel's hand. (Rev 8:1–4)

Who would believe that after the soul has arrived and has been put in truth, there is still a seal to open? It seems like everything is done. It is true that everything has been done to the soul, since she is annihilated, but the truth has not been heard in her. There is still a seal, which is the mission to manifest this truth to others. Before this happens, the soul is placed in a new state of silence. There is a profound silence and an increase of peace throughout the soul.

The seven trumpets are *given to seven angels who stand before God,* designating the facility which is given to the soul to announce truth on the earth. Then she is given the mediation to pray and intercede for others through her interior prayers. Our brothers and sisters on earth should see that the saints and angels intercede for us through prayers to God.

The saints offer the prayers in a *golden censer*, which means a pure will holds the prayers. Before God, these *prayers are accompanied* by continual sacrifices, like *incense* and perfume ascending to God. This is like Genesis 8:21 when the Lord smelled the pleasing odor of Noah's sacrifice before leaving the Ark. The will contains this state of sacrifice and prayers. By means of pure love, the will melts and dissolves like incense gum over fire and mounts continually before God. This is what the bride says in Song of Songs 3:6, *What is that coming up from the wilderness, like a column of smoke, perfumed with myrrh and frankincense?* *The Spirits before the throne of* God re-unite these prayers made in different places by different people. This is the communion of the faithful, whose prayers become united. All the prayers are *offered to God on his* altar because they are all in his will. This prayer is a pure and simple prayer. We content ourselves with bringing everything together in God's will by recollection, or rather, by the abandon of faith itself into the hands of God. The fire of God's love melts and dissolves almost all that is in the soul that could prevent her from flowing into her God. When this is done, she *goes up to him* like *smoke* and is lost in God. This is true prayer that is made by abandoned and annihilated souls. This is why is it added, *The smoke of the incense, together with the prayers of God's people, went up before God from the angel's hand.* The soul rises in God through the union of sacrifice and prayer.

> Then the angel took the censer and filled it with fire from the altar and threw it on the earth; and there were peals of thunder, rumblings, flashes of lightning, and an earthquake. (Rev 8:5)

When God spreads his pure love on the earth, the *angel* who has this commission *takes the censor*, which is, the will and the heart of the human being who makes the prayer with a purified will. The angel takes the *fire* of holy love *from the altar* of the will of God, and *throws it on the earth*, which means, into the proper capacity of the praying soul. The *fire* spreads into the soul and then goes back to the altar of God, uniting the soul with God. This smoke rises even higher than the blessed spirits that hold the censor.

But what happens when these blessed Spirits throw this holy fire with loving smoke on the earth? It makes *thunders, rumblings*. Persecutions and strange murmurings start against interior and grace-filled souls. It seems as if everything is lost. The same soul trembles in the inferior part, to see so much damage, although her foundation is full of joy. However, Divine Savior, you told us, *I came to bring fire to the earth, and how I wish it were already kindled!* (Luke 12:49). It is always this way. This fire comes on earth and creatures murmur. O divine fire, which nothing can extinguish! Neither the noise of the torrents and rivers or the great waters have been able to kill you! *Many waters cannot quench love, neither can floods drown it* (Song 8:7). The noise thunders, cries, and talks, but we remain blessed to be consumed and on fire.

> Now the seven angels who had the seven trumpets made ready
> to blow them. (Rev 8:6)

God's fire on earth animates apostolic human beings to announce his truth and to unite with this fire to destroy the natural human. This happens to people who embrace supernatural human life. But if all these noises are made for a few people who embrace the interior life, how much more will it be when this Spirit is spread to all the earth? When will Jesus Christ command this fire, which he himself brings, to burn all the world? O God, what a disorder, a storm, thunder will happen at that time? All nature will shriek horrible alarms and arm itself to prevent this because this brings ruin. The demon will join with it to make a strange destruction, because the demon recognizes that if once the fire wins the whole earth, his empire is absolutely destroyed. The demon will then be chained and closed in an abyss. O, that this fire will burn! O mystery, mystery so close to us, in the midst of us! You are not known! The fire is already ready to fall and that is why we hear the excited noise. O nature! O demon! You will not be the strongest. O human being, what are you doing? You take the side of nature and demons while believing that you take the side of God! You fight for yourself against yourself. You are enemies of your own repose because you will never rest until these two enemies are destroyed.

> The first angel blew his trumpet, and there came hail and fire,
> mixed with blood, and they were hurled to the earth; and a third
> of the earth was burned up, and a third of the trees were burned
> up, and all green grass was burned up. (Rev 8:7)

When apostolic humans begin to preach and teach the truth, this fire will have to fall to consume all people, because the victory which Jesus won over all the princes of the world will have its full extent. When his pure Spirit and sacrifice spreads on the earth and when his truth will be announced, *there came hail* and storms. It will seem that the whole earth will arm itself to prevent this, and that *the fire*, or the wrath of those who persecute this spirit of sacrifice, will not be appeased. They will spread the blood of those who have God's Spirit. God permits this as he once spread the blood of the martyrs throughout the earth. This blood holds a seed of the interior Spirit that will be spread throughout the earth. This will cause very great damage because fear, dread, and torments will *burn up a third part* of those who have already received the first fruit of this Spirit of sacrifice.

When this day arrives generally in the world, those who live then will see it and if these writings still remain, those in whose hands they fall, will know that they have been told the truth. The same will happen also in the soul of those in whom the truth of Jesus Christ must be manifested. This *falls on them* like *hail* of exterior and interior suffering, yet these sufferings are very superficial. The world is alarmed about and against them. The faithful burn with a *fire* of love, but it is a *fire mixed with blood* in two ways. This fire breathes only repentance and we want to be in this breath. Yet this pure fire of God mixed with blood is not damaged by matter or mixed with the senses. However, this fire consumes the vigor of the senses little by little, which is like *green grass. It burns* also *the trees*, which are the productions of the same earth. The fire of God burns and transforms the senses of human beings.

> The second angel blew his trumpet, and something like a great mountain, burning with fire, was thrown into the sea. [9] A third of the sea became blood, a third of the living creatures in the sea died, and a third of the ships were destroyed. (Rev 8:8–9)

When the first herald destroys the vigor of the exterior senses, the second herald destroys the vigor of the interior senses. *The fire* which has descended on the soul seems to win the powers but then is damaged in the sea, which is the will who *converts it into blood*. This blood is the abundance of tears caused by the vehemence of this fire, which produces a painful and crucifying love. Then the interior senses, which had been full *of life*, and increased the life of the powers, find themselves as dying and *dead*. The soul loses all ease of feeling, tasting, seeing, hearing, and touching. All is lost. This causes pain and begins the second death which is *a third of the ships were destroyed* which are *a third* part of the supports that she had in herself is entirely destroyed. This crucifying love is stronger than the other.

We need to know that the apocalypse is not only as one imagines, a revelation of the Last Judgment but is also a prophesy of what will arrive in the church of God, especially in the last times, where the church must spread through all the earth, where the scroll of the truth must be manifested all over.

The scroll is written both outside and inside, because it is the interior and the exterior of Jesus Christ and his church, that must be manifested everywhere. Therefore, when this interior and exterior truth is revealed to all human beings, the signs, so described, will be found in a literal manner but also according to the meaning that it pleases the Holy Spirit to give.[2]

---

2. I am afraid that it will be said that these things happen, at least most of it, in the literal sense. But, patience! We will see this arrive assuredly as I describe it. There is already a part of it arrived since the four years that this book has been written. October 1688.

THE APOCALYPSE OF THE APOSTLE JOHN

Before this time, *a mountain* of wrath and fury, *the fire* will be *thrown into the sea*. This mountain of entirely spiritual fire will be thrown into the church, which is the sea where St. Peter fished. Human beings who will be powerful in resources and in words will rise up and *change the third part of* the sea into *blood* of carnage, tears and afflictions. Then *a large number of living creatures will perish*, that is to say, one-third will die and leave the way of God and live only in themselves. Yet those who are not dead will be neither shaken nor corrupted, but the third part of the support will perish that they had to sail on the sea. O God, this will be for your glory. Those to whom your light is given will be seen. These are the first two heralds of truth.

> The third angel blew his trumpet, and a great star fell from heaven, blazing like a torch, and it fell on a third of the rivers and on the springs of water. [11] The name of the star is Wormwood. A third of the waters became wormwood, and many died from the water, because it was made bitter. (Rev 8:10–11)

As soon as the third herald of truth *blew his trumpet*, then *a great star fell from heaven* which had served as guide and way. This is the time of the death of propriety, when human understanding and knowledge fails. The rivers of graces and consolations change into *bitterness* and sorrows. This is still only *the third part bitter*, however it seems that everything is turning bitter. Yet the spirit of propriety will never die except by the fall of this great star.

When the third herald of truth speaks then a *star*, which is a great light in the church, *falls* and all changes into the bitterness of persecution of the church. The rivers, which are abandoned souls, are filled with bitterness because this star is called *Wormwood*. The star must fall on the soul's *rivers* and torrents, who by a total abandonment constantly run to their end. It falls on her *springs*, which are always full of the water of grace to distribute to others. All will be *changed into bitterness* and gall, because of the fall of this star. *A great number* of souls will die in these bitter waters. The persecution will cause many to leave the way because the rivers and springs will be in bitterness. O God, support your church!

> The fourth angel blew his trumpet, and a third of the sun was struck, and a third of the moon, and a third of the stars, so that a third of their light was darkened; a third of the day was kept from shining, and likewise the night. [13] Then I looked, and I heard an eagle crying with a loud voice as it flew in midheaven, "Woe, woe, woe to the inhabitants of the earth, at the blasts of the other trumpets that the three angels are about to blow!" (Rev 8:12–13)

O God, what pain and what desolation the fourth herald of the truth brings to earth! You only illuminate by obscuring and destroying all human created light, so that they may enter into uncreated light of truth. All this must happen both to the individual soul and to the general church to be placed in the truth. But before this time, which is closer than we think, O God what sorrows, what strange reversals we will pass through! O Love, would you allow me to say this? Yes, the sorrows will be appalling. God will deprive the sun, moon, and stars of a third part of their light, so the saints only show the light. The fire of their self-centered light will be obscured. However, it will only be a third part and the eclipse will not be entire. The lights of the church will be darkened for a little while, the same for a third part of the sun, but the rest is always bright and brilliant. But these other parts will not give light in this darkness, neither to those who are in the light, nor to those who are in darkness.

As for the soul, to whom the fourth herald announces truth, the three powers of the soul are placed in obscurity. Not quite everything, but a third part but it seems to the self to be everything, though there is still a lot of brilliance that she does not discover, though she has neither light or understanding, that represents the *day*. Neither has she the *fire* of the will, which means *night* because of her blindness. She has neither the fires of light nor the sacred darkness of the faith. But if these disgraces seem great, those that follow will be much different. The earth must experience the last extremity of misfortune before enjoying the height of all goodness.

> And the fifth angel blew his trumpet, and I saw a star that had fallen from heaven to earth, and he was given the key to the shaft of the bottomless pit; [2] he opened the shaft of the bottomless pit, and from the shaft rose smoke like the smoke of a great furnace, and the sun and the air were darkened with the smoke from the shaft. (Rev 9:1–2)

The stars falling from heaven are those persons who are elevated and dignified who illuminate others. God uses their fall to make the strongest crosses and the hardest persecutions for his servants. The angel is *given the key to the shaft of the bottomless pit*. The fallen people are given the power to slander others that causes a horrible *smoke* of murmurings and gossiping. By divine permission, the demon through slanders and calumnies raises a smoke that *obscures* even the truth. Smoke fills the air, and everyone believes these slanders. The faithful in the church, the sun, are obscured by a host of false accusers, who rise up against these persons. O infernal well, you throw your last fire, and my Master permits this for the strong, until all the misfortunes that must fall on the earth do so and it is filled with the goods that will arrive to finish this.

This star was a remnant of the light of abandonment, faith, and trust, which was in the soul, and was following God's way. What happens to this soul when the last remnant of abandonment falls? Now there is no light left, and *she was given the key to the shaft of the bottomless pit.* This well has only infamous and stinking smoke of infernal fumes of the most dangerous temptations. It seems that the angel has become a demon. Everything is on fire. This is a *furnace* of miseries of nature and concupiscence who attack the body. Fumes of this kind ossify the reason filling both the body and the soul.

> Then from the smoke came locusts on the earth, and they were given authority like the authority of scorpions of the earth. [4] They were told not to damage the grass of the earth or any green growth or any tree, but only those people who do not have the seal of God on their foreheads. (Rev 9:3–4)

From our human perspective, it seems that God wants to destroy everything. O God, you seem to extinguish the truth, far from establishing it. This is one of the Master's blows and in this way you act most like God. O human, you are blind, yet you imagine that you penetrate and understand the way God conducts souls. We claim understanding of God but actually treat God worse than the most ignorant of people by our ignorance. What do we see in this scripture? God makes out of the well of the abyss a species of *scorpions* with blows and spikes worse than death. And what seems harsher in this conduct of God is that he gives new life to the human senses and to these operations, which he had caused to die from the beginning. But by a stroke of God's infinite an adorable mercy, the locusts only damage people who are not *marked by God's seal.*

Human beings have two aspects, the natural and animal or the spiritual and divine. The latter aspect bears the characteristics of God and is in the superior part of the soul. This superior part has God and is marked by the character of Divinity. This person marked with the seal of God is composed of three powers of understanding, remembrance, and will. In this state, the person, absorbed in God, lives the superior will, which is the sovereign power. These locusts are not allowed to attack this soul in any way. These people remain pure and integrated in God which is being marked by the seal of God. But for those humans who are in the animal (the corrupt and sinning Adam) will not be saved. O, these locusts will strangely ravage the earth! Ah, they will damage the church of God! But if the servants of God suffer in their bodies and nature, their Spirit will never be freer than in the most overwhelming of evils.

> They were allowed to torture them for five months, but not to
> kill them, and their torture was like the torture of a scorpion
> when it stings someone. 6 And in those days people will seek
> death but will not find it; they will long to die, but death will flee
> from them. (Rev 9:5–6)

People who have passed through these types of states are ravished to see descriptions of these sorts. Is there anything more expressive and real? They are *allowed to torture* them because the time *five months* is a mystery meaning a long time. But, O God, you have to treat people with so much rigor before showing them your truth. A person may be put in the truth only by the experience of these things. Yet You do not give power to the demon and the corrupt nature *to kill him,* which means, to let him sin mortally, yet you give them power *to torment* and feel their stings. The grand herald of your truth, Paul, bore this torment. The wounds are similar to the *scorpion's* wounds because they cause pain to the person, yet the venom can be made into a medicine. The pain is like that to death without dying. He feels this wound continually, without the pain being appeased by death.

But how are spiritual wounds *similar to that of the scorpion?* In the same way of the venom of a real scorpion, the venom of sin passes to the heart and attacks the will yet the sealed will is not damaged. This venom can only cause extreme *pain,* without being allowed to spread to a place within, and without infecting the noble part of the soul. Also, the scorpion's venom when applied to the wound serves as a remedy. The same goes for the sinner when converted; he has the pain and confusion caused by his sin, yet the sin also brings the remedy. God makes the very wounds of sin become marvelous ointments that heal the wounds of pride and self-sufficiency. These sins are the ones most opposed to the truth and need more pain to destroy them because vanity is directly opposed to the truth. Truth is entirely in God and nothing of the creature. Vanity tears everything away from God and there can be no truth with vanity. The remedy for vanity is that the person knows, feels, and experiences who and what he is.

In those days of desolation and ordeal, those who are attacked *long for death, but death will flee from them.* O God, what consolation will it be for a person in this state of dying! She fears displeasing God more than death, and more than ten thousand deaths. She secretly hopes that death will deliver her. Yet because killing herself would be a mortal sin, she does not do it. Sometimes her pain is so great that it does not allow her to reason.

The soul purified of any self-interest does not worry about herself, but the sinner does worry. Because with this evil, the more one asks for deliverance, the more the evil increases, unless the soul abandons herself to God for the rest of her life.

This will also happen to the servants of God in his church. They will be *stung*, wounded by poisoned language which will raise unconceivable crosses. They will be *allowed to torture them for five months*, which is a number of months and years, but God will save a many of them. God will allow them to be excessively afflicted but not killed. As Paul says, *We are afflicted until death but not killed* (2 Corinthians 6:9).

> The locusts looked like horses prepared for battle. On their heads they wore something like crowns of gold, and their faces resembled human faces. [8] Their hair was like women's hair, and their teeth were like lions' teeth. [9] They had breastplates like breastplates of iron, and the sound of their wings was like the thundering of many horses and chariots rushing into battle. [10] They have tails like scorpions, with stingers, and in their tails is their power to harm people for five months. [11] They have as king over them the angel of the bottomless pit; his name in Hebrew is Abaddon, and in Greek he is called Apollyon. (Rev 9:7–9)

Two perspectives exist here. First, we see what will happen in the world before the reunion of all people under one Master. The second perspective is what happens to a particular soul whom God afflicts with evil before giving grand and eminent graces to the person. The animals, or those people who must torment the servants of God, are like *horses prepared for battle* because certainly this is the most terrible war ever. Their persecutors are losing all human characteristics. Only the appearance of the face remains human. They have *crowns*, to show that these powerful people employed to persecute the servants of God consider the ill treatment of others as a victory. The crowns *of gold on their head* also show that the combat is under the pretext of the glory of God. However, they only have the passion and love of themselves in their actions. *They have a human face* because these people pretend externally to have pity on the people whom they mistreat.

Their *hair* was *like women's hair*, which pretends an artificial softness, which seduces souls and ties them up. All who are with the locusts will be disgraced. The soul does not see that *their teeth were like lions' teeth* and without pity for the innocent souls they despise.

Their hard cruelty gives them *breastplates of iron* since they are covered with pretexts that make them invulnerable to others. When they attack and wound, they strike without fear of being damaged themselves. The *sound of their wings*, their renown, flies everywhere *like the thundering of many horses and chariots rushing into battle*. It seems to everyone that these people are armed with zeal to defend the cause of God. They are widely known and publicize their success with others, and others join with them believing that God gives them success in their initiatives. But they do not see their tails, even if their face appears human. *They have tails like scorpions,* which cause the world's most savage wounds, even mortal wounds, if God did not stop their poisoned malice from having its effect. Ah, these animals have venom in their tail, cover themselves with human appearance, and yet are dangerous! What harm they will do, since *they have the power* of God to do all this evil to his servants in order to sanctify and put them into truth?

But even though they have the power of God, who animates them to do these things, and who makes them do them, they have their *king,* who is the *angel of the abyss,* the *killing angel,* who wants to kill the servants of God because he sees the good that they will do one day. The killing angel sees that God wants his servants to serve him by extending his kingdom and destroying the empire of Satan. The *killing angel* makes every effort to destroy and remove God's servants from the earth but instead of killing them, the killing angel destroys in God's servants what is opposing God and makes them obedient to his will.

The demon and locusts attack particular people and seem to win continual victories with their cruelty. Yet their victims can neither attack their enemies nor defend themselves. All of this seems to the attackers to be a *human* and natural situation; they find something sweet and flattering in this situation. But alas! Their *lion's teeth* makes the cruelest martyrdom. The appearance of these animals' faces promises something agreeable, yet they wound with a sharp point. They bring together terrible *noises,* terror, persecutions, cries, and a thousand other things. O God, this is hard and cruel, and these tortures would be sweet if they gave death! But we must live without hope of ever dying!

> The first woe has passed. There are still two woes to come. (Rev 9:12)

Who does not want to see all the evils pass away and be at the end? We would be very happy if we came to the end! O God, You appear to be cruel but this is only an appearance. Behind this appearance of cruelty is hidden an infinite mercy and what seems to be the cruelest is filled with sweetness. In contrast, the evil appears to be soft but its poisonous venom wounds.

> Then the sixth angel blew his trumpet, and I heard a voice from the four horns of the golden altar before God, [14] saying to the sixth angel who had the trumpet, "Release the four angels who are bound at the great river Euphrates." [15] So the four angels

were released, who had been held ready for the hour, the day, the month, and the year, to kill a third of humankind. (Rev 9:13–15)

The *sixth* herald is that of death. What previously happened prepared for death, but it had not arrived. But without this death, truth will not be manifested to human beings. *The voice from the four horns of the golden altar*, announces the last of the sacrifices, the most strange and terrible of all.

O Justice of my God, how you appear to be cruel! Yet who is put in the truth, adores, blesses, and loves God's justice, which is only under apparent cruelty and gives her a great good. O Justice, O Truth! I only think of you and I am transported into pleasure! What appears to be cruelties seems to me the height of happiness. You have a harsh and cruel approach, but your cruelty only gives a torrent of delights. O mystery of cruelty! Mystery of love and gentleness! Who will comprehend that whoever has found your favor is happy to find the truth? The one you spare the least is the most content and happiest. Ah Justice! You are only cruel to those who oppose the kingdom of pure love! But you are sweet and friendly to those who are not opposed to pure love. O pen, who cannot and will never be able to write how the hearts feels, understands, loves, and adores the Justice of my God! Justice, the character of my God, is pure love. You alone can give pure love. You only communicate pure love to any soul through rigors and sacrifices. O Justice! Whoever fears you is far from the purity of love! O Justice! Who loves you with the most extreme passion, is disengaged from herself and self-centeredness. O Justice, I can say nothing because I have so much to say! O Love, O pure Love! Where are you, where are you? You are only in the heart who understands that divine justice holds only charms and sweets. For these souls, love has shared sweetness. Others think that love has only rigors and they complain, but it is quite the opposite. The greatest sweetness of love is to have no sweetness. O divine Justice, how can I be your herald as I am your supporter?

All the afflictions that occurred until now could not cause death, because the *angels who are bound at the great river* were not released. Until now, abandonment has always been maintained with vigor. She desired death and yet abandoned herself to God to die or not to die. The fruit of a long and constant suffering was to be abandoned and in perfect indifference. When the soul has arrived there, sorrows cease from the blows. She believes that she is delivered forever from all sorts of sorrows. But she is astonished at how little release she has, because this has only served to prepare her for another fight, which is all the harsher to her because she had tasted the sweetness and tranquility of repose. It is an astonishing thing that lengthy troubles are not unbearable. We finally get used to them.

What makes these sorrows harder is that she recovers her sense of pain. God requires the loss of our propriety. The soul rages, resists, and revolts as it experiences these evils, yet this makes the tests even more distressing. This resists the abandonment. We then experiment to the measure we can to surrender ourselves to these evils and they diminish and end. God delivers us from our pain.

Yet then our abandonment becomes expanded. This first abandonment, which destroyed propriety, now becomes a powerful river carrying and leading us. We are on a ship that loses land but saves from drowning. Yet this ship must inevitably be lost, drown, and die. Without this, we will never leave ourselves.

After the destruction of the ship, we lose ourselves in God. We sail and walk on this immense ocean with abandonment. We no longer have the former sorrows and rages. To the contrary, the more we lose ourselves, the soul becomes annihilated and less attached to the senses. Her pain is only pain because we attach to it in order to keep ourselves.

God *releases* the power to make us lost in God. But when and how? *In the hour, the day, the month, and the year* that God destines and intends. My God, these words show God's providence and perfect timing! A soul who lets herself be led unreservedly finds the desires of her soul being fulfilled. O, it is good to release ourselves to this providence! All the pitfalls of the spiritual life come from the fact that souls want to put themselves into states, because they have heard of them. We need to wait in patience for God's hour, time, and moment. When it seems that everything is destroyed and lost, we will see that God has acted in an admirable manner.

> The number of the troops of cavalry was two hundred million; I heard their number. [17] And this was how I saw the horses in my vision: the riders wore breastplates the color of fire and of sapphire and of sulfur; the heads of the horses were like lions' heads, and fire and smoke and sulfur came out of their mouths. [18] By these three plagues a third of humankind was killed, by the fire and smoke and sulfur coming out of their mouths. [19] For the power of the horses is in their mouths and in their tails; their tails are like serpents, having heads; and with them they inflict harm. (Rev 9:16–19)

The evils that come to overwhelm these souls multiply almost to infinity. This *army* gets bigger every day. Surrounded on all sides, our ills double and multiply like sands of the sea. Each day we see more ills born, grow, and multiply by those who oppose us. People harm us without knowing why. It will seem that nature, hell, and people are banded against souls abandoned to God. Those who fight have *breastplates the color of fire* because they are to pass for having a true zeal. However, this fire and sulfur is only infernal zeal. The breastplates have the color of *sapphire* to pretend the color of the coat of justice. The demon is the *horse* they ride. His *head of a lion,* full of force and fury, aims to destroy the servants of God. Their infernal mouth of fire issues only *fire,* rage, *brimstone,* and *smoke,* which causes death. This *fire* and the *brimstone* of persecution only comes from hell. The fury of their smoke of lies and of persecution gives rise to artifice. *Their tails like serpents, having heads,* cover the blows that they give with a thousand artifices.

Some individuals experience persecutions from both hidden and domestic enemies who attack with fury. God gives power to the demon which exhausts the soul. This infernal fire, covered in the appearance of some pleasure, brings real pain. Pride and other sins seem to come to tear down this soul. She is surrounded by all the evils and deprived of all goods. This is a face of the lion and *a tail of the serpent* with rage and the artifice. The fury of hell seems to be unchained. On whatever side we turn we cannot avoid being devoured or stung. It seems that by avoiding one evil, we are taken into a more violent one. O God, from which side to turn? We must die. There is no way to escape. But what makes one die? It is fire, smoke, and sulfur. O happy those who then turn around without help and without support! Because they truly die and are annihilated. O, if we knew the harm we do to the souls not to leave them pure and full in the hand of God! Because in thinking we save them, we lose them.

> The rest of mankind who were not killed by these plagues still did not repent of the work of their hands; they did not stop worshiping demons, and idols of gold, silver, bronze, stone and wood—idols that cannot see or hear or walk. [21] Nor did they repent of their murders, their magic arts, their sexual immorality or their thefts. (Rev 9:20–21)

When these things happen, the world will be in a time of the strangest depravity and malice will be at its height. One purpose is to remind the unfaithful of the faith and to convert sinners. Another purpose is to destroy propriety and to make human beings truly spiritual.

The demon works to make idolaters more stubborn, sinners more hardened, and spirituality destroyed. To the measure that the demon opposes the good, evil will be augmented. The more we see the good servants of God persecuted and destroyed, the more evil is strengthened and multiplied. At the designated time, God will finish the evils of his saints and the crimes of their adversaries.

Two types of people idolaters and sinners *still did not repent* what they are and *the work of their hands*. The sinners and the *idolaters* will see terrible wars before their eyes, strange evils, horrible famines, extraordinary evils, and wonders because all the universe will be in trouble. However, most will harden in their evil. Those who are proprietary appear to be further strengthened in this by the persecution of the saints. They prefer their own interests to those of God and the lie to the truth. They *worship the demons*. Some are interested in *money*, others honor, others themselves, others perfection through imaginary virtues, and worship *idols that cannot see or hear or walk*.

The world *did not repent* and will be in the height of malice with many murders of the body, soul, and honor. There will be *poisonings*, enchantments, *sexual immorality*, and thefts. They pillage the property of others with impunity. Yet do not all these things happen in this century? O God, what depravity! Have pity on our church! We destroy the altar of the true God in our heart and that of our brothers and sisters and instead put in vanity, lies, and self-centeredness. They persecute those who adore God in their heart, yet support those with an impure heart, envy, adultery, and resentments. They think only of establishing themselves in the minds of others and applaud their own work, but their hearts are empty. Yet society esteems and applauds these people. Those who burn with pure love for God and despise the esteem of people are decried and maltreated as the most outcast of people. O God, in this century we call the good, bad, and the bad, good.

> And I saw another mighty angel coming down from heaven, wrapped in a cloud, with a rainbow over his head; his face was like the sun, and his legs like pillars of fire. [2] He was holding a little scroll, which lay open in his hand. He planted his right foot on the sea and his left foot on the land. (Rev 10:1–2)

If the evils have been cruel and strange, they are the source of all good. When the evils are the most desperate, we are the closest to the greatest goods. The servants of God and the partisans of truth appear to be destroyed by those who triumph and reign with the lie. They had been saved from the first evil and then suffer a crueler pain. The perversity of the whole universe seemed to be its ruin. Sinning became stronger and the virtues were lost. Death devoured those who practiced virtues. However, in this time of desolation we are closest to happiness. O death, pain, losses, and hopes, you cause good! You bring life, pleasures, joy, possession, and salvation. This strong and powerful *angel* who follows death is the Herald of truth. There is nothing stronger than the truth. All the other powers in comparison are very great weaknesses. This truth is finally *descended from heaven* a second time by the pure effect of divine *power*. O Jesus, now you manifest your truth to all the world. The time has come. The *scroll* of truth is not only open in heaven, but has come down to be revealed on earth. O Truth, ignored, buried, and tied up until now, you will be manifested.

This angel *wrapped in a cloud* lets us know that the manifestation of truth in this life is always accompanied by a cloud. It is not the same in heaven. The angel with a *rainbow over his head* is a sign of a general reconciliation of invariable, immobile, and perfect peace that God makes with humanity in his manifestation of the truth. All the evils of people came from not knowing the truth. All the goods of people have come from knowing the truth. Errors and lies have attracted God's anger to the earth. Truth will bring peace, tranquility, and joy. O Peace, so fought against, so decried, how much more will you be triumphant!

The face of the herald of the truth *like the sun* chases away the darkness of error and lies, like the sun chases away night and shadows. Now the sun of day brings its presence. In the same way, all errors, wanderings, darkness, and ignorance come from the absence of the truth, as the light come from its presence.

His legs like pillars of fire show that truth is based on a firm and inviolable charity.

The scroll which lay open in his hand manifests truth that must be made to human beings. This is a new language. The scroll is *small* because of the simplicity of truth yet it contains all that is most grand. His *foot on the sea* and the other *on the land* shows that this truth must be manifested throughout the world, without reserving anything. The truth must be manifested for the exterior and for the interior. All peoples will know and worship the true God in spirit and in truth.

> He gave a great shout, like a lion roaring. And when he shouted, the seven thunders sounded. ⁴ And when the seven thunders had sounded, I was about to write, but I heard a voice from heaven saying, "Seal up what the seven thunders have said, and do not write it down." (Rev 10:3–4)

O Truth! You will be announced with strength by the voice of a *Lion* chosen to manifest truth. There is not a corner in the earth where you will not be heard. O Truth, your day is close. O, all people hear your voice! O great Truth, you reveal things in our heart to whom you manifest your voice! But at the same time of this announcement, there are *seven thunders* of the truth. But even though the noise of seven thunders is heard everywhere, God manifests the distinction of their voice and what they express to John and only a very few people.

There are two things in this admirable truth. First, truth must be published, known, preached, and announced to all the world. Secondly, truth must he *sealed* and hidden, because the world is not capable of it. O Truth hidden in the most profound mysteries, who can hear this? And if you are revealed and announced, who can hear you? Those to whom are you manifested, keep you locked away in the bottom of their heart. There are *seven voices* of the truth which must not be revealed to human beings, although God will reveal them one day when the time has come. For now, the truth must be hidden because of the corruption of human beings. But when this corruption is purified, the seven voices of truth will be manifested.

> Then the angel whom I saw standing on the sea and the land raised his right hand to heaven [6] and swore by him who lives forever and ever, who created heaven and what is in it, the earth and what is in it, and the sea and what is in it: "There will be no more delay, [7] but in the days when the seventh angel is to blow his trumpet, the mystery of God will be fulfilled, as he announced to his servants the prophets." (Rev 10:5–7)

The *angel* swears and protests *there will be no more delay* for the manifestation of truth. The *last* herald of truth *has sounded the trumpet and manifested the truth.* O Truth, O *mystery* of the same truth, when will you be revealed? But, O Truth, give the intelligence of what you announce. You are not now known and heard. "I will be known," says this Truth, "but I will not be heard. Then I will be heard and not understood. Then I will give understanding and I will give the intelligence of my mystery when the time has come. I will be known, heard, and understood. The time to make myself known is close. The time to be heard is far. The time to make me understood even farther. But the centuries will not pass without me being known, heard, and understood."

This is consistent with the word that Jesus Christ said, *Heaven and earth will pass away, but my words will never pass away* (Matt 24:35). His words are truth. The heaven and the earth will pass away, but the truth will remain firm and unshaken.

> Then the voice that I had heard from heaven spoke to me again, saying, "Go, take the scroll that is open in the hand of the angel who is standing on the sea and on the land." (Rev 10:8)

All the voices that are speaking up to the voice of the sixth trumpet are voices of elders or angels or animals. But this last voice is the one who comes out of the altar of sacrifices and comes from God. O voice, you are altogether sweet and charming! This same *voice* commands John to *take the scroll that is open in the hand of the angel.* Here is an order and a mission to publish and reveal the truth. O God, you are going to make heralds of your truth. But what persecutions will they not suffer?

> So I went to the angel and told him to give me the little scroll;
> and he said to me, "Take it, and eat; it will be bitter to your stom-
> ach, but sweet as honey in your mouth." (Rev 10:9)

The truth to be manifested to the soul must be eaten by being understood. This truth must be received in the soul before it can be manifested to oth-ers. This tells us that we need to be placed in truth before we teach it to others. Like John, we need not only to have known and heard the truth, but to have understood the truth. This means we eat the truth, before manifesting it to others.

But as soon as we receive the truth, *the stomach is filled with bitterness but sweet as honey in the mouth.* The truth is so sweet in the will, which is her mouth through which it is received, and delights her soul. One cannot believe the joy and contentment a soul receives to whom truth has been communicated. Yet the stomach is put into bitterness. This is the difference between the truth that is communicated to the soul only for herself, and the truth that is communicated for others. The truth communicated only for herself is sweet after the passage of the terrible states that preceded this. But when truth is communicated for others, O God, stomachs are full of pain of childbirth and the repercussions of the unfaithfulness of the children. What pains and fatigue! What calumny! But all this is nothing compared to the interior pains that must be suffered to produce the truth. The passion of Jesus Christ is like this bitterness of the stomach that John suffered. Paul also suffered this, when he assured them that the dear spiritual infants in his bowels were going astray, *My little children, for whom I am again in the pain of childbirth until Christ is formed in you* (Galatians 4:19). I wish all people would understand these pains, even if they do not experience them.

> Then I took the little book out of the angel's hand and ate it, and
> it was as sweet as honey in my mouth. But when I had eaten
> it, my stomach became bitter. ¹¹ And he said to me, "You must
> prophesy again about many peoples, nations, tongues, and
> kings." (Rev 10:10–11)

John confesses that the reception of truth within himself is a very great *sweet-ness.* But after receiving, *eaten,* and understood it, he needed to announce this to the others, and he *suffered* inconceivable *bitterness in his stomach.* He was told to *prophecy about the nations* and to manifest this same truth in many places, *about peoples and about kings.* After having received the truth, it is no longer general pain, but it is the fruitful pain of childbirth. All the suffering that saints have gone through before arriving at the knowledge of truth cannot compare to what these apostolic people suffered when they were destined to help others before and after the reception of truth. God gives them light about their experience, so they do not misunderstand how to guide other souls. God has them also pass through rigorous states intended for their sanctification and increased discernment. They have borne all their own weakness and are not surprised to see weakness in others. Jesus Christ took our nature, because to have true compassion, one must feel the same weaknesses of others.

> Then I was given a measuring rod like a staff, and I was told, "Come and measure the temple of God and the altar and those who worship there, ² but do not measure the court outside the temple; leave that out, for it is given over to the nations, and they will trample over the holy city for forty-two months." (Rev 11:1–2)

It is necessary that the apostle be given *a rod for measuring* all things with equality, otherwise it would be very difficult to understand. True justice sees both the fault and the good. Until this rod is given to measure all things as God sees them, we often judge souls by appearance and by what we feel and do not feel. We frequently misunderstand and declare the proprietary soul good, rather than the one in the greatest purity and poverty.

The soul in truth is given *this rule* to judge souls in the same truth; she cannot do otherwise. In the beginning, this brings some pain, because she believes that she lacks charity in her judgment. She makes some effort to change her feelings and sentiments and accuses herself of presumption and a lack of charity. This though destroys peace and she is obliged to let the judgment of God remain in her as God has made this. The soul placed in truth may only judge according to the truth. Often a soul who is considered less than other souls is actually the most perfect and has the heart of God. She is measured on the temple of God and on the grandeur of the *worship* of God.

But the *court* or exterior is *not measured* because it is often *given to the nations* and Gentiles. It seems that everybody has the right to mistreat the faithful people with torrents of crosses and persecutions. God permits persecution, so these souls suffer and are annihilated. God gives power *to the Gentiles to trample on them* and to profane *the holy city for forty-two months.* The times for forty-two months is three and half years, an extended period of time, and the persecution can last for several years.

> And I will grant my two witnesses authority to prophesy for one
> thousand two hundred sixty days, wearing sackcloth." ⁴ These
> are the two olive trees and the two lampstands that stand before
> the Lord of the earth. ⁵ And if anyone wants to harm them, fire
> pours from their mouth and consumes their foes; anyone who
> wants to harm them must be killed in this manner. (Rev 11:3–5)

Everything in the scroll of the apocalypse happens down to the letter before
the entire manifestation of the truth. John does not describe here the last
judgment, but the advent of Jesus Christ's reign in all souls and the earth
to show what must happen before and during this time. Because, O God,
here is the height of your glory. Until now, the redemption of Christ has
been bound and captive and has not have had its full extent. But now, O
God, redemption must be without limit or measure and in superabundance,
not only in a few souls, as it was formerly, but in all the world. Jesus Christ
will come to destroy and ruin the demon's empire throughout the earth.
The demon has ruined God's kingdom in many hearts and will of creatures.
Now Jesus Christ has extended the plenitude of his redemption. The time
will come and is closer than we think but will come only after the demon
has exercised all his tyranny, and then will be banished from the earth. Jesus
Christ will extend his kingdom in all the extremities of the earth, as it is
written, *Ask of me, and I will make the nations your heritage, and the ends of
the earth your possession* (Psalm 2:8). Jesus Christ will be loved by all hearts.
Then all those who truly reign as kings in their freedom will choose Jesus
Christ as king. The wolf and the lamb will live together (Isaiah 11:6), people
will be together, and there will be no malignity on the earth. The well of the
abyss will be forever closed (Rev 20:3).

All this therefore will be executed. God will choose *two witnesses* in
particular to put strength and power on them to announce the truth. These
witnesses will *prophesy a thousand two hundred and threescore days* with a
nondescript exterior. However, these *two lights* will be *standing* before the
One who must have the universal power on all the earth, in front of the
divine Pastor.

These *two witnesses* of the truth precede everything and are in all souls
to whom truth is manifested. These two witnesses are faith and pure love,
which are the prophecy of sacrifice and care. Faith lives only as sacrifice, and
pure love as care. When these two witnesses are in the soul, they are two
candlesticks, or two lights, who are *standing before the God of the earth*, who
is the One who has the right to judge souls.

*And if anyone will hurt them, fire pours from their mouth and consumes
their foes.* The two witnesses' strong and efficacious words cause everyone

who opposes them to fall and compels their enemies to enter into the truth and not pursue them. Or if these people do not enter into the truth, God will soon be present but is patient and concealed. It seems initially that he favors the part of his enemies. But the time come that God will destroy their enemies *by the words of his mouth* through his servants whom he chooses to give testimony (Isaiah 11:42). *And then the lawless one will be revealed, whom the Lord Jesus will destroy with the breath of his mouth, annihilating him by the manifestation of his coming* (2 Thessalonians 2:8). These words of fire are their only weapon.

Particular souls also have no other weapon for their defense against oppression than the effects of their love and faith, which serves as testimony and slays their enemies. God gives them words that no one can resist or contradict.

> They have authority to shut the sky, so that no rain may fall dur-
> ing the days of their prophesying, and they have authority over
> the waters to turn them into blood, and to strike the earth with
> every kind of plague, as often as they desire. (Rev 11:6)

Those who are given the power to testify to the truth of Jesus Christ *have authority* over souls, bodies, and the elements which is surprising. Signs prove their announcement of truth. O God, what power do they not have? They have the power to *shut the sky* to prevent the *rain* of consolations for people not in grace. They *change the waters* of grace and softness *to blood* and carnage. There is only suffering, misery, and astonishing disasters. They *strike* the interior life *with every kind of plague, as often as they desire.* These heralds of truth have a great power over the souls who are dependent on them. They change, as it pleases them, their interior dispositions, and often the exterior. If they say, "Remain in peace," they enter into a profound peace. If while in this profound peace, they enter into sorrow, they enter into a strange sorrow.

> When they have finished their testimony, the beast that comes
> up from the bottomless pit will make war on them and conquer
> them and kill them, [8] and their dead bodies will lie in the street
> of the great city that is prophetically called Sodom and Egypt,
> where also their Lord was crucified. (Rev 11:7–8)

When the two witnesses finish making their testimony to the truth, they are beaten by the *beast from the bottomless pit.* They suffer death, because the beast wages a cruel war through lies that destroy the reputations that they have acquired by their virtue and words. They will be absolutely *killed* in the spirit by all human beings. *Their dead bodies will lie* in the world and there will be no hope for many days to recover their reputation. These bodies rest in a *spiritual Egypt*, in a *Sodom* where God is not known and is dishonored in the strangest manner, in the place and in the circumstances that they killed my Savior.

The world is only an *Egypt* because of the multiplicity of combat and lack of unity. It is a *Sodom* because of the disorder that they commit. What will I say, O Love, to those who compose their church? Combat between Christians and Catholics? The church is presently a place of multiplicity and a Sodom. Most children dishonor it. But the corruption of the children has been prophesied, and they have not been able to change the church's holiness or integrity.

It was the children of the world who *crucified our Lord.* It will be the children of the church who will be dying as faithful witnesses of the truth of the church. But if they die, their bodies will remain to serve after their death as a testimony to the world's cruelty. O, here is the reign of Satan and the time that he will make his efforts to destroy the church if he can! But alas! The poor church will stay alone without consolation. Her children will despise and abandon her and prevent the actions of the Spirit. The church carries within herself Jacob and Esau and her unfortunate children will be at war in her womb against the true interior Jacob. But if Esau has the advantage of appearing first, Jacob will have the right to minister and to have the blessing of his Father. O church, you mourn the loss of your Father! Loving Rachel, you mourn, and you cannot be consoled, because your children are no more. But be consoled, the time will come when your children will be brought from all the extremities of the earth. You will see them all at your table eating bread that you give them. They will no longer rebel. You will have twice the number of children according to the Spirit and not according to the flesh. O very holy church, your tears will change to cries of joy. You will see the nations that did not know your Mother. I confess that you will suffer pain. You will even say these words, If *I carry war in my womb, why did I become a mother?* (Genesis 25:22). No, no, mother most holy. You are now carrying war in your womb but despite the malice of your children, you will give birth to peace. I confess that it is your children who are at war. That within you Esau persecuted Jacob but you will soon give birth to Jacob. As God loves him from eternity, you will love him for all centuries. He will finally be your heir. He will cover himself for a time in the skin of Esau but will have the voice of Jacob. Also, your Isaac who was immolated on Calvary, you give an eternal blessing that will never be retracted. Therefore rejoice, O church! The time of your joy approaches. Your sadness will be finished. You will triumph throughout the world. Your Jacob will be victorious. It will seem for a time that God fights against him. If he remains lame in the fight, it is for a sign to posterity of his victory. In Jerusalem, the holy city, held for so many years by the infidel, there will come a time when you see in your enclosure the children of the Lord. Jerusalem, Jerusalem, you will be the flourishing city of the house of our God! The beast destroys and kills for a time this testimony of truth but it does not last long.

> For three and a half days members of the peoples and tribes and languages and nations will gaze at their dead bodies and refuse to let them be placed in a tomb; [10] and the inhabitants of the earth will gloat over them and celebrate and exchange presents, because these two prophets had been a torment to the inhabitants of the earth. (Rev 11:9–10)

Almost *all the peoples of the earth* will speak against the two witnesses. Everyone *will rejoice at their* apparent *defeat* because nothing in the world torments sinners like the truth. Humans cannot suffer the truth. They say that the truth is unsupportable and because of this, banish truth from the court of princes as well as in conversations among circles of people and in the streets. No one follows or even suffers the truth.

Pilate listened to Jesus Christ with pleasure but withdrew as soon as he heard him speak the truth. Truth came from heaven with Jesus Christ but after finding no place to live on the earth, it went back to heaven. This truth must come again to the earth with thunder and light, but humans oppose this with all their strength. The two witnesses of the truth are made to suffer intolerable pain. Lies seem to overcome truth yet if truth's witnesses appear destroyed, it is only to come back and resurrected with more force.

> But after the three and a half days, the breath of life from God entered them, and they stood on their feet, and those who saw them were terrified. [12] Then they heard a loud voice from heaven saying to them, "Come up here!" And they went up to heaven in a cloud while their enemies watched them. [13] At that moment there was a great earthquake, and a tenth of the city fell; seven thousand people were killed in the earthquake, and the rest were terrified and gave glory to the God of heaven. (Rev 11:11–13)

After the three and a half days when truth appeared defeated with the death of the witnesses and the triumph of falsehoods, *the breath of life from God enters into them.* This is the Spirit *sent from God.*

Those destined to give testimony to the truth must have the same strength and must die. When they have been dead *three and a half days,* when they will have the death of the sensible, the powers, and the foundation, heaven sends a life-giving Spirit. After this resurrection, they are *received in heaven* to God *in a cloud*. This is the difference between the presence of God in this life and that of the other life. And it will be in the *sight of their enemies* who are the demons and the flesh, who can then never attack them.

The Spirit of life enters therefore *into* the two witnesses. God will give them the life that the father of lies has taken away. It will not be the same life, but it will be a new life of the Spirit of truth that enters into them, the spirit that the world cannot receive. So they *went up to heaven in a cloud while their enemies watched them* because they will be freed forever from their pains, persecutions, and travails. After their resurrection, the truth will be entirely manifested.

But in the time of these marvels, there was a *great earthquake* because of the fear of destruction. The inferior part trembled because the natural life has been taken away, and this pleased her more than the spiritual and divine life that she did not know.

In the quaking of the earth, *a tenth of the city fell*, which is a tenth of the church falls. The soul arrives here knowing her propriety has been torn off, but she is not upset because sin is destroyed forever. The number seven marks the seven mortal sins, and seven *thousand* more sins follow. A sin produces a thousand more sins. O ineffable happiness! Sin will be forever banished from the earth by sin itself; the truth will be known instead of the lie. O state of the world, you will be a felicity! O God, you will no longer be offended or dishonored! O nature and sin, O demon, your empire will be destroyed by the same things which you believe establish it.

> The second woe has passed. The third woe is coming very soon.
> (Rev 11:14)

Misfortune is no longer a misfortune when it is passed. What frequently seems like it will destroy us is what establishes us. A misfortune and a loss as long as it lasts but even if its time and duration are rough and grim, what follows is sweet and agreeable.

> Then the seventh angel blew his trumpet, and there were loud voices in heaven, saying, "The kingdom of the world has become the kingdom of our Lord and of his Messiah, and he will reign forever and ever." (Rev 11:15)

Finally, at the opening of the seventh seal, the seventh herald manifests truth and announces ineffable happiness. O pain, travail, and chagrin, you have been well compensated by the revelation of the truth! I am not surprised that Paul, who had been given such knowledge, said *The sufferings of this present time are not worth comparing with the glory about to be revealed to us* as recompense for these pains. O happiness! Ah century very happy, you have been preceded by very many disasters. O souls in whom truth is manifested, rejoice in your happiness! Your tears are many! The souls in whom the truth is manifested are proven invariably in the body of the church. The one who makes me write this makes me say the truth. There is not a word in the scroll of the apocalypse that will not arrive as it is predicted, not only in the exterior but in the interior. We will see the arrival of the destruction of empires in the manner that is written. Then we will see the revealed truth. The words that God in his truth is writing here will be known to everyone as very true, when we see what they mean. Yes, O truth, you will be manifested when the seventh seal is opened, when the seventh herald will announce the truth which will appear clearly.

But what is truth? This truth is no other than the interior and exterior reign of Jesus Christ. The souls in whom Jesus Christ reigns absolutely are placed in truth. The exterior reign of Jesus Christ will extend throughout the earth. Finally, in the same century happy enough to see the spirits of the earth submitted to the reign of Jesus Christ will also see all hearts submitted to his movement and will. They will follow all the motions of the Spirit. The will of God will be done on the earth as it is in heaven. Jesus Christ will reign over spirits and hearts, as he will reign in all centuries. Amen.

> And the twenty-four elders, who were seated on their thrones before God, fell on their faces and worshiped God, [17] saying: "We give thanks to you, Lord God Almighty, the One who is and who was, because you have taken your great power and have begun to reign. (Rev 11:16–17)

Nothing will give more joy to all the blessed and to all in Heaven than the fortunate moment in which the *reign* of Jesus Christ extends through all the earth in the way he has said. Only in this time does he take entire possession of his *great power*. All power was given to Jesus Christ on heaven and in the earth when he came to the world, but his power is only extended when this same power is exerted on the hearts of all human beings. This is why it is written, *The Lord* says to my lord, *Sit at my right hand until I make your enemies your footstool* (Psalm 110:1). Jesus Christ after the resurrection is seated at the right hand of his Father but his enemies are not yet the footstool under his feet. They will not become the footstool until all the rebellious wills and mutinous spirits who are his enemies are subjected to him and serve him under his stool, when he reposes in them as the most high. Therefore, when Jesus Christ reigns in this way, he enters into possession of his great power which will be the joy of heaven and the pleasure of the earth. What must happen in all the whole universe, happens in every soul, when the spirit and the will is entirely submitted to Jesus Christ. We must let Jesus

Christ lead, move, and guide us. This will make joy in the blessed and the greatest glory that God can receive from his creature.

> The nations raged, but your wrath has come, and the time for judging the dead, for rewarding your servants, the prophets and saints and all who fear your name, both small and great, and for destroying those who destroy the earth. (Rev 11:18–19)

After telling of the wonderful reign of Jesus Christ, John speaks again of what must precede this happy day. *The nations rage* against the reign of Jesus Christ and try to destroy the interior. But then *the day of the wrath of God arrives* and take vengeance on all his enemies of his reign and punishes them in a surprising manner. The time has come to judge both the literal and the mystical dead. The cruelty of people has caused the faithful the loss of honor and what they hold most dear, along with a thousand deaths. God will make it known to the whole world that his servants are in the truth and that if they seemed dead to the eyes of the senses, their lives were filled with their promised immortality and their portion is with the saints. Then God *rewards his servants*, showing them the truth of the words they had announced. He also rewards *his saints* by showing them that they have kept the true way. You manifest yourself, O Lord, to them.

It is time, Lord Jesus, to do this and *destroy those who destroy the earth.* It is necessary to destroy the self-centered spirit and will which continually oppose the reign of Jesus Christ. The spirit of self is idolatry, and the will of self is the source of all other sins. Also, Jesus Christ cannot reign absolutely and entirely on earth until these two enemies are destroyed. He opposed these two powerful enemies with faith and pure love by the two witnesses that are sent. When the time of Gods returns comes, *the temple of God will be open,* and all the nations will enter into the church of God and in the foundation of their heart. We will see the *ark of his covenant*, through which he unites all humanity. Ah God, you will reveal grand things to your poor creatures! But it will only happen after *thunders, noises, and lightning* wielding the power against those who now believe that they are doing a great service to God by opposing his kingdom. Paul is the figure of what will happen then. Those who have fought against the truth with the most passion will change the most.

> A great portent appeared in heaven: a woman clothed with the sun, with the moon under her feet, and on her head a crown of twelve stars. ² She was pregnant and was crying out in birth pangs, in the agony of giving birth. (Rev 12:1–2)

This *woman* has three different meanings, all equally true. First, truth must be born into the earth but it is not produced on the earth. The spirit of truth has been banished and must be newly born on the earth. Pure love produces the truth. Secondly, the church wants to give birth to this truth but truth will only come from the interior. The third meaning is prayer like the experience of childbirth.

This woman according to these three meanings *is* clothed *with the sun.* Truth like light must be manifested in this life. *She has the moon under her feet* because she is beyond inconstancy. The truth has stability, but the lie is full of inconstancy. When souls are established in truth, they no longer vary and change in substance.

She is *clothed* with the sun with its true, permanent, and lasting light. She is separated from inconstant and variable lights. She is *crowned with twelve stars* which are the twelve fruits of the Holy Spirit. Because the soul is placed in truth she possesses everything. She possesses joy, peace, patience, and kindness. Also, when truth is on the earth and lies are banished, charity reigns because the Holy Spirit is true and loving. Where truth is, charity is also.

She is pregnant and wants to produce her fruit of justice in the world. But alas, what pains and birth pangs to produce this! In extreme pain Jesus Christ produced fruit on the cross. This interior truth must be produced in newness on the earth. *God is spirit, and those who worship him must worship in spirit and truth* (John 4:24) which gives God the justice that is due him. Truth produces justice and lies make injustice. Until now injustice reigns on earth because the lie, and the father of lies, brings injustice here. In this way, human beings rob God of his glory to attribute to themselves things they should attribute to God. It is through this injustice, that all evil comes on earth. But truth only produces justice, so that all people will restore to God what they owe him. God will be known for who he is and the creature will remain in annihilation.

The second explanation is the church is ready to give birth to the interior Spirit. *She is pregnant* with this Spirit, which is like the second coming of Jesus Christ. *She is crying out in birth pangs, in agony* to produce the fruit, which will cost her all the more pain to bring forth this very precious fruit. The church has not yet produced the divine motion in her children but there have been some who have been sprouts and have been part of the divine filiation, explained in Paul. But they are very rare. However, all Christians have been called to this vocation, but they do not respond. To the contrary, they are opposed to this. But as the church extends its reach throughout the earth, all people are animated by the Spirit, and must hide themselves under its shadow. At the same time, the church wants to produce the Spirit of abandon and divine motion in all its members. It is designed in the bosom of God but does not bring forth a child. This church, a female portent, is *clothed in the sun* and in the light of truth. She has *the moon under her feet* that shows her constancy. She is crowned with the twelve apostles, like so many *stars* who served to support her.

> Then another portent appeared in heaven: a great red dragon, with seven heads and ten horns, and seven diadems on his heads. ⁴ His tail swept down a third of the stars of heaven and threw them to the earth. Then the dragon stood before the woman who was about to bear a child, so that he might devour her child as soon as it was born. (Rev 12:3–4)

The *dragon* of self-love and pride, the father of lies, directly opposes pure love, a mortal enemy of the truth. The devil even in *heaven* preferred the world to God and wanted to attribute everything to himself rather than God. He *swept down* with him *a third part of* angels. The same dragon today sees that the truth coming into the world, *stands up to devour it to* prevent the truth from appearing. This woman who is mother of justice and pure love banishes absolutely pride and propriety. The dragon is *red* because it is against pure love. The *seven heads* are the seven deadly sins which entered the world through the dragon's way. The *ten horns* are the violation of the law, which he inspired by introducing sins, because without sins there is no point to the law. The seven heads are *crowned* to show that the dragon reigns in the world by the sins that he has introduced and that these seven sins are the source and the origin of other sins.

The dragon *swept down a third* of humanity because he makes them fall; they only see his malignity after his tail throws them down. He uses finesse and cunning. The horrible dragon *stood before the woman who was about to bear a child, so that he might devour her fruit*. The dragon Lucifer sees that the justice and truth which he had banished will be reproduced. Because the truth will banish his lies from the earth, he makes efforts to devour the fruit and swallow the mother. The dragon gives a spirit of trouble, multiplicity, and division, while the church is ready to give birth to the interior spirit, the spirit of peace and equity. Now the church wants to produce the Spirit in the whole universe, she is in *pain* and strange birth pangs *in agony*. The dragon is incessantly before her *to devour her fruit* at the time of her birth. But, O God, his efforts are rendered useless! Truth triumphs over the lie, pure love over pride, justice over injustice. The dragon is also continually *before the woman* in whom God wants to manifest the truth and to make Jesus known in a more particular way than he was known before. But as Jesus Christ and the Spirit of Jesus Christ must bear fruit in the following centuries and in all the earth, his efforts will be rendered useless in the world.

> And she gave birth to a son, a male child, who is to rule all the nations with a rod of iron. But her child was snatched away and taken to God and to his throne; [6] and the woman fled into the wilderness, where she has a place prepared by God, so that there she can be nourished for one thousand two hundred sixty days. (Rev 12:5–6)

However, truth does not fail to produce its fruit, as it was seen and predicted by David. *Steadfast love and faithfulness will meet; righteousness and peace will kiss each other* (Psalm 85:10). In this happy meeting, mercy, faithfulness, righteousness, and peace meet. Where there is justice, there is peace; where this is injustice, there is trouble.

Therefore, the fruit is he who in the future will *rule all the nations with a rod of iron*. None can be found who can resist him. All the peoples will worship the true God. Submitting their spirit to his truth, they submit their heart to his wonderful leadership.

But her child was snatched away to God, or rather, he will be. Because God himself will preserve the justice that all nations must render to him.

At God's throne all nations will recognize him as their God, as the One in whom is contained all the power and all the merit, as the One to adore and let lead. To him it is necessary to make a complete resignation and a surrender of the heart and spirit, so that they please him. The creature will then recognize her error, weakness, misery, and uselessness. She will give to God all the justice that she owes him.

Before the time that this fruit appears on earth, (because it will be something that happens) he will be carried away to the throne of God for a time. During the dragon's time, the truth will be *in the desert*, it will be banished from the earth. The truth however will be in solitary places, in hearts who are prepared, but it will have to be so secret that no one can discover it. It will be *nourished*, cultivated and maintained *one thousand, two hundred and sixty days*, which is the time that the truth remains hidden before it appears on the earth.

O mystery most true that the truth will shine, you pass now for fables and fairy tales for little children, for reveries, and, even worse, for evil things. But the time will come, that you appear in all of your light and your words will be regarded with respect because people will see that they come from my God. O truth unknown by those with whom it lives! O, the day comes when you will be manifested, you will be put on the edge of the sea like a lighthouse, who reaches all extremities by its light to enlighten those who navigate. O truth misunderstood and now considered the execration of the earth, you will one day receive admiration, beauty, and luster. This spirit, which our whole mother is ready to give birth to, and from whom she now suffers pains and convulsions, will be for whatever reason *removed*. O God, it will remain unknown on earth. This heavenly Mother, which is doctrine and the truth of her principles, will be banished. *The woman fled into the desert* because only empty hearts will receive this spirit. Those who seem to be banished will find this a true place of refuge. It is there that she will be *nourished* and cultivated until the time when the faith (the essence of religion) will spread its branches all over the earth. Alas! Alas! There is no more faith in the world. There is *simulation* of faith, like David's wife Michal who pretended that David was home to hide him from Saul, but it was only *the image of David who is in the bed*. David had fled to the desert (1 Samuel 19:16–18). Yes, this faith is only in deserts and in empty hearts. All others pretend and have only images of faith, but they have no faith. However, as faith will never be banished from the earth, God chooses a desert, where she can be nourished and cultivated. O dragon, all your efforts to devour the Spirit of faith are useless, because God protects her in a special way. He keeps her with him, so that it cannot be fully spread on the earth, until the dragon is shackled. The Spirit, which appears now as the abomination of the earth, will become its glory and support. You speak, O God! *For rebellion is no less a sin than divination, and stubbornness is like iniquity and idolatry* (1 Sam 15:23). However, human beings speak to the contrary and say that the Spirit tells us not to resist magic and we should be led by magic. Or that what we read in the scriptures is false and lies. However, there will come a time, when the truth is declared and seen clearly in your scriptures. One day the scriptures will appear brighter than the day.

> And war broke out in heaven; Michael and his angels fought against the dragon. The dragon and his angels fought back. (Rev 12:7)

The *war* that broke out *in heaven* is the war between pride and pure love. *Michael* is the angel of pure love. This is why when God wishes to introduce a soul into pure love, he gives Michael as a particular protector who fights against all the forces of pride and self-love in the soul so that only pure love can reign. The fight is strangely rough. It is why the soul is in heaven when this combat is done and suffers a lot. *The dragon* defends himself with all his might. This miserable self-love, which seemed to leave the soul in peace when one does not attack it, now gives violent blows, so that there is not a rougher combat in the world. O terrible and appalling attacks!

This combat was made in heaven at the creation of the world. Presently the combat rages both in the church and in all souls destined for pure love. Michael and all his supporters fight with all their force for them. The dragon defends himself as much as he can, but pure love will defeat him after strange wars.

> But they were defeated, and there was no longer any place for
> them in heaven. (Rev 12:8)

O self-love, you arm yourself as much as you can to fight against the church and the true servants of God, supporters of pure love. Self-love will be defeated, though it will not appear so.

This dreadful dragon no longer appears in an individual soul once Michael defeats self-love. But, O God, what time, suffering, and combats, before self-love is vanquished.

> The great dragon was thrown down, that ancient serpent, who
> is called the devil and Satan, the deceiver of the whole world—
> he was thrown down to the earth, and his angels were thrown
> down with him. (Rev 12:9)

Once pure love takes the place of a destroyed self-love, *the devil is thrown out of heaven onto earth*. When there is no more pride, the demon loses its hold.

When the same combat between self-love and pure love which begins in the church of my God will be finished, the dragon will no longer have power over the servants of God. They will be placed in a state of wonderful innocence. O marvels that will arrive in the church of my God! The serpent now present on the earth exercises his empire but soon this empire and the princes of the world will be destroyed like chaff. Jesus Christ has victory over the dragon. The time is closer than we think. The demon will be chained in the abyss but now he is fighting with all his strength.

> Then I heard a loud voice in heaven, proclaiming, "Now have
> come the salvation and the power and the kingdom of our God
> and the authority of his Messiah, for the accuser of our com-
> rades has been thrown down, who accuses them day and night
> before our God." (Rev 12:10)

Heaven has inconceivable joy when the dragon no longer has the power to tempt or accuse human beings. One may speak with truth now that the dragon has been thrown down and pride destroyed, *salvation and the power and the kingdom of our God* is established in our soul. When the dragon is destroyed, O God, this is when you reign as sovereign.

The will of God was made perfectly in heaven since pride was banished and Satan was thrown out. But this will has not been accomplished on earth and will not be until the dragon is entirely destroyed.

When the church of God, in heaven and on earth, sings with power, *Now have come the salvation,* God's will is realized. Until now, salvation was not universal because the dragon knocked an infinite number of souls into the abyss. But when the dragon will be overthrown and destroyed, the *reign of God will be established.* Also, hell will be there until the time of the Antichrist. There will be a long space of years before the whole face of the earth will be renewed because Jesus Christ sends his Spirit, as it is written, *When you send forth your spirit, they are created; and you renew the face of the ground* (Psalm 104:30). This new state of innocence of redemption is so abundant that we will taste the fruits with astonishment and surprise.

In this time the *strength of our God* will be shown with the light of his power. Now, O my God, you will be king and reign as Sovereign. Your reign will be a reign of peace, full of delicacies. Until now, O my dear King, you have not reigned absolutely but now you are going to reign. O God, it seems that you had no power and that the demon had an almost invincible power, because he was born of pride. But the demon's power will come to an end, because there will be only pure love. O salvation, you are great! O day of salvation written so clearly about in the prophets! I pray that those who read these writings fall into God's hands, if they only hear what they contain. If what is written there seems to them so bold and surprising, do not let them judge poorly. Keep them on the mark and let them arrive well at what is written. The Lord assures us that this is the truth, and he will not let any point pass that is not fulfilled, according to the promises of Jesus Christ. Yes, without doubt, O God, your reign will come. You will be known, worshipped, and loved by all the nations. As the prophet Isaiah says for everyone on earth, *every knee will bow* (Isaiah 45:23).

> "But they have conquered him by the blood of the Lamb and by the word of their testimony, for they did not cling to life even in the face of death. [12] Rejoice then, you heavens and those who dwell in them! But woe to the earth and the sea, for the devil has come down to you with great wrath, because he knows that his time is short!" (Rev 12:11–12)

Pride will never be *defeated* except *by the blood of the Lamb.* The efforts of the creatures are useless in this enterprise. But how is it done? *By the word of their testimony to Jesus Christ* and to his divine power, they confess him for what he is. When *love* that humans have *for life* does not cause them to cling to an ordinary *death,* but they committed themselves without reservation to suffer thousands and thousands of deaths. *Rejoice then, you heavens*, that is to say, O superior part of the soul, because the dragon will not harm you. But you, O *earth*, O inferior part, fear. Because he has come down to you with great wrath because *his time is short.*

To explain this well, we need to know that when the division of the superior and inferior parts of the soul is done, the devil is chaff and pride. The demon has some access to the inferior part but no access to the superior part. The inferior part will only be healed in time. The demon takes revenge on it with fury and reduces it very often to a deplorable state. But even its stinging pain is the mark of the next deliverance.

The demon had the power to *rest in the air*. As Ephesians 2:2 reads, *In which you once lived, following the course of this world, following the ruler of the power of the air, the spirit that is now at work among those who are disobedient.* The demon's power is *the spiritual forces of evil in the heavenly places* but now he is banished from the air (Eph 6:12). He has fallen on *the earth*, where he has only a short time to exercise his cruelty and tyranny. It seems that the world must perish. Pure love is almost banished and it only lives in some in solitude in a few souls chosen over all the others.

The dragon exercises his cruelty with more strength than ever. He has taken nearly all human beings for his supporters. But if the desolation is great and he makes great pain for human beings, we must rejoice, because the time of our general and permanent deliverance approaches. O if the souls whom the dragon hate with fury, understood that they are close to their deliverance, what joy would they have! But alas! They are convinced that this time will not end. However, it never ends when we expect it.

> So when the dragon saw that he had been thrown down to the earth, he pursued the woman who had given birth to the male child. 14 But the woman was given the two wings of the great eagle, so that she could fly from the serpent into the wilderness, to her place where she is nourished for a time, and times, and half a time. (Rev 12:13–14)

The dragon made the cruelest war that he could against the truth, but the woman is given *two wings* like *an eagle* to surmount all the others. She *flies into the desert*, to souls separated from the world, in deserted places. It is there that she is cultivated and *nourished* ready to appear in the day.

The children of the church persecute her but she *flies* into a place where she is not known. The spirit of faith and truth that animates it is hidden for several years. The interior spirit, which is its main ornament, appears extinguished. After this, it appears in all its luster. It is the Spirit of the church which must bring forth the interior in all hearts. And as the dragon sees that this bride of Jesus Christ is going to extend the kingdom of Jesus Christ through all the earth, he arouses the greatest persecutions against them. The church is divided against herself because all her children are at war with *division* that causes quarrels. The loving hearts with the *most God* are those fighting the cause of division. And where does that come from? It is those who stop between *two times* and do not strive to come to an end. Jesus Christ says that the world will pass away, but all that is written about him will not pass away. He accomplishes all of this without doubt and in a manner that fills the hearts with joy.

> Then from his mouth the serpent poured water like a river after the woman, to sweep her away with the flood. ¹⁶ But the earth came to the help of the woman; it opened its mouth and swallowed the river that the dragon had poured from his mouth. (Rev 12:15–16)

The *serpent poured* a river of lies against the truth. He wants to engulf her by this horrible river's torrent of vanity and lies. But *the earth opens* itself *to receive the horrible river* within itself. The dragon throws again the river of heresy against the church, and the most dangerous are perhaps the most secret. All heretics have never done so much harm to the church as bad Christians who from within persecute the church from within and fight against the Spirit under the pretext of supporting its doctrine. They try to destroy it by pretending to establish it. You only, O Jesus, know the malice of these people, who cover themselves with the skin of a lamb but inside are a ravishing wolf pretending to establish your kingdom. O my King, they ruin your kingdom to establish themselves. However, the ones making cases against Christians are valued today. The dragon uses them and though them vomits his river of pride and poison to devour the church and truth, faith, and interior spirit. But his efforts are useless. Truth triumphs over lies. The interior spirit of the church will win. For the dragon will not be able to damage the *woman*. *The earth opens up* all of this and she is not submerged in water. He vomits again from his infernal mouth his venom to destroy her, but he can do no harm. O God, before whom everything is present, the truth is already verified.

> Then the dragon was angry with the woman, and went off to make war on the rest of her children, those who keep the commandments of God and hold the testimony of Jesus. 18 Then the dragon took his stand on the sand of the seashore. (Rev 12:17–18)

The dragon, seeing that he could do nothing either to the truth or to the church, *makes war on the rest of her children* by starting a general persecution against all interior souls who love the truth. Many will be shaken in this tempest and fear. There will be attacks on the real church who *holds the testimony of Jesus Christ*, which is none other than to have in them the reign of Jesus Christ.

> And I saw a beast rising out of the sea, having ten horns and seven heads; and on its horns were ten diadems, and on its heads were blasphemous names. (Rev 13:1)

Pride produces this frightening monster who makes eternal war on all human beings. It climbs out to appear on this stormy sea of life and makes a war more open than the first. He has *seven heads*, which are seven rejections of malice, inseparable from him and his pride. His *ten horns* are ambition, hate, jealousy, contempt of others, gossip, injustice, murders and quarrels, usurpation, luxury, revenge, and impiety. From these are derived many others. These ten horns have *crowns*, because there is not one that we do not give a crown. Ambition passes for honor; hatred and jealousy for the signs of spirit and discernment. Pride passes for courage. Nothing is so opposed to God as self-interest and pride. If one dethrones God, it would be to put himself in God's place.

> And the beast that I saw was like a leopard, its feet were like a bear's, and its mouth was like a lion's mouth. And the dragon gave it his power and his throne and great authority. (Rev 13:2)

Self-interest is *like a leopard* because outside its skin is beautiful. In the same way, self-interest is covered with the beautiful appearance of the world, with its exterior charm. But *his feet were like a bear's*, to climb and rise above all that oppose his reign. His feet are very ugly, because his actions are opposed to what he appears outside. *Its mouth was like a lion* because it devours everyone as food, such as the poor, widows, and students. The *dragon gave it his power* because all the power and malice of the demon is contained in pride, son of self-interest.

A soul without pride is an annihilated soul, in which the demon has no power. She who has pure love cannot have sin.

> One of its heads seemed to have received a death-blow, but its mortal wound had been healed. In amazement the whole earth followed the beast. (Rev 13:3)

When the head of this infernal monster appears dead, it is raised with violence and fury. Until propriety is entirely destroyed, all the other vices renew themselves and revive when they seem the most extinguished. *All the earth is in amazement*. Love of self and ambition is a rule that all human beings *follow* inviolably, with even spiritual people doing this. Where do you find one who does not search for her own interests? Scripture reads, *All of them are seeking their own interests, not those of Jesus Christ* (Philippians 2:21). Also, *All have turned aside, together they have become worthless; there is no one who shows kindness, there is not even one* (Romans 3:12). The greatest good on heaven and earth is the honor of God alone. But where do we find who has only the interests of God? Alas, it is a deplorable thing that we cannot find them! In the heart of leaders, we find the desire to please the king and to advance their own interests! In war, the desire to acquire glory and own interests! In merchants, the desire to acquire and amass wealth and own interests! In priests, frequently they desire to enter into the priesthood and hierarchy! There is no place where own interests lodge better than in the cloisters. Self-interests outside, self-interests inside, in all that they do; if they receive others, it is about their own interests. They do not work for the glory of God! This is like the skin of the leopard by which we cover all that we do. The preacher preaches about the glory of God, while searching for his own glory and applause. The missionary seeks success, while looking only for brilliance and fruit. The confessor is looking to be in vogue. Those who do not have such a gross interest, search to acquire virtues, to become perfect, searching for salvation, yet they look at themselves in all things. Where are those who look at God alone? A few look for God alone and abandon themselves and find strange crosses, dirt, and filth. Yet they remain in an inviolable sacrifice, O these people are rare! The fruits of pure love are contrary to self-love and interest. But in this century, all run after their own interests and in one way or another. Those who do not run after their interests but the interests of God alone, pass for fools and heretics. They seem the execration of the world and nature. O God! Your children are today the horror of people.

> They worshiped the dragon, for he had given his authority to the beast, and they worshiped the beast, saying, "Who is like the beast, and who can fight against it?" [5] The beast was given a mouth uttering haughty and blasphemous words, and it was allowed to exercise authority for forty-two months. [6] It opened its mouth to utter blasphemies against God, blaspheming his name and his dwelling, that is, those who dwell in heaven. (Rev 13:4–6)

All people who still live in themselves are idolatrous with self-love. They *worship* the dragon and share his fate of destruction. They say, *Who can fight against it*, to oppose their reason and their self-wisdom? They also say in their hearts, "Who will stop me from sinning?" They justify themselves by condemning other people. They glorify themselves in their prosperity, because it seems success and applause are everything to them and they put waste, misery, and condemnation on the saints.

They are *allowed to exercise authority for forty-two months* and oppress the servants of God. These people animated by self-love *blaspheme* against God. With a frightful audacity, they blaspheme *God's name* and condemn the unction of his grace which they regard as an error, an illusion, and a deception. His name is written in scripture about the outpouring of grace. This is described like the spouse who is beginning to feel the effects of an interior grace, *Your anointing oils are fragrant, your name is perfume poured out* (Song 1:3). Yet these people have the insolence to condemn experiences they do not have. These self-interested people *blaspheme against* the interior and *against God's dwelling*, the interior dwelling in peace and tranquility, as in a true *heaven*. The *tabernacle of God* is interior and extends throughout the soul, where God lives and makes his home, as Jesus himself promised, *Those who love me will keep my word, and my Father will love them, and we will come to them and make our home with them* (John 14:23). However, they fight against this interior tabernacle and tolerate all crimes and disorders. It is now, O God, that this prophecy is fulfilled.

> Also it was allowed to make war on the saints and to conquer them. It was given authority over every tribe and people and language and nation. (Rev 13:7)

Self-interests make a continual *war* against the *saints* who give glory and tribute to the greatness of God, even when stripped of everything. All the world is armed against the saints, yet those who serve the beast find approval and pass for saints and for geniuses. The saints are *defeated* and oppressed, after which, the time of truth will come. *He will not break a bruised reed or quench a smoldering wick until he brings justice to victory* (Matthew 12:20). The saints will be removed from oppression and God will give them back what they lost with advantage. However, all the rest of humanity will be dominated and possessed by the spirit of self-interest. As it is written, based on Psalm 38:7, *Every living man is an abyss of vanity.*

> And all the inhabitants of the earth will worship it, everyone whose name has not been written from the foundation of the world in the book of life of the Lamb that was slaughtered. (Rev 13:8)

No century was ever so corrupt and depraved as this one with its artifice and hypocrisy. Vices take the name of virtues. The virtues that can alone bear this name, which are pure charity, bare faith, hope without support, full annihilation, and true humiliation. These are the essential virtues, without which we have only the name and appearance of a Christian but not the heart. This is why scripture has no difficulty saying, *They worshipped the* beast, since worship and idolatry is their preference. In every century, there is corruption. However, there are also many interior people who are of God, marked with the seal of the *Lamb* and marked with the Lamb's character.

The *Lamb was immolated at the origin of the world*, that is to say, the origins of the interior and Christian world. The Lamb in his immolation changed by his death and blood the book of death into a *book of life*. Because after Adam sinned, it became a book of death, protesting against all human beings but the Lamb by his immolation brought us from death and changed the decree, giving us a general absolution and changing the condemnation of death into a promise of life. Jesus Christ obtained this life and imprints his character on all those who would like to live with his life and let him destroy death within them.

All souls in whom Jesus Christ lives and reigns are those marked by his seal and are freed from their tyranny by the blood of Jesus Christ. But those who are not animated by the life of Jesus Christ, and have not submitted to his empire, are not marked by his seal. The beast has power over them.

But, some say, all Christians are marked with the seal of Jesus Christ. I confess this is true, if she lives the life of a Christian, and her interior and her conduct have relationship with his name. To be a Christian, we need to live the life of Jesus Christ and to be animated by his Spirit, to be as Paul says, *And those who belong to Christ Jesus have crucified the flesh with its passions and desires* (Galatians 5:24). They are *a new creation: everything old has passed away; see, everything has become new!* (2 Corinthians 5:17). *All of us*, he continues, *who have been baptized into Christ Jesus were baptized into his death* to have a part in his new life. Then *For all who are led by the Spirit of God are children of God* (Romans 8:14). But where do we find them? They are many but are unknown. Or if they are known, they take on the character of Jesus Christ.

> Let anyone who has an ear listen: [10] If you are to be taken captive, into captivity you go; if you kill with the sword, with the sword you must be killed. Here is a call for the endurance and faith of the saints. (Rev 13:9–10)

This passage should be well-feared. Interior souls will be attacked with the fury of an unchained lion and suffer punishments and outrages. The attackers will have some victory, because God permits them some time so his servants will be annihilated and tested. As Ecclesiasticus 2:5 says, God's servants will be tested in the *furnace of adversity* as *gold is tried in the fire*. We are purified at the same time. But after God serves his servants by purifying and annihilating them, he punishes and burns with rods those who have chastised his children.

Let those who triumph today *and hold them captive* be persuaded that they will be themselves *reduced* one day *to captivity* and will have the same misfortune they made others suffer. O Justice of my God! You appear to be without eyes or ears but the time you avenge your servants will come. But you, O oppressed servants of God, rejoice, because you show your faithfulness to God. This time is only for the testing of your faith. God tests you as he did Abraham, to see if you will retain your faithfulness, trust, and abandonment in your suffering. Yet when you are oppressed, afflicted, and tormented, you re-double your faith, abandonment, and patience.

Let anyone who has an ear listen to the truth. The time has come when the lie triumphs over the truth, and where the lovers of selfishness triumph over the lovers of Jesus Christ. But the time will come, Jesus Christ will come, when the face of things changes.

> Then I saw another beast that rose out of the earth; it had two horns like a lamb and it spoke like a dragon. [12] It exercises all the authority of the first beast on its behalf, and it makes the earth and its inhabitants worship the first beast, whose mortal wound had been healed. (Rev 13:11–12)

The *other beast* of propriety is held in less suspicions, but actually does more harm. This one has a very beautiful appearance, full of its own interest in a hidden manner, that makes it difficult to discern because *it had two horns like a Lamb*. The horns of the Lamb are justice and divine strength. The horns of the beast are self-interested justice and strength. This is why they *rise out of the earth*, because it comes out of corrupt nature, instead of coming from the Lamb above. But how to know this terrible monster? Its voice speaks like the dragon. The word of God is always fertile, a speech only regarding the glory of God and the good for human beings, as he himself says, *Yet I do not seek my own glory, but that of the One who sent me* (John 8:50). But the beast seeks his own glory and profit

This frightful beast *exercises all the authority of the first beast*, all the tyranny of self-interest, and makes others *worship* and esteem the advantage of self-interest because it is propriety that sustains and fortifies it.

> It performs great signs, even making fire come down from
> heaven to earth in the sight of all. (Rev 13:13)

Propriety covered with the appearance of piety has power to perform *signs*.
It *makes fire come down from heaven,* a false light that resembles heaven to
inflate the pride of this beast and give him a new power over human beings.
If a proprietary human being undertakes something, he succeeds at everything. The success swells up and makes them more proprietary. Troubles
annihilate the other group and make them sink more and more into God.

> And by the signs that it is allowed to perform on behalf of the
> beast, it deceives the inhabitants of earth, telling them to make
> an image for the beast that had been wounded by the sword and
> yet lived. (Rev 13:14)

This propriety *deceives the inhabitants of earth,* those who live in self-
centeredness. It blinds them so much that they are persuaded that the true
good is bad. They *make an image of the beast* to wear. This *image* resembles
self-love, because self-love counterfeits pure love and the image of self-love
appears to be pure love to those who do not know.

This beast is wounded but though it appears deadly, it is still full of
life. She who has pure love, truly dies by the force and wounds made against
her. To the opposite, self-love becomes even more alive. Yes, all the world is
deceived and blind on this point. What are you pretending with the image of
the beast that passes for signs in the world! These signs feed people to attract
souls to the beast and worship themselves rather than to worship God. The
idol shepherd makes them idolize and worship the idols (Zechariah 11:17).
Finally, everything is seduced by propriety.

> And he had power to give life unto the image of the beast, that
> the image of the beast should both speak, and cause that as
> many as would not worship the image of the beast should be
> killed. (Rev 13:15)

This *image of the beast is animated* by propriety. O that we know those who
belong to self-love and those who belong to God! One is animated by propriety and the others are annihilated and are animated only by the Spirit of
God. This propriety is *worshipped* at the present throughout the world and
appears great on the earth. O what blindness! Now only propriety has the
right to *speak* and alone is listened to. A few good and simple souls hear
the language of pure love, yet all other people are stone deaf. They only
hear the language of the beast. To them the language of pure love appears
strange and barbarian. To them the Spirit of the church and Gospels seem

a suspicious spirit. All the world listens to the language of the beast which seems natural to them. Propriety, the enemy of pure love, will try to destroy, *kill* and extinguish pure love. This is why it oppresses *all those who do not submit* to it. O truth as clear as the day, how are you not understood?

> Also it causes all, both small and great, both rich and poor, both
> free and slave, to be marked on the right hand or the forehead,
> [17] so that no one can buy or sell who does not have the mark,
> that is, the name of the beast or the number of its name. (Rev
> 13:16)

Is it not today that self-ownership is acted on in all the world? Ah, there is not a person on the earth who is not led by *self-interest*. It is the *character* that is received *from the beast* in which one thinks only of one's self. They will not act for faith. All human beings act in this way, except those marked with the character of the Lamb to have no other interest than that of God alone.

The character and mark of the servants of God is *a mark on the fore-heads, God alone* in all things, God and his cross. We act for God's glory and interest alone, and not for all that pleases us: goods, honors, friends, children, salvation, eternity, perfections. For God alone. This is the seal and character of the Lamb with the Lamb's voice and language. The other people are contrary. Whatever you propose to them, they consult their own interest of honor, glory, reputation, family, money, and self-advancement. They regard themselves in all things. The most perfect are those who look upon the interest of their salvation. God willing that all are reduced to this! Self-interest is therefore the character and language of the beast.

> So that no one can buy or sell who does not have the mark, that
> is, the name of the beast or the number of its name. [18] This calls
> for wisdom: let anyone with understanding calculate the num-
> ber of the beast, for it is the number of a person. Its number is
> six hundred sixty-six. (Rev 13:17–18)

Those who do not bear the character of the beast, and in whom their own interest no longer reigns, are rejected by their communities and hated by their relatives. They are not suitable *for commerce*, they say, because they do not know how to lie or deceive. But, O God, they are only hated by the world because they do not have the character of the world. They are not like other human beings, because they carry the character of Jesus Christ. Although they are the gentlest and kindest of people, people run away, fear, and hate them, as if they are refuse. What did this person do to you whom you do not know, to hate as you do, to talk about with such contempt? All we can say it that we will not bear the character of the beast, because its actions and its words are different from ours. We are not like the others. O abuse!

Somewhere in the world are found the souls marked by the character of Jesus Christ, who do not speak the same language and act in the same way as those marked by the character of the beast. *This calls for wisdom*, to be able to discern the character of those marked by the beast or those marked by Jesus Christ. The beast's strength is in his number but his time will end soon, soon.

> Then I looked, and there was the Lamb, standing on Mount Zion! And with him were one hundred forty-four thousand who had his name and his Father's name written on their foreheads. (Rev 14:1)

The Lamb is on Mount Zion, which is none other than the center of the soul marked by his seal and engraved with his character. *With him were one hundred forty-four thousand* who are those marked with his seal. These one hundred forty-four thousand are reduced in annihilation and are in perfect unity, forever *with the Lamb*.

The Lamb is also in the church in a continual immolation and in a state of annihilation. These annihilated souls are united with a unity of spirit on the altar of Jesus Christ in a perpetual sacrifice and a continual annihilation, in a state of death. These are the souls who are the victims of Jesus Christ, who is immolated for them. Their union with Jesus Christ is extremely grand on the altar, because they carry his state. We will only see in heaven the grandeur and the nature of this union. We carry in ourselves in the supreme part of our spirit the character of the Divinity. O happy souls, who participate in the happiness of Jesus Christ! You are hidden, dead, and annihilated with him. You suffer outrages, affronts, calumnies like he did, in a perfect silence. But the time will come, when you will be raised out of your oppression and moved into the wedding of the Lamb.

> And I heard a voice from heaven like the sound of many waters and like the sound of loud thunder; the voice I heard was like the sound of harpists playing on their harps, ³ and they sing a new song before the throne and before the four living creatures and before the elders. No one could learn that song except the one hundred forty-four thousand who have been redeemed from the earth. (Rev 14:2–3)

A voice from heaven like the sound of many waters is the voice of abandoned souls like *the sound of loud thunder*. However, it is like the voice of *the sound of harpists playing on their harps* because it is in harmony and all their wills are voluntary, submitted, and dependent in continual accord with the will of God. O, if we knew the glory that God sends upon the souls who become one with God's only and unique will. They have perfect accord and admirable union, all the creature with the Creator that is shared among them. Because they are entirely animated by one Spirit and they have one and indivisible will, which is that of God.

These souls *sing a new song that no other can learn or sing* because it will never be understood except by annihilated souls, who have no more propriety, self-spirit, and will. They are given a divine language which only God can teach them to sing and a *new song* of Jesus Christ that he sang at birth. He said, *I delight to do your will, O my God; your law is within my heart* (Psalm 40:8). Also, *Then I said, "See, God, I have come to do your will, O God' (in the scroll of the book it is written of me)"* (Hebrews 10:7). It is *new* because no one ever sang it and cannot sing it, except those who are annihilated. It is unknown to all others except those in whom this canticle is sung. It is new for those who sing it after their complete destruction and after having been *redeemed from the earth.*

This redemption is understood in two senses. One, these redeemed souls have had taken away from all that is proprietary and terrestrial from Adam. The other redemption is that God has exempted them from the common way of annihilation, having privileged them even before their birth. It is good to have both annihilations and the annihilation will not fail to be manifested one day. O God, you reveal your grand things, and manifest things now to my heart that cannot be expressed because they would not be heard.

> It is these who have not defiled themselves with women, for they
> are virgins; these follow the Lamb wherever he goes. They have
> been redeemed from humankind as first fruits for God and the
> Lamb. (Rev 14:4)

The *virginity* of the body contributes to the beautiful walk that shows a great courage. With such a singular advantage, O God, what crosses, reversals do not happen to them? They appear the most unfortunate of human beings and yet they are the most blessed.

They *have been redeemed from human kind.* They were brought out of corrupt nature, propriety, and separated from all that is of Adam. They have been redeemed from human kind *to be the first fruits for God* and to be his particular sacrifices. The souls of this type are not removed from the world, but they are in the bosom of God. But if God gives to the soul such a singular grace by removing her from propriety, she is to become an offering and sacrifice because God makes these souls perpetual victims, in whom he immolates their will in an admirable way.

> And in their mouth no lie was found; they are blameless. (Rev 14:5)

These annihilated souls are put in truth. They do not say *lies*, since the slightest deception would be for them a thing unsupportable. Their words are truth, since all their words are only to show all of God and the nothingness of the creature. They give God what is due to him and delight in him. As such, they *are blameless* and are like a mirror reflecting the sun of justice.

> Then I saw another angel flying in midheaven, with an eternal gospel to proclaim to those who live on the earth—to every nation and tribe and language and people. (Rev 14:6)

The eternal gospel is none other than the gospel of the will of God, who has always been and who will always be. This is the gospel of his truth known in eternity where your will is perfectly accomplished. You accomplish it yourself in yourself for your creatures and angels. But, O God, rebellious humans used their freedom to oppose you with all their will. Your will is always infallible and they do not fail to be punished who use this freedom to revolt against your will. If the angels could aspire to something, it would be to have this freedom, so that they would freely choose the will of God. However, foolish and insensitive human, O reckless and ungrateful human, you use this freedom to oppose God, however useless this is. Instead, use your freedom to submit in justice and to do God's will.

This *eternal gospel* is therefore the will of God, which *is proclaimed to those who live on the earth*. O God, yes: this is true as scripture says, *This good news of the kingdom will be proclaimed throughout the world* (Matthew 24:14). The gospel, which we almost do not know, which seems to be a very particular language, will be the common and universal language. O divine language, you will be the happiness for people on earth! What made humans unhappy was disobedience to God. What makes people happy is accomplishing the will of God. Let the person does all she wants to make herself happy, when she possesses all the kingdoms of the world with pleasures and riches, she will only be perfectly happy in the accomplishment of the will of God. The least resistance puts her in trouble, pain, and suffering. When she only lets herself be what God wants of her, she enters into peace and an inconceivable joy. If she lives only for pleasure, she will always feel trouble and boredom inside.

What makes us fail to do the will of God is that we want to judge the will by our reason, and according to our own thoughts. This is not a good way to judge. Instead, let's judge by abandon and a total surrender to God which gives us peace, joy, and freedom. O eternal will, you will only be known by the annihilated soul O *eternal gospel*, you will only be practiced by the souls without propriety!

> He said in a loud voice, "Fear God and give him glory, for the hour of his judgment has come; and worship him who made heaven and earth, the sea and the springs of water." (Rev 14:7)

Almost everyone mistakenly understands the fear of God as the fear of being chastised, which is the self's fear of the truth and punishment. Pure love causes us to fear not pleasing God enough or of not doing his will. Chastisements are not to be feared because they come from God's justice. John says that we are to *give him glory, for the hour of his judgment has come*. The faithful soul loves God's judgment, however rigorous it may be. A usurping injustice withdraws creatures from God and from submitting their will to God. O Love, do make your judgments promptly! I love and worship you. I will always *give you glory*. This is enough for me without regarding myself or my own self-interest. Only your glory, O God, only your glory brings me pleasure. You will be glorified in your judgment. That is enough to please me. Even if I see my condemnation described, O God, you only are known, loved, and worshipped! But the time will come, the time will come, when the *eternal gospel* will be preached. It will be then that the language that is written here, will be heard throughout the world and will not appear barbarous and strange.

Is it not right, that we *worship* our *Creator*, who has created all things and whom we worship with a double admiration? This is why scripture reads *who made heaven and earth*, that is to say, the interior and the exterior, the inside and the outside. All Christians believe in worshipping God, but it is easy to prove that hardly any adore him. *Worship God in our interior* by giving homage to his sovereignty by our annihilation before him. *Worship God in our exterior* is to remain with a profound respect in his presence. But to worship in the exterior is not true if it is not supported by in the interior. Who is annihilated before God? Who is it who believes that he must be annihilated before God? Who is that stands before God with the modesty and respect that is due God? To see the Christians in the church of God is to see people in a market or in a fair. There is no person seeing this who can imagine that we believe that God is present, and that we only come to the temple to dishonor him. The Turks and pagans are a thousand times more respectful in their temples.

> Then another angel, a second, followed, saying, "Fallen, fallen is
> Babylon the great! She has made all nations drink of the wine of
> the wrath of her fornication." (Rev 14:8)

Babylon, a city of confusion, cupidity, pride, and sensuality, is the enemy of
peace and simplicity which caused the division of languages at the beginning of the world. It was she who wanted to dispense and rise above God.
Let's make, said the Babylonians, a tower that goes up to the heaven. They
did not obey God anymore. O Babylon, that makes confusion and multiplicity among human beings and changed their language so it differs from
God. And as God wants to establish his eternal gospel, which is his will, it
is necessary that he destroy and *overthrow* the self-will of Babylon. All sins
are committed only by the separation of our will from that of God. Adam
brought sin into the world, because he had a will contrary to the will of God.
If our will were united with God, we would never sin. Because God does not
want sin, we could want it no more.

Before God establishes his eternal gospel, he overthrows the self-will
but does not do this operation all of a sudden. The creature is too weak
to carry God's will quickly. But little by little, God accommodates to our
weakness.

This Babylon *has made all nations drink of the wine of the wrath of her
fornication.* There is hardly a person on the earth not full of his own will. We
do not wish to renounce our will in all respects. Scriptures rightly call this
fornication because our will was made to be united with God's will and to be
the same with God. However, people withdrew from God to give themselves
to the demon. Since that time, people have been in a continual revolt against
God. Human beings left the unity and the simplicity of God to enter into the
multiplicity of Babylon.

> Then another angel, a third, followed them, crying with a loud
> voice, "Those who worship the beast and its image, and receive
> a mark on their foreheads or on their hands, [10] they will also
> drink the wine of God's wrath, poured unmixed into the cup of
> his anger, and they will be tormented with fire and sulfur in the
> presence of the holy angels and in the presence of the Lamb."
> (Rev 14:9–10)

Those marked by the seal and character of propriety have rejected the holy
fire and pure love to be burned instead by the fire of cupidity. In taking
the name of pure love when they were full of self-love, they blasphemed
against the church. They have been led by their own inclination and unregulated and corrupt will. They have taken *the character of the beast* on
their forehead, and their spirit is only full of themselves, regarding their

own pleasure, glory, and avarice. They have also received the mark of the beast *on their hands* and consecrated all their works to serve their own love, interest, and propriety.

Those who only want to drink from the cellars of the divine Spouse will let themselves be drained of themselves. Jesus Christ's sweet and strong wine begins as both wine and milk, but afterwards he gives charity within us. May it be that this heart can burn only with pure love and no other artificial fire! As I say, those who refused this pure wine mingled in the loving chalice of Jesus Christ will drink only bitterness. They leave behind the useful and delectable. Instead, they will *drink the wine of God's wrath, poured unmixed into the cup of his anger.* They will drink it with bitterness, even in this life. The one who drinks pure love, which is strong and delicious, and full of peace and pleasure, is fully satisfied. The one who drinks the wine of the wrath in filled with trouble and chagrin. The more he drinks it, the more he is changed, because it is not his natural drink. The human being has been born to love God purely, and this makes her happy and satisfied. But those with the beast have a heart filled with the poison of the serpent, which is a strange love which becomes his hangman destroying and burning continually. To the opposite, the blood of the Lamb is a drink refreshing that quenches our thirst and warms and changes us. The wine of self-love, which is a wine of anger and not of love, *torments* those who take it, changes continually, and never quenches their thirst. The torment they have in this world is only weak in comparison to the one they must suffer in the other world. That will be a continuation and intensification of evils. They drank wine of *fire and sulfur* which is the *wrath of God* for their cupidity. They will drink in the other life with long strokes of sulfur fire.

It is not that anyone who has propriety is not saved, but they *go through the fire* (1 Corinthians 3:15). The gross and carnal sins justly frighten us. Yet sins of propriety are monsters a thousand times more appalling yet they do not cause fear. We follow, love, and tolerate them as if they were nothing. Are there in the world such dreadful beasts as are described here? However, we are afraid of other beasts, who are not as dangerous. This horrible beast causes such great misfortune. O blindness, blindness! But where does this blindness come from? The light of truth is chased away and hidden in the desert in solitary places dedicated to pure love. All other people walk in the light of a false light, which dazzles them without enlightening them, which makes them see precipices as mountains and mountains as precipices, which assures them that their feet are in solid and firm places, and instead they step in mud and water. O God, send the light of your truth. You will send it, O Love, when the dragon will be killed and destroyed, and Babylon completely overthrown.

> And the smoke of their torment goes up forever and ever.
> There is no rest day or night for those who worship the beast
> and its image and for anyone who receives the mark of its
> name. (Rev 14:11)

Those with propriety *worship the beast*. O God, some of these people pass
as having merit! O God, your sacred fire knows well how to purify what
is yours and reject what is not. Surely proprietary people suffer in this life
very great torment with *no rest day or night*. Their regrets gnaw at them,
their ambition devours them, and they suffer from inconceivable torments.
But if they suffer in this way, the torments prepared for them in the other
life are much stranger.

The servants of God suffer a large quantity of crosses, pains, and afflictions but they are full of immortality. They bring to the soul that suffers
a certain peace and a profound joy. When the exterior appears the most
desolate, it is then that the interior tastes a most profound contentment.
So that the crosses and sorrows of the saints should not properly pass for
crosses and pains because of the consolation they bring. However, these
sweet sorrows that love makes its lovers feel are rewarded with an eternal
weight of glory. However, the partisans of self-love suffer grievous sorrows
and unsuccessful pains followed by eternal torment. It is said that there is so
much pain in being saved. But for me, there is much more pain in getting
lost from God.

> Here is a call for the endurance of the saints, those who keep
> the commandments of God and hold fast to the faith of Jesus.
> (Rev 14:12)

In this time, one sees *the endurance of the saints*. Saints need a great patience
to live with the sinners who torment them. Even when the saints do no
wrong, others treat them as if they do wrong. The sinners, the proprietar-
ies, and others persecute the saints. These torments are a strange force like
carnivorous wolves coming after them. However, these persecutors pass for
the most just in the world. But the time of truth arrives, when the eternal
day comes to light and things will change. However, O saints, do not be
weary of suffering persecution, when it seems to you that God is opposed
to you. God conceals your suffering but does not ignore it. God uses this to
increase your crown by giving you matters for your *patience*. You note that
God increases your patience by the measure of the crosses that he sends
you, so that through your suffering, you become insensible to suffering. This
patience is given to those who follow the will of God and who place all their
trust in Jesus Christ.

> And I heard a voice from heaven saying, "Write this: Blessed
> are the dead who from now on die in the Lord." "Yes," says the
> Spirit, "they will rest from their labors, for their deeds follow
> them." (Rev 14:13)

My God, these beautiful words! How consoling they are! There are two types of *dead in the Lord*. The first must necessarily precede the other. To die in the first death in the Lord, it is necessary that the person lose all that he has of himself, all that is of the sinner Adam, all that is natural and human, all propriety, so that he is in God. O truly happy death! You wipe away all pains. O fortunate death, in which the soul leaves herself, to be received into God, and finds joy in an inconceivable happiness. O death, the source of a true life! John speaks about this death that has a relationship with all other states. Because without this death, the soul will never come out of itself and its propriety. O fortunate death, who places the soul in God! Only you can do that. After this death, natural death is an ineffable happiness because it gives a perfect joy and light, which we enjoy under the veil of faith. Without this first death, the second death is always a bit to be feared because it does not always put the soul in God, but into the flames of purgatory, where it will be according to what remains of propriety. But the soul that is truly dead, when death consumes, is received into God himself.

The souls taken to God in the passive way have a strong tendency to union because of the intimate and delectable qualities of this state. Her joy is only in perfect repose. Yet she feels some impurities that separate her from God and wants to be more united and lost in the abyss of God. However, the union does not always feel consistent. Sometimes instead of union, she feels division rather than a union. This torments the soul. She experiences a passionate love which makes her desire death because she does not understand that she can be united to God in this life. She wishes to be delivered from the prison of her body, like Paul says to be separated from the body to be united with God. Then that we experience this great and violent desire for death, which seems to reduce the body to a tomb and to give the soul the happiness after which she sighs. Many saints and holy people have died of love and for love.

There is a time following this when the soul loses her first ardor and enters under strange influences. Her state seems entirely reversed. In place of desiring and hoping for an intimate union, she only waits for punishments and tortures. It makes death all the more terrible because it seems that the same day that ends her natural life will begin her eternal death.

Following these frights and terrors of death, she enters into another state that is a new desire to die. She does not dare to hope anymore but she wishes for death to be delivered from this body and life of sin.

When she passes through this state, frequently the fear and fright of death is taken away, until finally she is truly dead to all sentiment, interest, propriety; she rests in supreme indifference for this life and for death. She has no choice, no inclination, and no tendency for death. Now she has neither fear nor desire. She remains dead in the state where God holds her, without wishing to leave or fearing the state.

She is then in perfect *repose* because her union is in the center. Although she no longer distinguishes herself, she is much more real. She has found the perfect repose where she has no choice, penchants, and tendencies. This is the infallible mark of union which is in the center. In this perfect indifference, the soul cannot tend, will, or wish for either death or life. All is equal, and it is then that she says with Paul with indifference: *If we live, we live to the Lord, and if we die, we die to the Lord; so then, whether we live or whether we die, we are the Lord's* (Romans 14:8). This is enough.

When the soul has been a long time in this sincere and general state, she is put for some moments in a strong and pure love, in which she desires to die. This is unusual and better to experience than written about. She says in her soul: *Father, the hour has come; glorify your Son so that the Son may glorify you* (John 17:1). This shows the perfect indifference and effect of consummation. These souls are no longer for the earth and the earth is no longer for them. Such souls will only remain if they are destined to help others. When they are in this disposition, which fills the souls, they are ready to spend eternity on the earth, or even in hell, if this pleases God. Pure love burns within and consummates the soul in secret yet manifests itself outside. These souls as a rule are not well-known because God likes to hide this from themselves and others. O if we see the fire that burns with purity and cleanliness! We would be ravished. But God takes pleasure in covering this with a poor exterior, so that those who judge by the exterior, ignore them. Paul says, *But if I wish to boast, I will not be a fool, for I will be speaking the truth. But I refrain from it, so that no one may think better of me than what is seen in me or heard from me* (2 Corinthians 12:6). God has hidden these souls. *They will rest from their labors*: there is more for them. They carry everywhere the reward of their work, which is all made in God.

> Then I looked, and there was a white cloud, and seated on the cloud was one like the Son of Man, with a golden crown on his head, and a sharp sickle in his hand! [15] Another angel came out of the temple, calling with a loud voice to the one who sat on the

> cloud, "Use your sickle and reap, for the hour to reap has come,
> because the harvest of the earth is fully ripe." (Rev 14:14–15)

O Jesus, you who *reap the earth* to harvest it in your love or in your anger! You came, O Love, and gave your life, so that the weeds sown by the enemy, will be changed into the purest form of good grain. However, these weeds wanted to preserve their nature despite your care and your goodness. You will reap by your *sickle* and take to yourself the good grain and throw the other into the fire.

When the wheat is *ripe*, Jesus Christ reaps and places it in his granary. He attracts the soul to him, and has her die when her work is finished, unless he destines that she help others in a particular way. Your only love is that this soul does your will and is content to live in this strange land where we know you so little. O God, what does a creature do on this earth who is so consumed with love for you? Your will only. She cannot find anyone who suits her on earth. However, she remains abandoned, without consolation either in the interior or the exterior. O Love, you consummate us, hold us in this way, and will consummate us day to day. One may say that these souls are *ripe* for heaven, as the others are *ripe* for hell.

> So the one who sat on the cloud swung his sickle over the earth,
> and the earth was reaped. (Rev 14:16)

In Judgement Day, God will reap the rest of humanity. There are two times of reaping. In one it seems that God *reaps* all the servants in the cities and in the kingdoms, because these cities and kingdoms are unworthy. At another time God reaps all the sinners and leaves only the righteous. This is also the way he acted in the time of Noah and in the time of Lot. There will come a time when God reaps his enemies, because he wants to leave on earth an assembly of righteous people and saints. It will be then that God wearied of the torments which the impious and unjust inflict on his servants delivers them from oppression. The reaping is the harvest of the saints.

> Then another angel came out of the temple in heaven, and he
> too had a sharp sickle. [18] Then another angel came out from
> the altar, the angel who has authority over fire, and he called
> with a loud voice to him who had the sharp sickle, "Use your
> sharp sickle and gather the clusters of the vine of the earth, for
> its grapes are ripe." [19] So the angel swung his sickle over the earth
> and gathered the vintage of the earth, and he threw it into the
> great wine press of the wrath of God. [20] And the wine press was
> trodden outside the city, and blood flowed from the wine press,

as high as a horse's bridle, for a distance of about two hundred miles. (Rev 14:17–20)

The harvest is the horrible vengeance God will visit on the enemies of pure love. It will be a terrible justice and a strong carnage when the enemies of the church are subjected, and when all idolatrous nations and heretics are brought under his shadow. In this strong carnage, the enemies of God are finally defeated.

When God annihilates a soul, he uses this soul. All who participate in self-love, designated by the *inhabitants of the earth*, are thrown in the great wine press of the *wrath of God*, because they are not pardoned.

Those who have spread your blood and that of your servants, wanting to destroy your Spirit, tests your vengeance, O Lord.

> Then I saw another portent in heaven, great and amazing: seven angels with seven plagues, which are the last, for with them the wrath of God is ended. (Rev 15:1)

O vengeful God, how awful and terrible your vengeance! O it is hard and terrible to fall into the hands of the Living God! What, has the earth not suffered enough from plagues to appease your anger? O God, what more do you need? No, no. God is not entirely content. The earth must suffer these last signs of the wrath of God. But when the *seven last plagues* are passed, there will be no more to suffer and the earth will be at peace, and the servants of God will be delivered from oppression.

If this is for the general world, this is also for the particular human destined to be annihilated. It is necessary that the ungrateful earth, this rebellious nature, suffer these *seven plagues*, after which there will be nothing more for it to suffer. Because once these are passed, the wrath of God is finished and the creature annihilated. O God, as long as there is something of Adam's living nature, your wrath is illumined against it, and you do not let him rest. This is for the souls that God wants to annihilate and destroy and not for others. For the souls God chooses, there are only rigors as long as they have the least life. For the others there are only caresses.

> And I saw what appeared to be a sea of glass mixed with fire, and those who had conquered the beast and its image and the number of its name, standing beside the sea of glass with harps of God in their hands. (Rev 15:2)

The *sea* is Divinity, in which all annihilated souls are submerged and engulfed. But to come there, we must be like the sea, pure and transparent, which can only be done by the loss of propriety. The clarity and cleanliness of the sea is *mixed with fire* which is pure love. All the saints are reduced to their origin and become once again with God. They are like many droplets in the sea and are indivisible both with each other and with the sea itself. They are one and the same thing with God, although their being is very distinct, as the droplets have their being and their particular subsistence. They are the saints who are perfectly delivered and exempt from self-centeredness, propriety, and self-interest.

They have *harps of God*. These are not particular harps, but the harps of God. This is to say that they no longer have their own will, their will being lost in God. Having the will of God, they now have the most freedom. O admirable advantage of the loss of all will! Their harps resonate incessantly with the harmony God gives, who charms the heart, and fills the poor souls with joy.

> And they sing the song of Moses, the servant of God, and the song of the Lamb: "Great and amazing are your deeds, Lord God the Almighty! Just and true are your ways, King of the nations! ⁴ Lord, who will not fear and glorify your name? For you alone are holy. All nations will come and worship before you, for your judgments have been revealed." (Rev 15:3–4)

The soul of this kind is *singing* the *Canticle* with a wonderful harmony that God makes in her, having put her in a perfect order in his creation.

But what am I saying? Even more perfect than his creation, she sings a double *song*, that of *Moses*, which is a canticle of deliverance. The second song is that *of the Lamb* which is a canticle of redemption, showing how beneficial redemption is. O if we understand well the mystery of the Lamb's redemption, a Christian would let herself be sacrificed thousands and thousands of times.

But alas, the great mysteries of our religion are taught as we teach parrots. Many people preach and teach them to others, yet do not understand them. Those who want to understand better, believe that it is a question of considering them, and of much reasoning about them. They think they understand everything when they have exhausted their powers and that by dint of having tired their spirit, they have come to some subtle and delicate thought. O what poverty! Work your mind as long as you want to study, consume all your days. Occupy yourself in as much consideration as you please. You will never comprehend or understand the great mystery of annihilation. In an annihilated soul, without thinking or considering, the soul receives the pure knowledge of the mysteries of religion, of all that regards the faith of God and God himself. If we do not study, we miss nothing that others have done with a great deal of fatigue. Instead, with this pure and clear way, it seems that we are already in the full day of God's glory. Ah! Love, love truly and purely, you will understand more than any other way.

But what is the song that the saints sing? If we understand all the words, we easily see the purity of their words and the eminence of their knowledge. *Great and amazing are your deeds, Lord God the Almighty!* They are given the knowledge of the works of God. Both the interior and exterior operations of God are revealed and manifested with an inconceivable ravishment. They see everywhere and in all things the character of the *power* and grandeur of God. This fills them with joy.

After having spoken of the operations of God, they speak of his conduct and way. O God, your way and your conduct are admirable! But they are incomprehensible to the human spirit and no one can conceive of them if they are not manifested to them. However, people are so blind, they want to measure the ways of God by their own thought. Everything they do not understand seems impossible. O blindness and foolishness of humans! Doesn't the apostle say, wonderful are the ways of God, *How unsearchable are his judgments and how inscrutable his ways!* (Romans 11:33). However, when we believe, we understand them. Even more, we want to know God's ways and make them our way. But God's ways even if incomprehensible to the human spirit are however *just and true* ways.

Also, they are seeing the same justice and truth in their words. *Who will not fear you, O Lord,* they say. Who is the ungodly, the sinner, the wicked, who will not fear your wrath, since it is as formidable as we have described? But also, who is the righteous, who are your servants, who will not glorify your name and who will not give you glory for your works? Who could glorify himself, and attribute things to himself? He should know that he lives in error and lies. *You alone are holy* and there is no other holiness than you. You are full of mercy and goodness.

Then knowing the general conversion of the earth, and the reunion of all the empires in the kingdom of Jesus Christ, they assure, *All nations will come and worship before you.* Yes, O God. This will be verified after all the plagues that have to come, will come, and then will pass away. Happy are those who live in that fortunate century! They will only come to God in this way after God *reveals his judgments.*

> After this I looked, and the temple of the tent of witness in heaven was opened, ⁶ and out of the temple came the seven angels with the seven plagues, robed in pure bright linen, with golden sashes across their chests. ⁷ Then one of the four living creatures gave the seven angels seven golden bowls full of the wrath of God, who lives forever and ever; ⁸ and the temple was

> filled with smoke from the glory of God and from his power,
> and no one could enter the temple until the seven plagues of the
> seven angels were ended. (Rev 15:5–8)

In this beautiful and pure scripture, we are surprised that not everyone wants to see this revealed beauty and clarity. We know the grandeur and majesty of scripture reveals much meaning. Those who read scripture discover what it pleases God to manifest to them. There is a *temple of the tent of witness* in each of us. This temple is our heart, where we receive the testimony of the goodness of God and of his love for us and where we sing to God of our love for him. The *tabernacle* is in us like a holy temple. After God is pleased to give his testimony in the temple, as the proprietary creature lives and repents, what does God do? He sends his *seven plagues*, by which the soul is dispossessed of proprietary things little-by-little and annihilated. God in his mercy sends the seven *plagues of his wrath* to destroy the person's malignant nature and this unfortunate propriety. God saves the soul in this way. But alas, this does not appear to the soul as a good, but as the greatest of evils. This is why she has so much trouble complying with it.

But before the angels pour the *seven bowls full of the wrath of God, the temple*, into the malignant nature, the interior is *filled with smoke*. It seems that it hides the evil and fatal thoughts. But to our astonishment, this smoke painful to the soul and that she believes comes from the absence of her God, actually only comes from *the presence of God's majesty*. The *virtue of God* wants to have the effect to act as sovereign. The soul out of propriety wants to evacuate all virtues and strength. So if God lives in the temple with his majesty and virtue, God infuses the soul. Because *the entrance* is forbidden to her, as soon as this state begins, the soul is placed in powerlessness to return to itself, so that she is banished from the temple. This is what Thomas à Kempis says in *The Imitation of Jesus Christ* (Book 2, chapter 9, 1) that it is something to suffer the deprivation of all creatures. But, he said, to endure *the exile of the heart* is what is very difficult. Therefore, this exile of the heart in which the soul is placed is hard and terrible. Without the exile of the heart, all the plagues, rough as they are, would be for him indifferent.

Before the seven plagues come into the soul, there was a time when the interior is almost ignored. We cannot return in faith until this time is accomplished.

> Then I heard a loud voice from the temple telling the seven an-
> gels, "Go and pour out on the earth the seven bowls of the wrath
> of God." [2] So the first angel went and poured his bowl on the
> earth, and a foul and painful sore came on those who had the
> mark of the beast and who worshiped its image. (Rev 16:1–2)

People in general will be *hit* by sin (which is a foul and painful plague) for the punishment of their other sins. (Because God punishes sin in this life by punishing with the same sin.) However, this describes very well what happens to the soul in whom God wants to destroy propriety. First, God *pours out a shameful, malignant, and dangerous plague*, temptations of any kind all combined, which is surprising, especially because they least expected it. But, O God, do you not have other ways to destroy this miserable nature? No, says, God. These are the ones I have chosen. These are efficacious ways, otherwise she would feed herself and live only in my gifts, far from dying.

> The second angel poured his bowl into the sea, and it became like the blood of a corpse, and every living thing in the sea died. (Rev 16:3)

Even as the second plague is hard, it is very useful, even more than the first. The *bowl is poured* all over *the sea, on the soul*. These are strange miseries that fall on the person, so that reason cannot console her. This sea that has been a very long time calm and tranquil, now is only agitated, and even *becomes like blood* but blood that *resembles a corpse*, so we cannot distinguish if the blood is dead or not. There is an appearance that it is dead. But if this plague is terrible, it is at the same time useful, because *every living thing in the sea died* which are all the animal and brutal affections die. The human in this state believes that all her sentiments are sins. That is what makes her desolation inconceivable. But her excessive pain is an argument for her innocence.

This is also the second plague in which God hits the wicked. After the first punishment, which is a punishment for sin with the same sin, he punishes the second sin by stupor. The person loses almost all the spirit and remain as useless as if they were dead, because the blood is the *blood of a corpse*, which means everything seems to be forbidden.

> The third angel poured his bowl into the rivers and the springs of water, and they became blood. ⁵ And I heard the angel of the waters say, "You are just, O Holy One, who are and were, for you have judged these things; ⁶ because they shed the blood of saints and prophets, you have given them blood to drink. It is what they deserve!" (Rev 16:4–6)

The *third* plague is when the *springs* and sources where the worldly and the proprietary take their pleasures *become blood* and carnage, pains and suffering. The voluptuous find their death and pains in their voluptuous pleasures and the consequences they bring, the drinker in his wine, the miser in his avarice.

The true meaning is that people who cruelly persecuted the servants of God and who worked malice and who regarded as justice the evil they were making the servants endure, will be punished in the same way, sooner or later. These people swell in their vanity for the success they have in their slanders that they claim to be truth. O God, you allow this. But after this, the time will come when you give them the justice that they merit. The angels and saints rejoice, because they regard these poor persecuted ones as their brothers. They love them especially since they see in them the image of the King, and they themselves resemble him. *O Holy One*, says this tutelary angel, through whom God sends his graces on these people and has the right to keep them under his bowl, *you are just* to do this in this way. We cannot oppose your vengeance. It is just that they are treated in the same way they treated God's servants. They must drink *the blood that they have shed.* O God, your judgments are holy and fair! It seemed at the time that you lacked justice by letting your enemies oppress your servants without avenging you or avenging them. But your reserve vengeance for the day when you give them all the justice they can hope for.

When God send the *third* plague to the soul that will disengage her, it means that the *fountains, sources of consolation,* everything that once comforted her and gives her sweetness, *changes* to rigor, *blood*, and carnage. There is no more sweetness and peace but sorrow, misery, bitterness, and chagrin. However, God is no less fair and just in his judgments, than in the first. For it is necessary that this miserable nature of persecutors which has made the saints suffer, lose blood, and have strange pains, will themselves drink the blood of bitterness, rigor, and death.

> And I heard the altar respond, "Yes, O Lord God, the Almighty,
> your judgments are true and just!" (Rev 16:7)

O Lord, who would not say that? The soul prompted to speak will speak her heart. But then she is given neither eyes nor voice. It is then God appears in his power and equitable judgments. O people, you cover your war with God with a mantle of apparent piety. You say, that you give glory to God, and that you do justice doing what you do. *The judgments* of God are *true and just*, and we will see the truth and justice in them.

> The fourth angel poured his bowl on the sun, and it was allowed
> to scorch people with fire; [9] they were scorched by the fierce
> heat, but they cursed the name of God, who had authority over
> these plagues, and they did not repent and give him glory. (Rev
> 16:8–9)

Here is the difference between sinners and the just. The just accept the evils and receive them with resignation. The more violent the pains, the stronger becomes the resignation. But the sinners are the opposite. They get irritated and impatient against evil, entering into horrible blasphemies, angering God with their evil, far from appeasing his anger. *The sun*, who has only sweet influences in a temperate air, becomes burning hot and devours souls burning with the fire of concupiscence. At the end of their life, the sensual people will feel stinging pain. They usually die of violent evils. Some repent and convert, but some *do not repent*, entering into astonishing despair.

This *fourth* plague afflicts the soul who God wishes to disengage and brings a certain strange burning, often both inside and outside. This state puts the soul in a certain temptation of blasphemy that brings a much trouble. It often makes the soul terrified, without not being able to understand how. This state tests many people in the spiritual life. However, let them be persuaded that it is only because of their resistance to some things or dispositions that God wants from them. These things burn and afflict them. Instead of carrying them with resignation, submission, and disengagement from themselves, which is a great *glory* that they may *give to God*, they resist God and do not want to give God glory. They enter into horrible rages. God fights against this soul in order to destroy in it the malignant nature; he makes her suffer all the more because she is opposed to God's will. Nature feeling this oppression goes back and forth between rage and despair. She blames God. But she misunderstands this, because she has only her propriety to blame.

> The fifth angel poured his bowl on the throne of the beast, and its kingdom was plunged into darkness; people gnawed their tongues in agony, [11] and cursed the God of heaven because of their pains and sores, and they did not repent of their deeds. (Rev 16:10–11)

The fifth *plague* that God sends on the sinner is the affliction regarding his interest, goods, and honor. It is the *throne of the beast*. The human who reigned in the applause is now decried, whoever fattened on the goods of the widow and orphan is himself impoverished, and God joins poverty to pain. There the greatest grace of God may happen. However, sinners far from using it to convert, increase their rage and blasphemies *against God* and *did not repent* for the evil they have done.

This plague is the most terrible for propriety. Here the throne is reversed. Self-love is attacked in the source with the cruelest pain of the soul. The throne of self-love is *plunged into darkness*. There is no more clarity. But far from softening nature and making it pliable, the irritated person enters into surprising rages. It seems to be a possession of the demon, this being times of extreme violence. You did well, poor nature. You must perish and die. Your resistance serves only to increase and lengthen your torture.

> The sixth angel poured his bowl on the great river Euphrates, and its water was dried up in order to prepare the way for the kings from the east. [13] And I saw three foul spirits like frogs coming from the mouth of the dragon, from the mouth of the beast, and from the mouth of the false prophet. [14] These are demonic spirits, performing signs, who go abroad to the kings of the whole world, to assemble them for battle on the great day of God the Almighty. (Rev 16:12–14)

This *plague* appears inferior to the others that have preceded it, but it surpasses it. The waters were changed and turned into blood and do not stop until it was dried up. As we have said, nature is insatiable with nourishment and likes to nourish itself well and will drink the blood and carnage, rather than having nothing at all. The most proprietary souls despite having the most terrible states find in these states something to nourish them.

This shows a truth that I have never understood about disengagement and yet here is expressed quite clearly. Certain souls pass through states that should serve to disengage and make their nature die, and yet this does not happen. Even these states are therefore a support and nourishment. This is what John says they *do not repent and give God the glory*. Repentance in this state is to give God the glory by letting our corrupt human nature be severed. We will see in the great day of eternity that souls have passed through many states, as I have said, and yet become even more proprietary in these states. We will not know this by what people say of themselves either by judgment and ordinary reason but will know by the taste of the heart and by a supernatural light when God gives a perfect discernment of the spirits. This is not done by reason in advanced souls, but by a discernment of the heart. We do not discern these people by what they say, yet from a hundred leagues we will discern souls we have never seen. Nature needs to have died to have this discernment, otherwise we would mix pure discernment with personal inclinations or repugnance.

The souls who have been many years in a grand indifference find it impossible to sin any more either by hatred or by inclination towards any creature. I say that after the soul has been tormented for a long time by the inclinations and impressions, they are put either gradually or suddenly in a state of equilibrium so perfect, that they have no opposition or inclination, as if they were of stone or bronze. They are given a taste of the heart for cooperating with God's will which makes them have a strange burning. This makes a lot of trouble in the beginning for souls because they misunderstand what is going on and think of this as the effects of nature. Others oppose her with jealousy, oppositions, and natural dispositions. Everyone whom she tells what is going on judges her in the same way. This afflicts the soul because she fears not having charity for her neighbor.

She makes an effort, yet this redoubles her pain because she understands her discernment as a fault more dangerous than all the others. It seems to her that she lacks charity with her judgment of her neighbor and regards this as a fault. Yet this discernment is a light given to her because God destines the person for service to souls. In true discernment, she knows their state without being wrong. Resistance to this state of light puts the soul in pain. It pleases God to enlighten her. She sees now that it is actually the great grace of true discernment. She does not judge the souls by reason but by the taste and grace of God.

A soul bonded with God will experience suffering. We regard these gifts of discernment with the eyes of nature and think we are envious or jealous of others, but instead, this discernment is a divine state in annihilated souls. Later we see that God gives her knowledge and discernment of things with a discerning light. Also, when a soul surrenders fully to the direction of God, she receives discernment of the subtlest things for herself or for others. We often though lack the faithfulness to declare it to others and the others lack the resignation of their spirit to let themselves receive it.

The gift of discernment can only happen for a perfectly annihilated soul and those whom God designs to serve others. People who are entirely in nature do not understand this and think that some states of grace are actually deception. God desires to purify them of the natural states of personal desires or hatred.

To come back to what I said, nature is so malignant, she likes to feed herself better on blood and ills, then to go without nourishment. Nature feeds on the hardest penalties. This is why the *drying up of the river* is a thousand times more sensitive to him than the changing of the waters into blood. The river is dried up *to prepare a passage for kings*. We understand this passage in two ways. To make a way for the princes of the world who are nature and demons coming forth. Secondly, this also makes a place for the gifts and graces of God. The *drying up of the Euphrates* is a drying up of all known graces and of all support and of all penalties whatsoever. This is a drying up of all who is and who remains, either in good or in pain or even in evil. This state is harder to bear than any other.

It is also certain that there will be a terrible war and *an assembly of kings*, who will fight against the conquering King Jesus Christ.

The three foul spirits come from the mouth of the beast and the mouth of the false prophet. The beasts and false prophet are self-love, self-interest, and propriety. All are most opposed to pure love. The three spirits are pride, ambition, and love of avarice. The three spirits spread rumors over all the earth about war. This will be a universal revolution, but all will be conquered and subjugated under the kingdom of Jesus Christ. But the war will be terrible because Satan will defend himself with all his might.

> "See, I am coming like a thief! Blessed is the one who stays awake and is clothed, not going about naked and exposed to shame." (Rev 16:15)

O God, you *come like a thief,* when you catch the sinner in his sins, when you want to fill the soul with joy, after you have tested it with so many evils. Because when she least expects it, and she believes that her happy days are past, you fill her with joy and contentment.

The same happens when you come in your wrath or when you come to fill the world with joy at your second coming, you *come like a thief.* You come when we least expect it.

But the one who watches and pays attention to you will be *blessed* because she will not be surprised or, if she is surprised, it will be an agreeable way.

The one who *is clothed* is the one who keeps the Spirit of Jesus Christ. At baptism, the Christian is clothed with Jesus Christ. Following this, she either keeps or loses her clothing. If she keeps it, she will be happy but if stripped of it, she will have misfortune and a confusion. She who preserves the spirit of Jesus Christ in a spirit of disengagement and poverty, although she is *naked* of everything, is very well-clothed because she is clothed with what she must have. But those who appear to be well-clothed, and have no disengagement are naked and will be sooner or later seen in nudity, by those who even believe her to be well-dressed. The world reverses the meaning of things. They call disengagement as nudity and call propriety being well-dressed. However, propriety, which appears be clothing, is nudity and not wearing Jesus Christ. The one who is a complete beggar is perfectly well-clothed being dressed in Jesus Christ.

> And they assembled them at the place that in Hebrew is called Harmagedon. (Rev 16:16)

Here there is war between those who are *kings.* Some who are kings because Jesus Christ reigns in them and through them. They are truly kings because they are perfectly submissive to God and are put in independence of creation. Others have the will of God in them. There are people who use their power to do only what God wants.

These kings are *assembled* to fight against the other kings, who are the princes of the world, who believe they are kings but are actually slaves. Those who believe that they are the freest in the world are the must subject. Those who are free with the freedom of Jesus Christ fight only with the weapon of trust in God, abandoning themselves to God, sacrifice, and patience. The weapons of others though include anger, passion, pride, arrogance, hate, and strength.

> The seventh angel poured his bowl into the air, and a loud voice came out of the temple, from the throne, saying, "It is done!" [18] And there came flashes of lightning, rumblings, peals of thunder, and a violent earthquake, such as had not occurred since people were upon the earth, so violent was that earthquake. (Rev 16:17–18)

The last blow is the blow of grace, which consumes all the evil and which ends all the troubles and begins all the good. The angel *poured his bowl in the air* because this occupies all the capacity of the soul. A *voice came out of the temple* which is the foundation and center of the soul. The voice seems to come from God himself *saying, It is done!* These words mean that all hope is absolutely taken away from the soul who has no more resources. This state is the most terrible and the most disastrous. Until now there was some hope. But now all hope is absolutely taken away and does not remain anymore. It is at the present, the voice says, *It is done*. My misfortune is consumed. There is no more salvation for me. It seems that God confirms and makes the soul hear this.

Until then she was well convinced of her loss but now it is another thing. The first conviction was only superficial. She still had a hope for landing even in a state of weakness. However, now there is more evidence of desolation, and there is indeed more desolation and the loss is real. This loss is needed. We are put in an abutment and a hardening. However, the conviction is more real. Then nature has the last blow of death, after which there must be no more life for it. She enters into frightful terrors and horrible trances, into such horrors, that *had not occurred* before. God participates and seems to threaten her with *lightning*. All the moments of life are moments of waiting for this loss, and that becomes a visible punishment. But the loss more terrible than all the others is a one nature cannot express. You have to burst and die in this way. If this state has the greatest misfortunes, it is also the last.

When it will please God to send his spirit to the world, he will only send it when it is only about to be banished. When things will have the greatest despair and when the world condemns the truth, will be when the truth appears with the most clarity. But alas! Before this time, bursts of *thunder*, of terrible *lightning*! All the world assembles armed for combat to extinguish the truth if possible. Even those who will be filled with the truth will feel terrors and strange frights. All nature will be in strange fear because of the evils that threaten it. Things will be in entire despair. All appears *done*. But patience. It is true that it will be a consummation. But this consummation will be the end of pain and the ruin of the enemies of the truth. This last persecution will be the strongest of all.

> The great city was split into three parts, and the cities of the nations fell. God remembered great Babylon and gave her the wine-cup of the fury of his wrath. (Rev 16:19)

The soul appeared *divided in three* with an entire and perfect division of the superior and inferior part, and the spirit itself divided out. So it seems to the soul that there is in it two spirits acting. One chooses one thing and the other condemns this choice. One condemns and the other finds itself condemned, seeks why it is condemned and does not find it. It seems to be done in this spirit as an army of reasons fighting each other, killing each other, and being born again. This division of the spirit against the same spirit is a very great torment.

In the combat, the soul does not know the meaning that the cities of nations, the refuges of the world, were lost and *fell*. She cannot find her strength any more. In the combat of spirit, it seems that is a spirit that pleads in its favor and often has the upper hand. However, in the end it is destroyed and defeated by a total sacrifice and a perfect immolation. It is then that nature has no more hope.

However, in the combat, she uses her own liberty to defend and save herself, like a drowning person uses the little strength left to protect herself against death. This effort, though, only serves to kill her more promptly. Because having exhausted herself, she is swept away more quickly by the waters. She suffocates more quickly as she is out of breath. *God remembers* the selfish will of *the great city Babylon*, the mother of trouble and confusion which are the enemies of peace, tranquility, and simplicity. God remembers and gives her to drink wine of his fury and anger. Ah God, what wine! It will be very pure and God will tell her: "You did other things that I did not want. You rebelled against me. I will do to you now what you do not want, but with much more violence than you had in rebellion to my will." God uses the same weapons for combat and the *fury* of God becomes more irritated against her, as she resists.

O *Babylon*, Babylon, who now troubles the whole universe by its confusion! There will come a time when you will be overthrown! You will be destroyed but in a way that will amaze the whole earth.

> And every island fled away, and no mountains were to be found.
> (Rev 16:20)

There is nothing left that is not destroyed. Everything that elevates the soul and supports her, is not found. She finds neither grandeur nor baseness. The soul who was once elevated is now much reduced. Because when a person is tested, we know that the soul has no greater support than when it is ensconced in a profound humiliation.

> And huge hailstones, each weighing about a hundred pounds, dropped from heaven on people, until they cursed God for the plague of the hail, so fearful was that plague. (Rev 17:21)

If all supports were taken away from the soul, without God making her feel the *weight* of his indignation, it would be a little thing. But to carry the weight of the wrath of God is most terrible. There is lightning falling incessantly as thick and heavy *hail*. God joins all the evils and takes away all perceptible supports, whatever they may be, so that the soul is left (at least the inferior part) in the most extreme weakness. To this is joined persecution without any remaining consolation. To the contrary, it seems they are all united and in concert to torment us. To turn to any side, we only see oppressions from all sides, and with it *the hail* of indignation of the wrath of God that is discharged without mercy. This is not a mediocre wrath but a strange anger. O God, who can support your anger? The soul in this state would be reduced to a powder if God did not support with his invisible hand. When nature is strong and propriety large, nature enters into strange rages to see oneself in this state, that she would tear herself apart if God did not send help. Some give up and let themselves be destroyed by these blows. Others arm themselves and resist with violence, so they suffer great penalties, in which they sometimes die. Or else, by force of effort, they get out of this state and do not reenter it, but also never have a real peace. Unlike the others, others after having these punishments do enter into peace and are no longer lost.

The great Babylon, city of trouble and confusion, provokes the wrath of God. Strange misfortunes will come to it. The throne of the Sovereign will be taken away and will be put in the holy city Jerusalem. The throne of Jesus Christ will be in the temple of peace, the city of David. His cradle will be his sepulcher. But Babylon will not however be destroyed or lost. To the contrary, it will be sanctified and consecrated to the Lord for many centuries, the abomination that reigns will be removed, and God alone will reign there.

> Then one of the seven angels who had the seven bowls came and said to me, "Come, I will show you the judgment of the great whore who is seated on many waters, [2] with whom the kings of the earth have committed fornication, and with the wine of whose fornication the inhabitants of the earth have become drunk." (Rev 17:1-2)

O Babylon, you must be *condemned* and destroyed. You are *responsible* for the multitude of sins and the *many waters* because you rest in pleasures which are fluid like water. You are a *great prostitute* because you were created to be united to the will of God and to submit to him. You left your legitimate spouse to be prostituted to the demon and nature, who have used you to bring iniquity into the world. In your sinning, you nurtured iniquities that caused rebellion and found repose in agitation and the inconstancy of the waves. You overflowed with torrents of iniquity and your corruption spread through all the earth.

The *kings of the earth have committed fornication* with you. All people would have been kings if their will had always been submitted to God, but through you, O miserable Babylon, the kings have been corrupted and become slaves. Instead of tasting the pure and chaste immortal delicacies for which they have been created, you have attached them to brutal and insane pleasures, and have lost the delicacies of the spirit. All the earth is full of this corruption and deprivation. But you are condemned to die by the same poison you have given others. God will use your wine that you gave to establish your empire for the destruction of the same empire.

> So he carried me away in the spirit into a wilderness, and I saw a woman sitting on a scarlet beast that was full of blasphemous names, and it had seven heads and ten horns. (Rev 17:3)

The selfish will is *a woman*, a female adulterer separated from her bridegroom by prostitution. She who was destined to sanctify all the earth, corrupted it. She is *in a wilderness*, because she cannot sympathize with any good. She is *sitting* on self-love, which is the *scarlet beast* because it counterfeits pure love. Is it not she who makes and produces all sins, since she serves them as their creator? Because without her, no sins. These sins are as red with malice as *scarlet*. She is given the freedom to commit all these crimes, because she wants everything she likes. Because she is malignant and the source of sins, she hides well sometimes, so we cannot discover her. She is *full of blasphe-mous names* because she incessantly denies the attributes of God and claims them as her own. She is always rebellious and opposed to God. All I can say about her malignancy is only a shadow of what it really is. The malignant will is worse than all the devils. The devils cannot do any harm to human beings without her. The sins on which she has gone up are not as malignant as she. The monster on which she sits has no malignity other than that which she communicates. O malignant will! If I could describe it, everyone would understand it as an abomination.

> The woman was clothed in purple and scarlet, and adorned with
> gold and jewels and pearls, holding in her hand a golden cup full
> of abominations and the impurities of her fornication. (Rev 17:4)

This unfortunate will, with all her malignity, has a terrible ruse to hide her-self. She is covered and *adorned* with the appearance of all the virtues. She fools the strong and catches people in her nets. She uses everything to rule and rests on her vices. She holds *a golden cup full of abominations and the impurities of her fornication*, without the golden cup preventing the malig-nity of its poison. When there is no self-will, there is no more malignity. This malignity is strong according to how strong the self-will is.

> And on her forehead was written a name, a mystery: "Babylon
> the great, mother of whores and of earth's abominations." [6] And
> I saw that the woman was drunk with the blood of the saints and
> the blood of the witnesses to Jesus. When I saw her, I was greatly
> amazed. (Rev 17:5–6)

This selfish will is a *mystery* that can be discovered in most souls. She will let them do all the austerities they want, provided she is allowed to live in rest. She is not opposed to the exterior practice of virtues. She feeds on all of this: Mystery! However, she is the *mother of fornications*.

She is the *mother of abominations*, since everything that comes from her is an abomination, as it was declared by the prophet, *Bringing offerings is futile; incense is an abomination to me. New moon and sabbath and calling of convocation—I cannot endure solemn assemblies with iniquity* (Isaiah 1:13). Out of her will she *is drinking the blood of the saints and martyrs*. When there is no more self-will in the world, there will be no more sin.

> But the angel said to me, "Why are you so amazed? I will tell you
> the mystery of the woman, and of the beast with seven heads
> and ten horns that carries her." [8] The beast that you saw was, and
> is not, and is about to ascend from the bottomless pit and go
> to destruction. And the inhabitants of the earth, whose names

have not been written in the book of life from the foundation
of the world, will be amazed when they see the beast, because it
was and is not and is to come. (Rev 17:7–8)

God must himself *declare the mystery* for us to be able to understand this
heresy *that has been* and *who is no longer*. It is certain that heresy has
reigned in the world as the sower of crimes. The beast *ascends from the pit*
because sin ascends from hell to the earth through the serpent's way. But
sin only rises *to go to destruction,* by the way of Jesus Christ's redemption
which he established with generous advantage. He reestablished grace with
more happiness than had been before. The damned and the devils *will be
amazed when they see the beast, because it was and is not and is to come.*
They are damned by the sin that was and is no longer on the earth, and yet
know that those who remain on the earth will not be damned. This fills the
damned with desolation and jealousy, causing them torments and tortures.
The devil will no longer have the power to tempt the faithful, when self-will
is banished from the earth.

This self-will is very much compared to Babylon as it causes trouble
and disorder in the soul. Union with the will of God is like the ark that saves
in the deluge. It is the center of peace and repose.

The self-will is hidden under a cloak of pretend obedience. I call us to
end self-will, when God puts the soul in such a posture that pleases him,
no matter how terrible, however staggering that state may be. When nature
is dead, there is no more resistance, and we are surrendered to God's will.
It is often surprising that nature is more resistant in the middle of the way
than at the beginning. At the beginning obedience is very easy. It seems
that we are in perfect submission to the whole will of God and to the tests.
However, at some point, we experience the opposite. It will be good to say
here the reason for the consolation of souls. It is that the self-will at the
beginning of conversion is again all in the heart, it occupies all the soul at its
most profound. By conversion, the rebellion of the will is taken away. There
is a difference between the sinner and the beginner. In the sinner, besides
the self-will is rooted in him in a very profound manner, entirely contrary
to God's will. But after conversion, he does not have rebellion that makes
mortal sin, but he does not fail to have a thousand wills opposed to that of
God's, although he no longer has the will to rebel against God to make an
open war against him. Following the conversion, God brings the soul into
knowledge, and a love of his will with sweetness, so that the senses and the
exterior feel gently led to the will of God.

Then the soul greatly desires to join the will of God. What does the
self-will do then? It sinks ever deeper into the soul and does not appear

externally. The self-will, I say, hides with all its might and does not appear, lest if it is revealed, will have a cruel war. Therefore, what does she do with this malicious will? She hides it and lets it sinks into the soul. Feeding on the delectable, she is not attacked and remains at peace

The soul then feels this sweet anointing and, finding no resistance in her, thinks she has no will. She has no more exterior will, but she has a very strong interior will that she never had before. Because once the self-will left the exterior, it entrenched herself inside with power. The soul now believes that she is exempt from self-will, yet she has a real and hidden will.

But what does God do, who has given so much grace to this soul to live? Would God let this monster live without destroying it?

God takes away the sense of sweetness and ease and comes into the foundation of this soul as a strong weapon to cut off the self-will. This will, which was believed dead and destroyed, is more alive than ever, now that God pursues it. It practices deception and makes strange disorder. Because the soul followed without resistance, she did not trouble it. The same, after the conversion and in the sweetness of new life, it did not appear much, because it hid. But when it is pursued in strength, it makes horrible disorders, until God finally descends into the foundation of the soul, where God commands and governs.

Here the soul perceives God more clearly from her nothingness. But this malignant will only seems to become every day more malignant. It is not that it becomes more malignant. To the contrary, it is already less dangerous because she is discovering herself. Now banished from the foundation, it becomes rebellious and puts all the senses in rebellion. Yet neither the foundation nor the supreme part of the soul will have any part in the malignant will and it does more harm to the external. Those seeing these strange revolts and see so little submission to God and creatures, are surprised at it, not understanding the mystery written on the front of this self-will.

After these rages of the self-will, she is placed in a state of great mortification. Finally, this will is so strong that it is obliged to leave the place and the will of God is substituted in its place and the soul has no more will. She no longer feels opposition for anything. She has the will of God, and yet resists grace, supposing that she has the total destruction of the will, not superficially but in reality.

It is good to warn here of two great troubles and pitfalls. One is for souls who are not entirely dead and annihilated, but they think they are because they desire to be and their exterior will has been extinguished. I say that these persons have said yes but still resist God and graces given to her. They also want to follow their inclinations, believing that they follow the will of God. However, as their will is alive, though hidden, they begin to follow only these penchants and yet are following the inclinations of nature which strengthen their self-will. Far from abandoning themselves, their self-will becomes stronger, yet they believe that they follow the will of God. Following their own will leads to very strange miseries; they are more irredeemable because of their persuasion that they are following the will of God.

The other trouble is that spiritual directors have ideas of virtue conforming to ordinary and communal rules. When a perfectly annihilated soul, which is very rare as I have said, presents herself to directors, they want to force her to violate her inclinations, yet they are the will of God for her. This puts her into suffering. She sees that God resists her. These cases happen less frequently with a beginning soul who does what others want with her. But, says the director, how do I know if the soul is annihilated? Or only beginning? Yes, if it is the first, it is the grace she follows. If it is the other, it is nature. Are both the same expressions? Ah that is easy to know! You will see the annihilated soul supple and pliable in the hand of God in all things. She does not change her conduct even with crosses or difficulties and reversals of creatures. The annihilated soul submits to let God lead by crosses and a strong providence. This soul must have experienced all the deaths and all the reversals, all the revolts and the rebellions of the will. She must have finally died to her will.

The other trouble only comes out of the world of senses and perceptions. She is full of herself and does not carry the cross and does not do the will of God but does her own will for the excellence of her own spirit. She also visibly resists God. However, she wants to be established in the will of God yet she never thwarts the will of nature, but she made great penitence out of self-will. All is self-will. Do not believe in her annihilation because her death is not real.

> "This calls for a mind that has wisdom: the seven heads are seven mountains on which the woman is seated; also, they are seven kings, [10] of whom five have fallen, one is living, and the other has not yet come; and when he comes, he must remain only a little while." (Rev 17:9–10)

The selfish will reposes in the soul on *seven mountains* on which she exercises her empire because this self-will is like a wheel that moves all the rest. There are *seven kings* who each want a throne, but the will is still their sovereign. There are seven mountains and seven sovereigns at the same time. She dominates and captivates all of them. The *seven mountains* are intelligence, reason, judgment, discernment, wisdom, power, and deliberation or choice. They all appear sovereigns. These make up the nobility and grandeur of the soul and with an excellence of spirit. However, each is subject to her will, and she dominates all of them. Her blind temerity drives everything. Jesus Christ has said in his gospel, *And if one blind person guides another, both will fall into a pit* (Matthew 15:14). This blind will itself finally falls over a precipice and ruins intelligence, offends reason, reverses judgment, obscures discernment, and destroys wisdom. That being done, the *five kings are dead*. There is *one* left and that is the king of deliberation. This remains the last with the domination of the self-will.

When God wants to destroy the self-will, he attacks the same things that she herself attacked, when she wanted to overthrow the throne and destroy his kingdom. First, he gives the light of intelligence, very different from the one she had. But he gives it to her with extraordinary brilliance only to extinguish it. He does the same with reason. God makes another reason in which she can see her error and deception, but it is only in order to destroy all reason in the future. God gives a just judgment, to condemn in her the self-will, but then she loses that judgment. She is given clear discernment in things and sees the abuses but then does with them all the more violence. She is given a wonderful wisdom, but it appears to others as folly. There is one left like force, which leads to blindness where the soul is reduced. The other has not yet come, which is deliberation and choice, which only lasts a moment. God gives wonderful power to the soul to resist the selfish will but this power changes into weakness. The choice, or deliberation, makes the soul give itself freely to God, but this choice, which although very brief, had been so advantageous to give herself to God. Yet in the future she seems to be lost because she has no choice left and instinct seems to be leading. This makes all the reversals.

> As for the beast that was and is not, it is an eighth but it belongs
> to the seven, and it goes to destruction. (Rev 17:11)

The beast is himself the self-will. *He was* because he subsisted in these things. He *is no longer* because these things are destroyed. He *is an eighth* because everything ends in it, and he is the end of these things. He is however the number *seven* because he is in the seven and particularly in the choice or deliberation, which is his main character, which seems to be attributed to his spirit. Because his will is blind, he cannot choose, and freely enter into action. A forceful action without choice or deliberation is an involuntary action.

> And the ten horns that you saw are ten kings who have not yet
> received a kingdom, but they are to receive authority as kings for
> one hour, together with the beast. (Rev 17:12)

These *ten horns* are the ten passions that joined with the beast make the eleventh which is self-interested love. Until then, the revolt of the passions *had not yet come.* But it is not so when they see approaching the destruction of the selfish will and their loss at the same time. Since the passions all reside in the will, which is their seat, particularly those of concupiscence, the others have no more goodness or malice than that which they borrow from the will. But the passions only appear *for a very short time* with fury, for as long as self-love still exists, they see its condemnation to death. That is what stirs it up and irritates all the other passions; therefore, it is king because both the simple and compound passions have no strength except what they borrow from love, either self or pure.

Love animates the desire for the possession of that which it loves. The possession of that which it loves makes the pleasure. He who loves himself finds pleasure in what increases his self-love, as those who love God find pleasure in God possessing him. The deprivation of this pleasure makes desire. It is the same with hate, the continuation of this, and pain. We become sad at the deprivation of that which one loves. We hate and experience deprivation. We despair when we do not see what we love. We become bold enough to undertake anything to possess it. We fear that we will not possess it or that we will lose this. Finally, the anger overwhelms us because we do not have what we love and all that is opposed to us getting this. It is the same with other passions. We are jealous of what we love and do not have. This suffices to show us that love is what excites the other passions. When self-love sees the will perishing, or perished, it is like a lamp that as it is extinguished, throws more light in the moment. This also ignites the other passions.

> These are united in yielding their power and authority to the beast. (Rev 17:13)

All together are *united* in one purpose. They have given to self-love all their strength and power and authority, so that self-love alone works between them all. Their self-will is still contained in them, but all of them finally yield their strength and rights to propriety.

> "They will make war on the Lamb, and the Lamb will conquer them, for he is Lord of lords and King of kings, and those with him are called and chosen and faithful." (Rev 17:14)

Propriety fights in a *war on the Lamb*, against the Spirit of Jesus Christ, against his reign and kingdom. This happens both in the general world and in the particular soul. What happens in the soul to establish the kingdom of Jesus Christ happens also in all the church to establish his kingdom. After a strange combat, and a terrible opposition from self-love and propriety against the Spirit, the kingdom of Jesus Christ will prevail. He will overcome and dominate all the passions, making them serve to his glory. Self-centered love will change into pure love, who will be the captain that consecrates to God all the other passions. Pure love gives the joy of God. The soul desires only God and God's glory and hates what opposes and displeases God. All other passions will change into service for God. Anger will be changed into zeal. Jesus Christ conquers in this way by using the same weapons that were previously used to fight him. Finally, having destroyed all propriety, those who will be him will be *chosen and faithful*. For he will use the soul only for his glory, and will confirm the soul in his love, giving him an inviolable faith.

> And he said to me, "The waters that you saw, where the whore is seated, are peoples and multitudes and nations and languages." (Rev 17:15)

All peoples, nations, and languages subject to their own self-will make all the evils and sins. The unruliness of the heart is the source of the unruliness of the spirit. Also, the disorder of the spirit augments and fortifies the disorder of the heart. If Adam had not sinned by his own will, idolatries would not have come into the world, nor all the other sins. The disorder of the will is therefore the source of all sins.

> And the ten horns that you saw, they and the beast will hate the whore; they will make her desolate and naked; they will devour her flesh and burn her up with fire." (Rev 17:16)

As I have already said, God uses the same passions to destroy the selfish will that they used to destroy the kingdom of Jesus Christ. Jesus Christ uses the same weapons to combat that were used against him. This is what Paul writes, *For just as you once presented your members as slaves to impurity and to greater and greater iniquity, so now present your members as slaves to righteousness for sanctification* (Romans 6:19) He also writes in another place, *Should I therefore take the members of Christ and make them members of a prostitute? Never!* (1 Corinthians 6:15) When we give ourselves back to Jesus Christ, we withdraw from the prostitute. We use the same weapons to fight against God's enemies that we used to destroy Jesus Christ in us.

The *hatred* and anger of the beast and ten kings are armed against her and *reduce her in the last* extremity and in the last *desolation*. They *make her desolate and naked*. They *devour her flesh* and annihilate her. The self-will was the mistress and devours all the good in the soul. Finally, *they burn it* and consumes it *in his fire*, so that none of it is left in the world. These things devoured are not left to subsist in the world or in the one who devours them. The self-will is devoured by the will of God. After this, pure love lives so that nothing remains of self-will, either in itself or in God. Because self-will is malignant, it corrupts if it could, the received will of God.

Ah malignant will, who can comprehend the malignity that is in you! It passes all that can be said. If you were not bound, we could say that you are as evil as God as good. All I can say is that you are the sovereign evil. I would rather be in hell without you, than in paradise with you. If all human beings knew the danger of the malignity of their own will, they would choose to be possessed by demons rather than to suffer them in their own self will.

> "For God has put it into their hearts to carry out his purpose by agreeing to give their kingdom to the beast, until the words of God will be fulfilled. ¹⁸ The woman you saw is the great city that rules over the kings of the earth." (Rev 17:17–18)

God has inspired these passions to annihilate the self-will. This is admirable. It is as was said before, God uses these passions for good to destroy the malignant will. God's good destroys this evil. So for awhile God appears to leave the unregulated passions alone, but this is the plan for the destruction of them. Self-love sees its destruction coming. Until at last the Word of God, which is the Word of life, the Spirit of the Word, finds the time to be *fulfilled* for all things, and its coming defeats self-will. O malice of self-will! For self-love purified by pure love serves God like the rest.

This is the wonderful economy of grace of the redemption of Jesus Christ, which cost Jesus Christ infinitely more than it costs the soul.

The self-will is Babylon *the great city that rules over the kings of the earth*. All the kings who command are subject to the self-will and slaves to their passions. They who dominate everyone cannot dominate because they are dominated by her. She compared to a *great city* because it contains noise, tumult, passions, sins, and commerce of creatures.

> After this I saw another angel coming down from heaven, hav-ing great authority; and the earth was made bright with his splendor. ² He called out with a mighty voice,

> "Fallen, fallen is Babylon the great!
> It has become a dwelling place of demons,
> a haunt of every foul spirit,
> a haunt of every foul bird,
> a haunt of every foul and hateful beast." (Rev 18:1–2)

This powerful and luminous *angel coming down from heaven* is the will of God that descends in the soul when the selfish will is banished.

The will of God descends into the soul to the extent that the selfish will has been banished. It descends first in the superior part and then the malignant will moves into the inferior. The will of God takes the place in the superior and the malignant will descends lower and lower. But what happens to this malignant will when it *falls* into the inferior part? It becomes *a dwelling place of demons, a haunt of every foul spirit, and a haunt of every foul bird* making all torments and *hatred* of human beings. Paul experienced this state when he said he felt *in his members a law which was at war to the law of his spirit* (Romans 7:23). He had a will that wanted and did the good and that was the will of God. He had another will that wanted and did the evil, and that was the malignant will. This malignant will at the lowest level becomes the *dwelling place of demons*. At some point the person seems possessed or obsessed. It is the *haunt of foul spirits* because one feels only miseries and impurities. The *foul birds* are the imagination and fantasies that seems to dwell in her with impure thoughts and ridiculous imaginations. The person in whom these things happen hates them as the devil and suffers a strange pain.

We must remark that what happens in a particular human also happens in the church. This miserable prostitute, the source of all evil, will destroy more, to the extent that she has been destroyed. The holy and pure church will have children who will indulge in impurity and all other vices and become the haunt of *impure demons*. When they are at the end of their reign, it will be then that the corrupt children of the church will attack the *birds* themselves who are people raised above the others by their spirit, knowledge, and devotion.

> "For all the nations have drunk
> of the wine of the wrath of her fornication,
> and the kings of the earth have committed fornication with her,
> and the merchants of the earth have grown rich from the
> power of her luxury." (Rev 18:3)

When Eve sinned, she made her own will triumph to the detriment of the will of God. Because Eve broke her union with God and joined with the devil's fornication, all humanity *has drunk* the *wine of the wrath of her fornication* from Eve's source. All human beings are born proprietary with a rebellious will. After baptism, some throw away the grace for rebellion. This self-will always remains rooted in the soul as a poison that penetrates the substance of the soul. This can only be cured by its antidote, which is transformation into the will of God.

The kings of the earth, who are all people, are born free and consequently kings, *have committed fornication with her* because there is not one that has not been reduced by this self-will, which makes them withdraw from the will of God. As the demon deceived Adam and Eve, all humanity does the same. This corrupt self-will takes its separated freedom. The self-will uses its freedom against the will of God who gave human beings a beautiful and noble freedom as a gift. Yet now corrupt human beings use their freedom only to oppose the will of God.

The merchants of the earth are demons and nature, who negotiate incessantly with human beings. They *have grown rich* with their spoils gained by self-will. They enrich themselves while impoverishing others. The true riches of pure love consist in having no other will than that of God or no other interest other than his. O Babylon, you are now a *superb city* where everyone is grown *rich* from the power of her luxury.

Then I heard another voice from heaven saying,

"Come out of her, my people,
so that you do not take part in her sins,
and so that you do not share in her plagues." (Rev 18:4)

Babylon, the figure of the self-will and of corrupt nature, is only corrupted by her own will. We are invited to *come out of* this *Babylon* and to leave ourselves. By losing our entire will, the soul *leaves* finally herself and the corruption of nature, which is propriety. We are all invited to be the *people of God* as interior and abandoned souls.

God wants his people to have the advantage of coming out of themselves. They *do not take part in her sins* of corrupt nature and the malignity of the selfish will and *do not share in her plagues*. Because all the *evil* allowed to happen to the soul destroys the self-will, unless the soul through faith carries the afflicted states of Jesus Christ. Those afflicted in this way carry his states after losing the self-will, and they suffer only then because they conform to the image of Jesus Christ, so that Jesus Christ may be born in those predestined for interior grace.

"For her sins are heaped high as heaven, and God has remembered her iniquities. ⁶ Render to her as she herself has rendered, and repay her double for her deeds; mix a double draught for her in the cup she mixed. (Rev 18:5–6)

God remembered the iniquity of the self-will with its miserable corruption. *For her sins* and malice are not content to remain in the inferior part of nature. Instead, here the malignant will is *heaped high as heaven* in the superior part.

In order to banish her absolutely from the soul, God begins to treat has as she merited. As she was brazen enough to attack God, therefore he is jealous to fulfill his will, because if God could be prevented from doing his will, he would cease to be God. The authority and grandeur of the Sovereign consists in this point that he can do what he wills. God sees that the self-will wants to attack all the way up to his throne and *remembered her iniquities*. But what happens then? God gives power to the ministers of justice to *render to her as she herself has rendered*. She wanted to rise beyond the will of God and has corrupted all of human nature. She needs to suffer all the pain that she has given and to *drink from the same chalice* and in the same way from the *cup she mixed* for other human beings to drink.

To drink from the *cup she mixed* means she is attacked in the same way that she attacked God. All the sins she has done are those served to her to punish and destroy her. The experiences the same excess that she used against God who punishes evils done voluntarily by the same evils suffered involuntarily. He does though make *her pay double* evil *for her deeds*. God arms himself against this miserable one and gives power to make her drink twice of the same nature of the things she has done. You who wanted to raise yourself to heaven will be cast down into the depths of the abyss.

All those in whom God wants to banish all the self-will experience it this way. God uses the same things in which they rebelled. David had felt this when he said to his God, *You have put me in the depths of the pit, in the regions dark and deep* (Psalm 88:6). This is the counter balance to elevation and pride. There are two parts to this punishment. We do what we do not want to do, as Paul said, *For I do not do the good I want, but the evil I do not want is what I do* (Romans 7:19). The other punishment is because of the insolence and elevation of his propriety, he falls into the most profound abyss of dirt and blood. If it were an abyss of water, he might hope that some tireless effort or force would help. But no hope exists for a profound abyss of dark and deep. O Prophet-King David, the deep abyss in which you were plunged tested you.

> "As she glorified herself and lived luxuriously, so give her a like measure of torment and grief. Since in her heart she says, 'I rule as a queen; I am no widow, and I will never see grief,' [8] therefore her plagues will come in a single day—pestilence and mourning and famine—and she will be burned with fire; for mighty is the Lord God who judges her." (Rev 18:7–8)

All the *torment* which God makes souls suffer in the spiritual life are only in *proportion* to their *pride*. The human nature, rising with pride, wants to rise above the will of God and is condemned to *pestilence and mourning and famine*. This is like the fallen angelic nature who had been condemned to hell because of its pride.

All the evil and pain that God sends to the soul are proportionate to its pride. Pride causes rage and despair. The selfish will is prideful and wants to raise itself out of the will of God. It wants to have all her *pleasures*. She cannot taste the divine will, which is only granted to those loving God. So what does she do? She aligns herself with corrupt nature, so she can taste illicit pleasures. She served corruption, as corruption served her.

But God, to withdraw the soul from sin and from the training of corrupt nature, sends into her heart the *fire* of his love. What will this malignant will do? It aligns itself with self-love. They unite together to feed on these celestial pleasures, since they find there even more taste than in carnal pleasures because celestial pleasures are forbidden. They fed and engraved on these divine tastes and served kings with their prostitution. O when seen in this way, what does this say about this miserable Babylon? *I am on the throne*, she says, since I eat spiritual goods, I am as *Queen*, and I am obeyed. With that, I have passed for the will of God. *I am no widow* because I am a prostitute. I will not miss a husband because if the pleasures of the flesh do not please me, I will taste pleasures in the spirit. If I lose those of the spirit, I will find others. *So I never see grief* or the devil.

But God who sees the audacity and insolence of the self-will gets even more angered against her, because of her malignity and corruption and the spoiling of spiritual things, that she had not done when in the carnal. Previously she used the weakness of nature to succeed in her evil designs and did not have so much malignity as now. This is why God hits her first with *plagues*. God covers her with the *devil* and afflictions: the *famine, will come in a single day*. When he says all will come *in a single day*, because of the promptitude and surprise with which it comes to overwhelm her, but it will not be finished in a day. O God, she would be happy if they were! She enters in a day into these things, as was said to Adam: *For in the day that you eat of it you shall die* (Genesis 2:17). His death did not end on that day. Also, all the evil of the prostitute did not end in one day. The plagues began as deadly plagues. One dies and yet cannot die because this miserable Babylon is riding on a beast that has seven heads and in all of these heads a quantity of lives. So that when one of these heads seems injured to death, she finds it lives with more force than it had before. *The devil* is in a continual death, because it is never finished and terminated by death. Then, the *famine*. These evils are united together because the selfish will is tormented at the same time by continual and double blows, by a famine, and a deprivation of all nourishment. All will be death in her and for her, until finally she is *burned with fire*

THE APOCALYPSE OF THE APOSTLE JOHN

and consumed *by fire*, so that there are no more traces or vestiges. The *mighty Lord God judges* and condemns this miserable creature.

> And the kings of the earth, who have committed fornication and lived deliciously with her, shall bewail her, and lament for her, when they shall see the smoke of her burning. (Rev 18:9)

The kings of the earth, who are kings of the superior part and freedom, *who have committed fornication* by their self and artificial will, see her torments of condemnation after having been rejected from the inferior part. The kings understand that they had a part in her disorder and rejection. They *wail* with all their force, fearing and believing to be wrapped up in her torture. The *smoke of her burning* rises up and seems to suffocate them. The smoke rises up to the superior part and seems to suffocate the spirit and envelope them in a fatal conflagration.

O God, this will happen on earth, so this wretch who seduces people, will be finally destroyed. Crime will not reign then; fire will consume it with sorrow and pain.

> They will stand far off, in fear of her torment, and say, "Alas, alas, the great city, Babylon, the mighty city! For in one hour your judgment has come." (Rev 18:10)

The more fire, death, and carnage attack the lower part, where the self-will has been rejected from the foundation, the more the superior part leaves and *stands far off*. The soul that experiences these things usually only knows these things after the evils are over. When they happen, she believes that the superior part will be enveloped in ruins. She cannot tell whether the self-will is rejected or not. This causes sadness because she confuses the smoke and burning. She believes that the smoke says the self-will remains in her. She is wrong, though, because there is no more division between the two parts than there is now. It is not the soul that burns but the self-will. However, her fear makes her strong, and drawing her away from herself, she cries, *Alas! Alas!* What desolation, what destruction! *In one hour your judgment has come*, when we least expected it.

> And the merchants of the earth weep and mourn for her, since no one buys their cargo anymore, [12] cargo of gold, silver, jewels and pearls, fine linen, purple, silk and scarlet, all kinds of scented wood, all articles of ivory, all articles of costly wood, bronze, iron, and marble, [13] cinnamon, spice, incense, myrrh, frankincense, wine, olive oil, choice flour and wheat, cattle and sheep, horses and chariots, slaves—and human lives. (Rev 18:11–13)

The merchants of the earth are the exterior and interior senses. Both are extremely distressed, because they see their *commerce* interrupted and all their pleasures stopped. They will not have any commerce with the spirit because it was self-love and the selfish will who were doing this business. The exterior senses trade only the things of the earth. The interior senses trade in feelings in a more delicate way because there is a sensual taste in the spirit, as there is a sensual taste in the body. There are ornaments, delicacies, touch, taste, intelligence, smell, sight, soul, and body. When the destruction of self-love and self-will have come, it seems to the interior and exterior senses that they will never have more pleasure. This is true that they will taste no more of the pleasures of self-love and self-will. Instead, they will be given a delicate and subtle taste by which, after the entire destruction of the unhappy Babylon, they will taste pure spiritual goods, without any part of impurity and propriety.

> "The fruit for which your soul longed has gone from you, and all your dainties and your splendor are lost to you, never to be found again!" [15] The merchants of these wares, who gained wealth from her, will stand far off, in fear of her torment, weeping and mourning aloud. (Rev 18:14–15)

To understand this passage, we must first look at what we have already said. The selfish will after having been removed from the foundation takes refuge in the inferior part, after previously having extended much further into the superior part. But when it is taken away from the superior part, it spreads into the inferior part and attacks this part with force and lives there with regret for its lost power. However, in the beginning, as it makes the senses taste some pleasures, it is received as a hostess with whom they trade what they own, each in their own way, and *get rich*. Yet finally the torments come to assail her, the *merchants* as witnesses of her pain suffer a great damage, leave her, and by moving away from her, she is consumed. The soul then remains forever separated and exempt from malignity. When the soul remains dead to all the selfish will and to all propriety, the soul lives in the will of God

The *merchants* had *gained wealth from her* in pleasures, abundance, the voluptuousness. Yet she brought them only gross and material voluptuousness which do not deserve the name of pleasure. Seeing the misfortunes of their own will, they keep away forever. They prefer a total abandon to the will of God to the grow pleasures that they tasted with her, because these pleasures enveloped them in strange *torments*. This misery remains alone consumed in the fire of the wrath of God and the senses are forever delivered. But before they get over this loss of their wares and the great city, they suffer inconceivable torments. They do what they can to conserve and retain the pleasures, because they believe that all their goods, treasures, and riches are in them. They mistakenly believe that they are the will of God because they mistake the sensualities that she communicates as spiritual goods. But seeing her punishment, they finally see the folly and go away forever. The selfish will only leads them into this and deprives them of all sorts of good. But this deprivation would be little, if not accompanied by the assembly of all strong evils.

> "Alas, alas, the great city, clothed in fine linen, in purple and scarlet, adorned with gold, with jewels, and with pearls! [17] For in one hour all this wealth has been laid waste!" And all shipmasters and seafarers, sailors and all whose trade is on the sea, stood far off. (Rev 18:16–17)

My God, what an admirable description of the self-will, both in her apparent triumph and in her destruction! Nothing is so *great* as the will of human beings; it is a sovereign that leads and governs all. Everything bends and obeys her. She is *clothed* and adorned in an excellent way. *The purple and scarlet* with charity is her principal ornament and everything given to her has nothing of the virtues, unless ordered in God's will. She has ineffable delicacies. But she will become the proprietor of these goods, misusing them. She abuses all the riches and dresses herself outwardly in the liberty of people; she compels this principal sovereign to defile herself with her. She wants to hide everything from God. In place of the charity to which she was united and which surrounded her with goodness and filled her with riches, she unites with self-love and interest, and introduces foreign usurpations. This miserable will unites with its god and becomes unfaithful. She prostitutes herself with the demon. God endures this for some time with patience but finally his wrath moves against her. In a moment this magnificence changes into ignominy. All those who noticed that this will with the faculties of the soul and the senses were previously united to God are astonished and *stood far off* from this misery.

If God did not do it in this way, his favors and graces, for from killing our selfish will and this malignant will, would increase this malignity, because she would use the benefits of God to become more malignant. But we need to know that when the malignity is most hidden, it is then that it is stronger. It is a ferocious beast which can never be tamed except by death.

> And cried out as they saw the smoke of her burning, "What city was like the great city?" [19] And they threw dust on their heads, as they wept and mourned, crying out, "Alas, alas, the great city,

> where all who had ships at sea grew rich by her wealth! For in
> one hour she has been laid waste." (Rev 18:18–19)

The selfish will is compared to a *city* because it is the will that contains all the operations of the soul, and in the city there are many operations. We have seen that all passions and feelings have their seat in the will. It is therefore a *city* and a city *where all the merchants become rich*. Because nature, demons, self-love, and self-interest navigate in the soul like on a sea to enrich oneself yet cannot be enriched except by the way of the propriety. But if this will be so malignant, and if she is an enemy of the soul in which she is contained, she enriches all her merchants only with the remains of the same soul.

However, this superb and evil city is *ruined in an hour* at the time destined by God for its ruin. The malignity of nature is a strange thing because as long as it remains and keeps its authority, malice and destruction grows. David is a good figure of what goes wrong. David was at the home of King of Achis (1 Samuel 27, 28, 29) and he ruined his kingdom. However, Achis thought David brought a thousand goods and regarded David as an angel of God. It is the same with the will as long as it remains in the soul. If we can understand the damage of the own selfish will in the soul, when the soul believes that the will brings a lot of good, they will be surprised. It is never more dangerous than when it seems most pleasant, useful, and necessary.

Then *the smoke of her burning* rises up to the height. Everyone who has known these people and the soul and see such surprising destruction, understand that such opposing states come only infrequently. It is surprising that after having apparently possessed so many great and elevated things, one can experience so many evils and miseries. However, the measure of the good that was possessed is the same measure as the evil they will have.

> Rejoice over her, O heaven, you saints and apostles and proph-
> ets! For God has given judgment for you against her. (Rev 18:20)

Nothing in the world is as beautiful and expressive as this. *Rejoice* therefore, *O heaven*! O church, rejoice you *over her* for all the disorders of your children for which you groan, are banished from your bosom, since the one who was the source is destroyed.

Rejoice you, O heaven. O supreme part of the soul, rejoice you when the inferior part which is the earth, seems to grieve more, for there is only good for you. Nothing will destroy your felicity any more, since your own self-will is destroyed.

And you, saints of the church, rejoice! Because the fruit of your apostolate will be fulfilled throughout the church. Your prophecies will be accomplished by the ruin of this miserable will because all propriety resides in it.

God has given judgment for you against her, the condemnation of your words was judged and ratified. God shows others by the loss of this city the truth of what you announced. And you, O humans who are *apostles and prophets* who announce the truth without ceasing, O noble power of the soul, *dwell in joy!* Because in the destruction of this miserable propriety *your judgment is judged* and there is no longer any fear, apprehension, and sorrow for yourself. By the loss of this city, your torments are finished, and your happiness is assured. In the city actions were all from the self-will. Without her, actions will be those of valor and goodness.

Your judgment is again *against her*. Because of her, we suffer torments. When propriety is destroyed, because one follows the other, the judgment for the soul is made. There is no other judgment than the joy of our God. O souls, rejoice therefore in your biggest disgraces because your judgment is contained in the condemnation of the self-will. If she is not condemned and destroyed, you yourself will be condemned to suffer in this life or in the next. But if she is condemned and destroyed, there will only be salvation, joy, and peace for you.

> Then a mighty angel took up a stone like a great millstone and threw it into the sea, saying, "With such violence Babylon the great city will be thrown down, and will be found no more." (Rev 18:21)

This *mighty angel* does the will of God, in condemning the self-will as its capital enemy. The divine will *takes and casts* out the selfish will after the judgment was made *into the sea* like a millstone, so that it may be found no more.

When the malignant will is condemned, and when its judgment is made, whoever admires it is burned in the fire. The division is made between the self-will and God. All propriety is destroyed. After this, the remaining will is entirely pure. To the same measure that propriety is thrown into the abyss, the good will is thrown into the will of God in God, and never leaves God again. Hell is where propriety is held never to leave again. But the bosom of God is the wonderful abyss where the good will remains forever more because it is where she is to be transformed into the will of God. O inconceivable happiness of the soul who comes here after passing through all these sorrows and troubles!

> "And the sound of harpists and minstrels and of flutists and trumpeters will be heard in you no more; and an artisan of any trade will be found in you no more; and the sound of the millstone will be heard in you no more; [23] and the light of a lamp will shine in you no more; and the voice of bridegroom and bride will be heard in you no more for your merchants were the

magnates of the earth, and all nations were deceived by your sorcery." (Rev 18:22–23)

O self-will, O malignant propriety, which like an evil spider took the spiritual and converted it into venom! Now you are rejected and destroyed, and spiritual harmonies *will be heard in you no more.* Trade artisans will be found in you no more.

Here is said two things about the one whose own will is the main food. First, the spiritual delights of the spirit in tastes, pleasures, and harmonies are sensible graces given from heaven. This is expressed in *the sound of harpists and minstrels and of flutists and trumpeters.* But secondly, the nourishment of evil propriety actually increases prideful delicacies of their spirit as seen in the works of the body and exterior penitence. This is explained in the work of the *artisan* and the *sound of the millstone.*

The light of a lamp signifies the demon partisans who claim credit and authority. As said earlier, the dragon gives all his power to this self-love and self-interest.

There is a certain liaison between the demon, nature, self-will, propriety, and self-interest that works together. The dragon gives all his power to the self-will is a great force and the demon transforms into an angel of *light* to give illustrations mistakenly regarded as great graces that fortify the soul into submission to this malignant will. The demon also counterfeits the interior words and dialogues of the Bridegroom and spouse. Frequently, God removes the soul from the dangerous effects of malice and sin by caressing this soul to hear the sweet *voice* of the Bridegroom. The malignant will corrupts this, so God takes away all his graces and favors. It is then that the demon counterfeits the *voice* and *lights,* giving him more taste and sensibilities, finally to hold the soul captive in propriety. But if propriety is not rejected, it forever deprives the soul of all goods and condemns it to all evil. When the self-will is divided from the will of God, each thing returns to its end and origin. Who belongs to God returns to him and is lost in God forever. But those who belong to propriety belong to the beast and are held forever in the abyss with demons who torment them.

The same thing happens in the church, the world, and in the soul. When God wants to disengage a soul, God divides the malignity from the good that is within him and sends the malignity into the abyss. Then all humans become saints because they are led into the will of God, while miserable propriety remains chained in the abyss. But, O God, when these chains are broken, they will be given a new power to harm human beings. With what fury will she not be able to avenge her prison?

The merchants of the self-will *are princes* because they use the most noble operations of the soul such as liberty to enrich and fatten itself. The princes *of the earth* are senses raised from the lower part to make merchants and maintain its commerce. In the general, human beings are sovereign of the earth because of their dignity and nobility but they may use the soul for unfair traffic by which she takes what is God's and sells it. There is no one who she has not *seduced by her enchantments*. But God will tell them of their malice and will take back what is his. After which, the merchants will be sent into the abyss.

> "And in you was found the blood of prophets and of saints, and
> of all who have been slaughtered on earth." (Rev 18:24)

How should this be heard? With unhappy propriety in the soul, one still does not know the damage being doing. To the contrary, one believes that all the evil and sadness come from not being faithful to it. As we try to be faithful to it, tyranny increases. It enchants and blinds the mind so well, that they believe more should be given to serve it with more faithfulness, thinking it will soften the evils. We never know that the evils actually come from it until after judgment is given. But after it is condemned and destroyed, we know and *find the blood of the prophets and saints*. God reveals that propriety causes all the soul's interior sadness and sorrows of the spirit, as well as the extinguished lights and banished holiness. Propriety is the cause of all evils.

> After this I heard what seemed to be the loud voice of a great
> multitude in heaven, saying, "Hallelujah! Salvation and glory
> and power to our God, ² for his judgments are true and just;
> he has judged the great whore who corrupted the earth with
> her fornication, and he has avenged on her the blood of his ser-
> vants." (Rev 19:1–2)

Heaven rejoices when propriety is banished because this will be the time for the *glory* and reign of God, when his will be done on earth as it is in heaven. The reign of Jesus Christ will never be perfect on earth without this. This benefits the servants of God because all their torments and suffering were caused by the sins of others due to propriety. So when propriety is banished from the earth, sins will be banished. This is what makes joy in heaven and with the saints on the earth, to see this miserable reality *condemned*. They admire the *truth* of God's judgments, his equity, and the means he uses to fulfill his plans.

The other *heaven*, the interior that is the soul's foundation and center, rejoices after the destruction of the proprietary and malignant will. This is

when the soul understands the great advantages that come with the destruction of the self-will and how *just* it is that she suffered all that she made
others suffer. In the profundity of this joy and ravishment, she cannot help
but *praise* God with thousands of thanksgivings for the wonderful ways he
leads us. "It is you," she says, "O God, who is due all *glory* and *salvation*
because you destroyed this unfortunate woman, who under the pretext of
contributing to our salvation opposes you continually. Alas! Without this,
what would become of our salvation? It looked as if our salvation was lost."
Then the soul entered with admiration and astonishment into the way of
God and *the truth of his judgments*. She is filled with joy at her deliverance
from her selfish will that had been an unfortunate prostitute after abandoning herself to the demon, *corrupted the earth with her fornication*. She knows
then that all the miseries that have happened only happened because of her.
Because of this misery God *has avenged the blood of his servants* which are
the *evils she made them suffer*.

> Once more they said, "Hallelujah! The smoke goes up from her
> forever and ever." [4] And the twenty-four elders and the four liv-
> ing creatures fell down and worshiped God who is seated on the
> throne, saying, "Amen. Hallelujah!" (Rev 19:3–4)

They *once more praise God* because one can only praise after such a great
good and admire his mercy after such a deliverance. It is true that God uses
painful means to destroy the self-will. As long as the operation lasts, the soul
sees nothing that is advantageous. To the contrary, she regards this as a loss
and does not know happiness until after her deliverance. But *the smoke goes
up from her* from this misery *forever and ever*, for there is still the memory
of life, according to the will of God.

Then *the twenty-four elders*, the saints, and the *animals*, who are great
and holy in their souls, *worship and adore God*. But how? By their annihilation, marked by their *prostration* and falling down. The soul cannot truly
adore God, or be perfectly annihilated, unless the selfish will is destroyed.
But once it is destroyed, she enters into true annihilation.

> And from the throne came a voice saying, "Praise our God, all
> you his servants, and all who fear him, small and great." (Rev
> 19:5)

O God, throughout eternity your *servants'* occupation is to *praise* you. But
to praise God according to God's merit, we have to become a child and be
annihilated and have a new birth.

We praise God in three ways in God's will. *Praise God who fear him*
from filial fear that makes us do his will at the slightest signal. We fear God

more than death and even more than hell. We want to do nothing that is against the will of God. The fear that is spoken of here causes no disturbance and no evil effect in the soul. Instead, this fear fills the soul with joy and trust. This fear of God is the door into the will of God without concern for human respect. This fear (which is an eminent gift of the Holy Spirit) praises God in God out of a profound respect and esteem for God. When we see a faithful person, we see one who fears God, giving birth to respect and love. This is not a fear that brings defiance and love of self. But where do we find people who will fear God in this way? This fear of God subsists in the soul when the self-will is destroyed.

The second type of praise happens in souls who have become simple again, like children without propriety. These are children who give perfect praise, as it is written: *Out of the mouths of infants* shall come perfect praise (Psalm 8:2). The infants know how to praise God and obey their Sovereign without reflection and resistance. A child without care or worry lets himself be led as it pleases his father. This is the praise that God wants from his children after the loss of their self-will. By the term *small* children includes those reduced to smallness by their annihilation. True praise involves the loss of the will.

Thirdly, the *greats* are here invited to praise God, we know that they are not great in themselves. People will never be able to praise God unless they know the secret of praising God consists in not having a self-will. As Jesus Christ has said, *I thank you, Father, Lord of heaven and earth, because you have hidden these things from the wise and the intelligent and have revealed them to infants* (Matthew 11:25). You want the fulfillment of your will; all secrets are hidden in your will. O God, when people are full of their own will, they are not in the state of understanding the secrets of your will. *The greats* are distant from their own grandeur and are lost in the will of God and worship him only. We do the will of God and *fear him* by being faithful and following his movements.

First, we do the will of God and *fear him* by being faithful and following his movements.

Secondly, we think only of the will of God while being oblivious to our personal interests but remaining in simplicity following God from moment to moment and doing what is given to do. We trust without thought, care, or worry.

The third state is for souls who pass through the first two states and grow out of the weakness of infants. These souls are destined to help others by leading them into ineffable secrets. They are also given the power to bear the states of Jesus Christ, and mostly the state of Jesus Christ crucified, which is the part of apostolic souls.

These souls are a paradox because they represent the simplicity, openness, and candor of a child, forgetting all that concerns them. However, they have the knowledge of the truth and this is manifested to others, so that the secrets and impenetrable routes are revealed. The state of childhood though is not a state of suffering, but a chance to be conformed in all things to the image of God's Son, and to be placed in an interior state of Jesus Christ crucified. Then Jesus Christ is revealed, as Paul explains in his writings.

The revelation of Jesus Christ is the most sublime state in this life. This revelation is not done by a light as some people imagine that Jesus Christ appeared to them. But if we follow what Paul says about the revelation of Jesus Christ, we understand this. First, Paul says, *I carry on my body the mortification of Jesus Christ* and hence repentance (2 Corinthians 4:10). Following this he says that *I carry the marks of Jesus branded on my body* (Gal 6:17). This is the conformity that is given to the states of Jesus Christ. As he says, *It is no longer I who live, but it is Christ who lives in me* (Galatians 2:20). Then Jesus Christ becomes the *true* life and animates the soul. Now the soul is in a new life following the new rebirth that Jesus Christ tells Nicodemus about. I say therefore, that the soul does not live anymore, but Jesus Christ lives within the soul. Before Jesus Christ is revealed in this way, the soul lives like a child, without knowing how he lives or what makes him live. He lives and that is enough but the manifestation of Jesus Christ is an entirely new thing.

This manifestation is a revelation done in the heart of the interior and exterior state. Finally, all is Jesus Christ not only for the individual but also for others. A few have this singular grace. God places the soul in a state of understanding the states of Jesus Christ through experience. Why does God do this? First, he annihilates the soul and separates her from any mixture, and places her in a state to feel no pain from all creatures and disgraces either interior or exterior. God makes this last like a rock. After having spent years in this immobility and powerlessness and suffering without pain, then God inflicts the most profound state of the pains of Jesus Christ. Instead, God's hand arms itself against this creature to whom he wants to reveal the experience of Jesus Christ. O, then God reveals to the soul the interior pains of Jesus Christ. They are other than we think. All that Jesus Christ suffered outside was only the image of what he suffered inside. The sight of these sufferings and his experience in the Garden of Gethsemane caused him to sweat blood. These sufferings were thousands of times worse than the passion. This state became worse when he was about to finish and he cried out, *My God, my God, why hast thou forsaken me?*

Let not the readers be mistaken that this state never operates except by a real death and annihilation. These are states that are discovered at the heart of the passive light.

Therefore, I say that the soul to whom Jesus Christ is revealed like Paul received makes the most sublime praise to God that can happen in this life. This is the sacrifice of praise and the most sublime glory that the soul can give to God. God gives this, and the creature receives the glory, praise, and sacrifice of God's Son. These are the dispositions that Paul, my dear apostle, describes as dying on the cross. He died in the same sacrifice of Jesus Christ. This is difficult to explain. Paul said, *In my flesh I am completing what is lacking in Christ's afflictions for the sake of his body, that is, the church* (Colossians 1:24). Paul was consummated in his dying and completed the passion of Jesus Christ. God chose Paul to express perfectly what no creature could express, as David had also shown this perfectly. Paul said that Jesus Christ had revealed himself in this manner.

All the sacrifices we had from God before the revelation of Jesus Christ in us and the profound experience of the same Jesus Christ, are inferior to those that he perpetuates in Christians that remain in him without reservation. This is the same sacrifice that he did on the cross and that he perpetuates in the church through the communion. He perpetuates in souls a profound annihilation. This sacrifice perpetuates and renews the soul and is the greatest glory that God can receive from his creature.

I say again that all the sacrifices that the soul has made up to then could not, however, be at the highest level because all other sacrifices are only a shadow compared to the sacrifice of the cross.

God cares for the soul, drawing from them all kinds of sacrifices until he has exhausted all the sacrifices of the soul, who no longer finds these sacrifices repugnant. He takes away until nothing of the self is left and then the soul has nothing in it to sacrifice. God then makes in the soul another sacrifice, more extended and painful than the other sacrifices. This is the sacrifice of Jesus Christ, which renews the soul in a wonderful way. She sees in persecutions the consummation of the same sacrifice of Jesus Christ.

This is the *praise* and the highest glory that God may draw from his creature. This is the ineffable mystery of the Christian religion and the state of consummation. But these profound virtues of our religion, this dignified worship of God, is ignored throughout the world. O truth, that will be manifested, all will be revealed but you will be manifested only by the loss of all will.

> Then I heard what seemed to be the voice of a great multitude, like the sound of many waters and like the sound of mighty thunder peals, crying out, "Hallelujah! For the Lord our God the Almighty reigns. [7] Let us rejoice and exult and give him the

glory, for the marriage of the Lamb has come, and his bride has
made herself ready." (Rev 19:6–7)

All the saints in heaven, the angels, and human beings *rejoice* when the infamous Babylon is destroyed and removed from the earth. For until that
time, God does not truly *enter* into his *reign*, and does not absolutely reign
in all the faithful, although he has reigned in some faithful. This kingdom
can never fully reign until the will of God is accomplished on the earth as it
is in heaven, as it says in the *Lord's Prayer*.

We have a beautiful sign of the accomplishment of his will in David,
the true figure of the interior and exterior reign of Jesus Christ, before the
revolt of Absalom. When the rebellious tribes of Israel reunited under
David in obedience, the reassembled flock filled him with joy. This is like
the church of Jesus Christ when the spirit and hearts are subject to Jesus
Christ. O Divine Jesus, on the day of the condemnation of the self-will, the
day when all the wills be submitted and there is no other will than yours,
you will be King of the Universe. But until now your kingdom has not been
established. O what *joy* for the saints in heaven and on the earth when this
day arrives! Inconceivable and inexplicable joy! But who can taste you, O
happy day! Passionate day for all the souls who love you, the day of your
sovereign kingdom! The whole universe will be full of joy. This will be the
end of evil and the beginning of good since evils come only because the
kingdom of Jesus Christ is not unified.

But notice the admirable expression of scripture. It does not say we
must rejoice because he is king, since he was born king, and as he says to
Pilate, he is the true king. But it says *Worship God because the All-Powerful
is entering his reign.* He was King but he was not in the total joy of his kingdom. O, if we knew the evil that self-will causes on earth! This is why Jesus
Christ does not reign over it. *Let us rejoice* therefore *and exult and give him
the glory!* Nothing may cause joy except the glory of God.

But what fills us with joy is the *marriage of the Lamb has come.* O
church, holy and without stain, you are the true *bride* of the Holy Spirit, but
until now the marriage of the Lamb has not been made in you. The Lamb
has come to marry all the souls. By the hypostatic union with human nature,
he wants a perfect union with all human beings. This is the ardent desire
of his heart, as he says before he dies, *As you, Father, are in me and I am
in you, may they also be in us* (John 17:21). Jesus Christ consummates the
marriage with the souls as his spouses. There are many interior and exterior
obstacles to this wedding. The exterior obstacles are the pagans and heretics.
The interior obstacles are the rebellion of the children in the church and the
unruliness of the corrupt self-will. The first obstacle presents this chaste wife

from extending her arms. The church, this mysterious vine, cannot extend its vines from one end of the earth to the other. Secondly, the sinful revolt of the children prevents consummation of the marriage, which can only be done in unity of heart and spirit. Those who withdraw from faith cease to be children. The ungrateful and mutinous children do not love. All must be reduced to unity, so that Jesus Christ reigns throughout the universe and that he consummates the divine marriage with human nature. Then there will only be the will of God.

The marriage of the Lamb are times of happy consummation with the greatest joy in heaven and the greatest happiness on earth. O day of your happiness, the triumph of the Lamb when he enjoys is coming to the faithful, when will you come? In this day truth will be manifested to all the earth.

His pure bride will be prepared by the loss and the treatment of all that was opposed to the Bridegroom. The church is then all purity and integrity.

But for the particular soul, when the selfish will is excavated and destroyed, she *rejoices.* She invites all the other souls to take part in her joy now *the Almighty reigns* in her with his will. Nothing in her resists God because she is entirely yielded to him. In the foundation of her soul are expressions of joy, because the reign of God has come with the *marriage of the Lamb* when all propriety is destroyed, as we see in the Song of Songs. The *preparation* for the marriage comes with the destruction of the self-will. O ineffable happiness! Who can comprehend this?

But note that we cannot come to such a wonderful happiness as soon as we think. What paths we must travel on and what work we must do! It is necessary that the self-centered will, which means propriety, must be destroyed. This happens through all we pass though. Then the soul is prepared for the marriage of the Lamb and the fruit of the marriage will be manifested as truth. O truth hidden and revealed, it is you who have made all the evils and all the goods that have been described. Everything is accomplished by the manifestation of Jesus Christ himself.

> "To her it has been granted to be clothed with fine linen, bright and pure"—for the fine linen is the righteous deeds of the saints (Rev 19:8)

The Lamb will only consummate his marriage when the bride is wearing her robe of innocence. Jesus Christ wants to give all human beings the robe of innocence and purity. After centuries of abomination comes centuries of innocence, centuries where all will be reduced to simplicity and the innocence of creation, where all will be in a natural state and all will be given to Jesus Christ and who will continue with the power of his redemption given to him by his Father to save human beings. The souls have *been granted to be clothed* with the robe of innocence and *candor* like an only spouse. This will not only be a simple state but one ennobled and enriched by thee virtues. This robe which will be given to the church, will be *justice for her* children. They will have a double justice in the exemption of sins for a time and in the true *righteousness* of choosing God and not the world. Without propriety, they will be free of lies and will be in truth. This happens in the reign of God and in the marriage of the Lamb.

With the marriage of the Lamb, God reigns in her soul as sovereign. But the Lamb without stain clothes his spouse with the robe of innocence, simplicity, and *candor, the robe* of the finest *linen.* This robe is original *righteousness,* that we return to God, the righteousness toward God, treating God as God, honoring God for the fulfillment of all his will, never hiding anything from him, as she stays constantly in her annihilation. I do not think that I speak too boldly that we will be put back in original justice. I say that it is wrong to doubt Jesus Christ whose redemption is sufficient and abundant. Jesus Christ merited redemption for us and reestablishes the human being in a state of innocence. Jesus Christ in his time will show the efficacy and truth of his redemption. He does this in souls in a hidden way and brings them happiness. So that many may say, I am in a state of innocence.

What is done in a few particular souls will be done in all the church. It will be the reign of God, the marriage of the Lamb, the triumph of truth. O century certain of happiness, you will come in the time chosen by God and you will come infallibly.

> And the angel said to me, "Write this: Blessed are those who are invited to the marriage supper of the Lamb." And he said to me, "These are true words of God." (Rev 19:9)

All those who participate in the marriage of the Lamb are *blessed* and are *invited to the supper* which is the mystical death called to the nuptial bed. No one will be allowed into this union who is not *invited to the supper,* which means was sacrificed, died, and annihilated, as was seen. O blessed supper, where the Lamb gives himself to eat to the souls he has taken for his spouses! *These words* and the promises of *God* by which we enter into the kingdom and celebrate the marriages of the Lamb are *true* and infallible.

> Then I fell down at his feet to worship him, but he said to me, "You must not do that! I am a fellow servant with you and your comrades who hold the testimony of Jesus. Worship God! For the testimony of Jesus is the spirit of prophecy." (Rev 19:10)

Souls not fully instructed might mistake the creatures for God. This is a fault ordinarily made from the state of light, where we mistake the gift for the giver and the servant for the Master. John did not do this by fault and was in the divine source yet surprised by the ways of God. We too want to be instructed about the faults we make on similar occasions. God stops us on our way and communicates these things to us. The angel teaches us by what he says to John, that we must stop at nothing less than God, no matter how grand and excellent it is. O human, if we understand even a little our dignity and no-bility, we would not desecrate ourselves with thousands of things base and undignified which we take out of pride. What are we proud of?

The angel assures us those who have the *testimony of Jesus* within them are as much as an angel and nothing else. We must adhere to God only in God's supreme majesty that makes us go past anything that would hinder us. Whoever worships an angel is in idolatry and worships an inferior thing. Also, anyone who stops at the gifts, graces, and favors of God are arrested at base things of the earth. *The spirit of prophecy* is the Spirit of Jesus Christ that is the testimony of the souls of faith.

> Then I saw heaven opened, and there was a white horse! Its rider is called Faithful and True, and in righteousness he judges and makes war. ¹² His eyes are like a flame of fire, and on his head are many diadems; and he has a name inscribed that no one knows but himself. (Rev 19:11–12)

The second coming of Jesus Christ is not the last judgment but the day of his manifestation. This *manifestation* of Jesus Christ will be on all the earth, in the church, and in the particular soul. But it will not be in the church until it is in full possession of the reign of God and after the marriage of the Lamb. O marriage of the Lamb that brings such good! The manifestation of Jesus Christ will then follow and will bring truth to all the earth.

Jesus Christ is *Faithful and True*. All that is not Jesus Christ is unfaithful and lies. He is mounted on innocence and justice. He brings justice and re-establishes the soul in a new innocence through his communication. He sits on justice because he renders just *judgment*, withdraws the human from the tyranny of the self-will, and puts the human in the order of creation, which entirely subordinates the soul to the will of God. He fights *justly* because he fights for the truth against lies. His being is truth and the full expression of God. As the Word of God, the truth of the Father is expressed entirely in the truth of his being, the Son having nothing less than the Father.

His eyes like a flame of fire show the perfect love that he sets afire. He is crowned with *many diadems* because a crown is due to him by his eternal birth, as well as crowns he has acquired by his victories he has won. His *name* is *known only to himself*, and his name is strength and power and he only knows the strength and power that God has given him.

He is clothed in a robe dipped in blood, and his name is called
The Word of God. (Rev 19:13)

Jesus Christ through his blood is *Word of God* in a *robe dipped in blood*
because humanity was like clothing on his Divinity. Through his death, Jesus Christ became victorious and the truth triumphed, destroying the lies
that held humanity captive. Jesus was then King of Truth, who brought the
truth on earth to banish the lie. However, this truth was only manifested to
some particular people in whom the lie was destroyed. In this fortunate and
happy day, the truth is manifested throughout the earth. O day of truth! This
is the second coming when Jesus Christ comes. Through the Holy Spirit,
truth will be spread throughout the universe. But the *robe* of *The Word of
God* that will be manifested is *dipped in blood* to show that through his death
he has merited this victory and has all rights as Redeemer. All power is now
given to him on heaven and earth. He is King and crowned as King, but he
had not yet reigned in all the universe.

There are three successive consecrations in which Jesus Christ became
king. The first time the reign of Jesus Christ was promised but not given. Jesus
Christ was born and came into the world as King. He was born *King of the
Jews* (Matthew 2:2). But alas! How many evils did he suffer? He did not appear as king. Jesus Christ seems to be king only to take the form of a servant
and a slave. The second consecration of Jesus Christ was by his death. He was
declared *King* (John 19:19) and he reigned truly as King at this moment, but
only for the Jews who were the faithful people. The people of Judah had composed up to now as his kingdom, which is the church, where he truly reigns
as Sovereign. In the third coronation, Jesus Christ appears in a robe dipped
in blood and reign over all Israel and the earth. He will then be confirmed as
King and reign also in the hearts and spirits.

We see in David a kingship like that of Jesus Christ with three different
coronations. In the first coronation, David also seemed to be crowned king
only to become more like a slave (1 Samuel 16:13). The second consecration
of David was only over Judah and after David suffered much evil (2 Samuel
2:4). David reigns in those who give themselves to him without reservation. But he does not reign fully in all human beings. He is not yet king of
all the hearts, wills, and spirits! It was necessary that he be declared king
for three times and that he enters fully into possession of his kingdom. All
people must be told of his blood and all must see and know that he is king.
O, tell all the souls, desolated by their rebellion, and did not want David as
king. *We have no portion in David* (2 Samuel 20:1). They said, *What are we
waiting for?* Why would they not give the kingship to him? Isn't he the true
and legitimate pastor? Isn't he the one who led us and delivered us from our

enemies? In his third consecration, David was only confirmed in his reign when it seemed most distant from him (2 Samuel 5:3).

We see that the manifestation of Jesus Christ in the soul is made only after the ruin of propriety, the reign of God, and the marriage of the Lamb.

> And the armies of heaven, wearing fine linen, white and pure, were following him on white horses. [15] From his mouth comes a sharp sword with which to strike down the nations, and he will rule them with a rod of iron; he will tread the wine press of the fury of the wrath of God the Almighty. (Rev 19:14–15)

Archangel Michael comes again with Jesus Christ to banish the enemy. All of *heaven's* army come to destroy the lies and establish the truth. All are mounted like their Captain *on white horses* to show their innocence, integrity, and justice which are the support of truth. They are *wearing fine linen, white and pure* to show that they are supported and covered by justice and innocence.

From the mouth of Jesus Christ comes a sharp sword with two sides. The sword is no other than his word and his word is the manifestation of the truth, as Jesus asked from his Father in the sight of this day that was to come. *My Father, Sanctify them in the truth; your word is truth* (John 17:17). Therefore, he comes with his sword of the truth to *strike down the nations* who are all those on the earth who oppose this truth. *He will rule the nations*, all without exception, *with a rod of iron* because he has full authority, doing all his will without anyone resisting him anymore. He rules in righteousness and equity. O God, until now your kingdom has been shared and in hearts on the earth, but the time will come when you reign on all the earth and you will reign in all hearts. Nobody will share your authority. You will guide and rule all souls according to your will because you will *tread the wine press of the fury of the wrath*. You will destroy with your justice all those opposed to your mercy. After having said he will rule with an iron rod, he says that he *breaks* all those who oppose his kingdom. O God, that day of your wrath will be terrible for your enemies, but it will be sweet and friendly to your servants!

> On his robe and on his thigh he has this name written: King of kings and Lord of lords. (Rev 19:16)

The name that Jesus Christ wears *written on his robe and on his thigh* shows the power he was given for becoming a human, and how God gives him the kingdom and power. This is the domain that his Father has given him. He only came to the world to be King. However, he had not fully used his rights throughout the kingdom. Here his kingdom comes, and *his name is on his thigh* needs to be King of kings because all the kings of the earth submit to him, not only externally in receiving the profession of his faith but in the interior in receiving the Spirit.

All the human beings aspire to be king and they want to rule. That is what makes all their revolts because they do not understand the way to rule. They can only rule through King Jesus Christ. When they submit absolutely to his spirit and heart, they rule truly since the reign consists of doing nothing against what he wants. Jesus will be the King of all people. He will be the King of kings and the Lord of lords because he will command and rule without any resistance.

> Then I saw an angel standing in the sun, and with a loud voice he called to all the birds that fly in midheaven, "Come, gather for the great supper of God, [18] to eat the flesh of kings, the flesh of captains, the flesh of the mighty, the flesh of horses and their riders—flesh of all, both free and slave, both small and great." (Rev 19:17–18)

This *angel in the sun* is the herald of truth. He will be seen in the day and *invites* all the human beings to come admire the light. But before this time, O God, what a horrible fight must be delivered on earth! God will use his supreme power and will arm people against other people. The birds are all good because they do the will of God. God in the last times, before the final combat and the entire destruction of the empire of Satan and the establishment of the reign of Jesus Christ, will raise a large number of servants like *birds* lost in God in bold flight. These *birds of the air* will be the ministers of the will of God, and *they devour all the flesh* of those opposed to God. They will *gather for the great supper of God*, the last sacrifice. In this surprising supper, which is the supper of the will of God, they *eat the flesh of kings* which the total destruction of the self-will. It is the destruction of the freedom to sacrifice others. They also eat *the flesh of captains* which means they eat the ways that the kings defended themselves. All self-will is stopped.

> Then I saw the beast and the kings of the earth with their armies gathered to make war against the rider on the horse and against his army. (Rev 19:19)

The *beast* of self-worship, declared enemy of truth, leads all human beings in opposition to charity and truth. This self-love *gathered together* people *to fight* with all their power against truth and pure love. Because they are on the point of ruin, they fight with all their power.

This happens both in the general world and in the particular person. Self-love never makes more effort than at the time of its destruction. Lies are never stronger than at the point when they will disappear, and truth will take its place. O God, with what fury the kings, all great, small, free, and slaves defend themselves and try to extend their empire, far from letting it be ruined? But their efforts are useless. The kings are without power and strength; nothing can resist the Sovereign King. They do not believe Jesus and it is against him they fight. But Jesus Christ knows how to fight against them and defend his cause.

> And the beast was captured, and with it the false prophet who had performed in its presence the signs by which he deceived those who had received the mark of the beast and those who worshiped its image. These two were thrown alive into the lake of fire that burns with sulfur. [21] And the rest were killed by the sword of the rider on the horse, the sword that came from his mouth; and all the birds were gorged with their flesh. (Rev 19:20–21)

The beast, miserable self-love, *is* finally *captured and with it the false prophet,* who with his artifices and *signs deceived* those who had not kept to the truth, but preferred self-love to pure love. But when Jesus Christ appears in his reign there will be combat, strange suffering, and inconceivable troubles; the beast must be caught. The monster recovers with fury because he is outraged at the half-victory won over him. But when Jesus Christ appears, the beast of self-love and the false prophet of lies are taken because Jesus Christ is charity and truth. O Jesus, when you come, the infernal monster, miserable self-love, cannot resist you! Its artifices and lies have deceived human beings and they have treated the beast with respect. They will be *thrown into hell* where they came from.

The horrible monster was returned to the abyss and the *rest were killed* by Jesus Christ by the *sword coming out of his mouth.* Jesus Christ saves his servants that are like *celestial birds* who will finish devouring *the flesh* of those who were killed. The birds by their strong and effective words will take away the impression that self-love and lies have made on their spirits and minds. This will happen assuredly in this way.

O God, now we live in the realm of self-love and lies. Come, Lord Jesus, come to destroy. The Spirit and the bride say, *Come!*

All the ways that God leads in the soul to establish the truth, will also pass in the church of God. There is much to go through.

> Then I saw an angel coming down from heaven, holding in his hand the key to the bottomless pit and a great chain. [2] He seized the dragon, that ancient serpent, who is the devil and Satan, and bound him for a thousand years, [3] and threw him into the pit,

and locked and sealed it over him, so that he would deceive the
nations no more, until the thousand years were ended. After
that he must be let out for a little while. (Rev 20:1–3)

The *angel who comes down from heaven* signifies divine power and has the
key to the bottomless pit. Jesus Christ has the power and the right to close
the abyss as well as open heaven. His blood has given a double advantage,
to open heaven to those who are washed and finally to close the abyss so
that no one enters it. Now the redemption of Jesus Christ is now extended
effectively to all human beings because all people were not formerly saved.
The fault is not the Redeemer's but the malignant will of human beings that
subsists in them that opposes the efficacy of redemption.

However, Jesus Christ planned for the extension of his redemption.
Heaven was opened at the time of his death and the *abyss* closed so it could
receive no one; what is he doing? He destroys propriety where it resides in the
spirit and the will. In the spirit, it causes error, stubbornness, and self-interest.
In the will, it causes a rebellious will and self-love. In Jesus Christ's second
coming he destroys all propriety, the horrible monster. This one monster in
appearance causes an infinity of monsters. Jesus Christ destroyed and sent
it into the abyss back to his father Satan, its father. He returns the demon to
its origin. The demon deceived the earth and is now banished. God *locked*
the *serpent* in whom resides the power to tempt people into punishment for
Adam's sin. God closes it *in the abyss* and *seals* it with his seal so that it may
never leave. During a *thousand years* (a long time) the serpent will have no
power to harm human beings. He will be locked up until the time of the Antichrist when the world will become perverse after having been good and then
he must be let out. O what harm there will be then!

For a long time, the demon will have no power over annihilated souls
and not have the power to tempt them. However, God before the end of
life allows exterior temptations in rough blows but the temptations have no
effect because God himself protects them *shortening the time* of the temptation. The way God leads us in wonderful. God delivers the soul from evils
and destroys propriety.

We see here the effectiveness of redemption to put the human being
in a new state of innocence. When we speak of original justice, the soul will
not be in a state of sin but will be entirely healed. The soul will be made
perfect in original justice. This does not prevent them from keeping the
scars of the wounds, but they are completely healed of the evil.

The advantage of the human being during these centuries beyond the
state of innocence is that the human has a time without sin. Many centuries

will pass in a time of candor and innocence; sin will be banished. Sin will have no strength until the devil *is released* again.

If sin is no longer on earth, if the heaven is incessantly opened with grace and receives souls, if sin is closed in hell, we conclude that this time will come infallibly when God will reign on the earth without anyone resisting him, where the marriage of the Lamb is consummated, where all human beings come to the banquet. *This time comes and it is closer than we think. Before this, there will be wars outside and* persecutions within. Jesus Christ opens his side on the cross as a sign that he opens heaven. He descends to earth to give us the knowledge that he will close the abyss and will do this but not when we think. Happy are the eyes who see this! The seven heads and the ten crowns of the beast signify the centuries of his reign and the time he has been given to fight against human beings before he enters into the abyss. When its time is passed, there will be a thousand years when human beings have no harm. This time is close.

> Then I saw thrones, and those seated on them were given authority to judge. I also saw the souls of those who had been beheaded for their testimony to Jesus and for the word of God. They had not worshiped the beast or its image and had not received its mark on their foreheads or their hands. They came to life and reigned with Christ a thousand years. (Rev 20:4)

Judgment is given to those who have left all to follow Jesus Christ. They left all the things of the earth and the self; to leave all that pertains to reason to embrace the faith; to leave all support and all assurance to live in hope; to leave all self-temporal interest for the eternal and spiritual. Grace *is given* to those who renounce all these things, so they *were given authority to judge* through the discernment that was given them. When it is said that *these souls had been beheaded,* this is understood of those who had been deprived of their natural use of their powers, so they would render testimony to Jesus Christ, to let him reign in them and be subject to him. Jesus Christ reigns in them entirely so that they lose their reputation and they are sustained by the words of Jesus Christ. They renounce self-love and have no idols. They *reigned with Jesus Christ* as he reigned in them. Because when Jesus Christ is king in the soul, he makes the soul a queen, and delivers her from all afflictions of self-love and corrupt nature. *She* reigns and *lives* because she lives the life of Jesus Christ. When this life comes into the soul, all other lives seem like death. This life is communicated through the mystical resurrection and has the name of life.

> (The rest of the dead did not come to life until the thousand
> years were ended.) This is the first resurrection. ⁶ Blessed and
> holy are those who share in the first resurrection. Over these
> the second death has no power, but they will be priests of God
> and of Christ, and they will reign with him a thousand years.
> (Rev 20:5–6)

The rest of the dead are the souls in purgatory and those in the state of mystical death. As long as the well of the abyss is closed, these dead will not enter into new life, but only those who have already entered. Because the reign of Jesus Christ is coming, he will enter into his reign with those who are prepared at that time. The others will be held back until the effect of his mercy, because their torments should have been eternal. At the moment of their death, God might have ended their temporal torment or it might continue until the end of the world. Some will not be taken at this time but will remain in their torment. For the others, who are in the mystical death, they remain in their death for the time that is destined and they will have no part in this life. The others, during this life will consummate their mystical death and enter into new life. O these are blessed! *This is the first resurrection*, mystical resurrection, of which we have written.

These are truly *happy* for many reasons. First, they are happy because sins have no power over them. Second, the natural death has no pain. It is for them a sweet sleep and not a death. Purgatory, which is a state of death for those who did not have a mystical death, will have no power over them and when the soul is resurrected, there will be no more *death* for her. When they enter a true resurrection, it is *holy and happy*. Outside of this there is no *happiness and holiness*. There will only be a shadow and an image of holiness and happiness. But these souls are rare!

God destines these as *priests of God and of Jesus Christ* because they enter into Jesus Christ's state of sacrifice to sacrifice themselves. *They reigned with Christ for a thousand years*. The thousand years means being placed in a constant state to reign with Jesus Christ.

O adorable reign, which extends throughout the earth, you will be like the reign that Jesus Christ will have throughout eternity. But if these times are happy, if these days are ones of mercy, O God, the days that will follow are days of mourning and pain, like the days that preceded this time were days of wrath! O God, you know how to glorify yourself in all ways! It is necessary that the reign of Jesus Christ comes and that Jesus Christ reigns over kings and emperors. The Ottoman Empire will be conceded to the reign of Jesus Christ. Satan also gives his empire to Jesus Christ.

> When the thousand years are ended, Satan will be released from
> his prison [8] and will come out to deceive the nations at the four
> corners of the earth, Gog and Magog, in order to gather them
> for battle; they are as numerous as the sands of the sea. They
> marched up over the breadth of the earth and surrounded the
> camp of the saints and the beloved city. (Rev 20:7–9a)

This event happens in history at the end of centuries, in the church and in
the soul.

After the soul has remained a long-time in a state of constancy, then
Jesus Christ reigns fully in her, and this soul reigns in him. The demons have
no power over her. The devil is given a few moments and arms all the earth
and all the soul against herself. His power seems boundless. *He surrounds*
in this way *the camp of the saints,* which is the supreme part of the soul so
beloved of God, but he is given no power except to surround. God has chosen
this soul to make her an eternal heritage. O God, there is no effort that the
devil does not use. He arms the cities and kingdoms against the soul, but all
his efforts are useless. God never protected her more, though he seems to
deliver her to her enemies. In the first attack, the soul defended itself with
all its might against its enemies, after which she was reduced to so great a
weakness that she gave herself in their hands and fell without being attacked.
But here is not the same. All hell attacks here yet she does not defend herself
or have any weakness. God himself is her strength and her defense. As Jesus
Christ will reign without resistance because of the loss of the self-will, he will
also reign without resistance. All will be reunited under the power of Jesus
Christ. All will make up a flock under only one pastor.

After the time of repose on the earth where Jesus Christ will reign
entirely and absolutely, then *Satan* will be *released* and spark the Antichrist,
who seduces all the people and arms all the nations. In the time that Satan is chained there was no more war but a profound peace. After these
happy times, the Antichrist will make a general revolt in the world. The
Antichrist's tyrannical reign will be the greatest evil in the earth, but it will
be short and followed by the eternal reign of Jesus Christ for centuries of
centuries, since God will have his power. Therefore, the times of the Antichrist will come immediately after this time of the reign of Jesus Christ and
the marriage of the Lamb.

> And fire came down from heaven and consumed them. [10] And
> the devil who had deceived them was thrown into the lake of
> fire and sulfur, where the beast and the false prophet were, and
> they will be tormented day and night forever and ever. (Rev
> 20:9b–10)

God destroys in a moment the mortal enemy of human beings. He seems to put him in liberty only to condemn him forever. The suffering God sends to the saints will be of little duration and will serve only to establish them forever in the eternal repose. Because after the last test and effort to *seduce* the servants of God, the devil will be eternally tormented in the flames that are prepared, never to leave them again. God, full of goodness, sees the weakness of the souls seduced by the rage of the evil one and is pleased to make these souls trophies of his mercy, while some serve as victims of his justice. What glory God gives us both in time and eternity!

> Then I saw a great white throne and the one who sat on it; the earth and the heaven fled from his presence, and no place was found for them. (Rev 20:11)

This is a wonderful figure for annihilation. Before God comes in all his majesty, heaven and earth remain. Heaven is adorned with stars and the earth with flowers. Then these stars fall from the heaven, that is to say, the divine virtues placed in the soul like a beautiful heaven, disappear, and the earth loses its ornaments in the quaking of the earth and in the misfortune that accompanies it because God, who lives in heaven, does not appear in all his majesty. After this, the heaven resumes its first brilliance, and the earth a new beauty. But as soon as God clothes the soul in its first innocence, he sits *himself on the white throne* that is prepared for his eternal rest. O, then the heaven and the earth *flee* and disappear and there was no vestige of them. Both the inferior and supreme parts of the soul must be lost before God alone. Nothing on heaven or earth is distinguished. The soul does not recognize a superior or inferior part. All is annihilated. She knows nothing but God and God rests alone in all glory and majesty.

This happens in the same way at the end of the world.

> And I saw the dead, great and small, standing before the throne, and books were opened. Also another book was opened, the book of life. And the dead were judged according to their works, as recorded in the books. [13] And the sea gave up the dead that were in it, Death and Hades gave up the dead that were in them, and all were judged according to what they had done. (Rev 20:12–13)

The Last Judgment makes it clear how those experiencing the mystical death will not be able to fear hell or sin. Before the soul is received in God, God makes a judgment of her to see if death has done its work. The death of the senses, the spirit, and powers, all appear and each must be judged *according to their works.* Those who are not annihilated suffer more fire and purifications.

All will be judged according to their works. Works are not good that are not made in the will of God. All works not done according to the will of God are done in malice.

The sea gave up its dead as purified and resurrected into heaven. For *Death and Hell* means the souls and bodies of the damned. But in the mystical sense, it is certain that Death, Hell, and the sea means their deaths that God makes in the judgment of the soul. The immense *sea* that absorbs the power and senses in lostness *gives them up.* The soul finds its lost powers and their use is returned as they enter into a new life. *Death* who held all the soul powerless *gives them back* to a new life in God. *Hell* which holds the soul in a state of suffering, sadness, and deprivation, also *gives up the dead* and they are given to the senses' participation in interior life. All is tranquil, peaceful, resigned, and abandoned.

> Then Death and Hades were thrown into the lake of fire. This is the second death, the lake of fire; [15] and anyone whose name was not found written in the book of life was thrown into the lake of fire. (Rev 20:14–15)

After the soul is released from this state, *Death and Hell are thrown into the fire.* There is no more death for this soul because Death and Hell are consumed. Now all is life and freedom. Those who have not experienced the mystical death, which is the first death, are tested in purgatory, which is a state of Death and Hell combined. This is the suffering of *the second death.*

Those not resurrected by grace and who are dead through sin will be condemned to eternal fire because they are dead eternally. This means that those who do not have a new life in Jesus Christ, who are the ones *written in the book of life,* are again burned in purgatory, where they suffer much sadness for the destruction of their impurities and proprieties. If we read the apocalypse with attention, we see that all the possible states in the spiritual and divine life are contained here.

> Then I saw a new heaven and a new earth; for the first heaven and the first earth had passed away, and the sea was no more. (Rev 21:1)

For the soul who has passed through the state described here, *the first heaven and earth* pass away. All terrestrial, natural, human, sensible, and carnal elements in the soul have gone. Instead, the soul has higher and spiritual things belonging to the Spirit. The gifts of God perfect these good things. But as soon as God comes with his majesty, everything must *pass away* and give God his place. David and all the prophets say that the earth and the heavens pass away before God. This is the right effect of the real presence of God in the soul. To those who know that God has come, there is the grandeur and power of God. As we see the mountains of snow melt and flow away before the face of the sun, the same happens with the majesty of God. It is necessary that the whole soul should vanish so that it no longer finds in it a substance that can conceive and distinguish either good or evil. Both are foreign to him. It seems that this is the entire destruction of all that is substantive within him and this is grace. David says, *I am utterly bowed down and prostrate* (Psalm 38:6). O God, since you have appeared, all that is within me of being or substance has vanished. I am annihilated so that you can work something new and form a *new* creature. There is nothing left in me from the world that was.

Therefore, when the majesty of God has the heaven and the earth vanish, he makes *a new heaven and earth*. This is the last consummation. All is made new. The former heaven and earth have passed away.

We do not however arrive here easily, and many do not do this. If we follow from point to point what to pass through, we'll see that it is rare. There will come a time before the end of the world where this will be more common. The soul remains a long time in annihilation before entering the state of a new creature. God takes pleasure in annihilating her beforehand. Annihilation takes time for perfection and consummation according to the capacity of the soul.

This annihilation is a disappearing of everything substantive in the soul but is different from mystical death. I will explain this with the grace of God. The nature of Jesus Christ is in annihilation when the Word is united with human nature so that the person's substance is the Word. This human nature though must have the Word of God as its only support and substance. The annihilated soul truly lives in this way. The soul must have the human substance taken away so that the majesty of God appears.

The difference between death and annihilation is that this *death* is done by an abundance of graces or by a subtraction of these same graces. One and the other cause the death. Sometimes one and sometimes the other, the excess of one or the other causes the death, which is an operation of God himself. This death happens passively. (The soul suffers the blows of death without contributing anything because everything she would do to try to increase or advance her death, would retard it.) Only the hand of God can operate and produce this death. The death prepares the place for the appearance of God's majesty. Mystical death is the death of all propriety, senses, and will. The soul is placed through death in a state of innocence that has nothing opposed to God. God comes to repose with this soul on a very pure throne. The soul is not annihilated again by this because the soul is dead. It is necessary that God appears with his majesty and all that is selfish within the soul disappears before God. It is then that the soul is placed in a state of nothing, so that God makes her a new creature. I do not mean here that the real being is annihilated as if the creature had never been. That is impossible. But a new substance and being is formed with her that could still make some resistance.

Therefore, God comes with his majesty and the soul has been made pliable through the will of God. But its suppleness does not make it capacity small because the annihilation changes the capacity. The soul is received in God who gives an immense capacity to the soul.

To understand this, we think of a hard stone, or a metal, which by fire can be made into the quality of wax. When the metal has lost all its resistance and made like a soft and pliable wax, it can take impressions. This effect causes the death that makes the soul lost all its resistance.

We need to know that propriety has three natures to destroy. First, is the destruction of the propriety of sin that has hardness and a malignant and rebellious quality that opposes all good. The rebellious soul cannot be bound to the hand of God. This malignity arms itself against God by the power that he has been given from the abyss. God is obliged to leave this soul. This is mortal sin. This first quality of revolt and rebellion of propriety is only destroyed by true conversion. Then when there is revolt in this soul, she remains like a strong rock without movement. God is content to chisel her to polish her a little bit in this life and completes her in the other life.

But for those of whom I speak here, where we see the destruction of the second nature of propriety, it is not the same. God is not content to hammer her but places her in a crucible and causes death. He uses many circumstances and suffering so that finally she loses the rock of human nature so that God can imprint her as he pleases. Happy are the souls who have come here! All the operations of suffering so strong and intimate have brought them here. Then God can make grand works; he raises, abases, and changes their character and tests them in all sorts of circumstances to see if they resist. Now she does not resist because she is supple and pliable in everything. She is annihilated well if in her annihilation she has lost the quality of being opposed to God and she has taken on the quality of sweetness and pliability through the death of propriety. It is good to know the truth of annihilation, but this is still not the consummation of annihilation. God is close to souls who are here! But alas! Those that come to this point are rare! God has caused their death through his operations, as we have noted, placing the soul in fire through diverse tribulations and by much suffering in the state of suppleness in his will. She has no will. God has reduced her to this point.

This operation mediates God to her through all kinds of crosses, angels, people, demons, and misery to reduce her to put the soul in a place where she does not resist. The first blows are the most difficult but to the measure that resistance is lost, the pain diminishes. If the pain increases, it is because resistance grows. The soul receives the blows without almost feeling them and her pain does not increase. God gives her relief and makes her new so that she is suppler so that finally she does not find resistance within her. God wants to impress on this soul in a hidden way and this is an intimate union. This soul is purified from all propriety, rebellion, and resistance and God comes with his majesty.

But then the third level of propriety must be destroyed, or this wax might have a subtle type of propriety. What does God do when his majesty appears? The soul melts in a moment. In God's presence, something sublime and transcendent happens and it melts into something pliable for God's will. The soul loses distinction and restriction. This is the effect of the majesty of God when God appears.

O wonderful effect! Then is made the admirable and divine will as in *that they may all be one* (John 17:21). Their union is an intimate union of substance. Then the bride becomes one with the Bridegroom. There is no distinction between them. She only exists in God. There is the consummation of her happiness where her perfect annihilation takes place and finds consummation. Annihilation begins when the rock becomes wax and loses the quality of hardness. She has a quality of suppleness and receives impressions. This annihilation continues when the wax melts. But it receives perfection when the she is remade and passes into the source where she loses all her consistency, quality, capacity, and distinction. Then she becomes one with God, and she loses herself in God never to be separated again.

These two different states are admirable figures in the book of the apocalypse. The first state is explained through *heaven rolling*. The soul loses its quality to take what God gives her, but heaven is still unfolding. The second state is marked by *heaven and earth passing away*. It does not fold and roll only but it vanishes and passes away before the majesty of God.

After the soul is lost, folded into, and united with God, she loses everything. She may have no exterior propriety. All her work, joy, and pleasure is here without being, life, and movement. But God, who wants her to serve others in his church, makes here a *new heaven and a new earth*. He gives her Jesus Christ who becomes her new heaven and earth. Jesus Christ makes his faculties and powers hers, giving an inconceivable advantage. She then never leaves the union. She is made a *new creature* in Jesus Christ. All is given in Jesus Christ and Jesus Christ is all in her. We do not need to speak of the former creature. She is entirely new and nothing remains of the former. He makes grand things in her. She is entirely recast in unity with his substance. He can do with her more than we can imagine. Most souls in recollection and their powers are absorbed believe that they are lost in God, but they are wrong. They have some absorption and know the unction of grace but of the happiness that I speak here, to be entirely lost in God, requires some patience. They will see that they are far away from it and may be more in themselves than ever.

When the souls are in the real state of being lost in the bosom of God, God makes them entirely one in him by their total flow into the original being. This is the end for which they are created, and they are astonished that God exists in unity and Trinity. God's Trinity flows constantly from his unity and returns to the same unity. We see also the same operations in the same soul. Then the Word and the Holy Spirit is produced within her. More than that, then God shares with the soul all the rights of his divinity without division or distinction. God is content with his interior operations associated with his unity and gives participation in the Trinity. God also carries the soul out of multiplicity into simplicity. All that God makes is grand. All that the Father makes comes from his Word and it flows incessantly. This same Word gives to the soul all interior and exterior operations. Jesus Christ came on the earth and was made man and passed into human nature with the nature of the Word. Also, he comes by incarnation into this soul and through her into others with his nature and operations. This is the right of Jesus Christ.

But to be united with Jesus Christ in principle and substance, the soul must entirely be annihilated and re-made in its original. Without this, although God's grace operates in the soul, it is not yet the immediate principle. God makes operations in the soul with the grace of the Redeemer.

Therefore, the Word is given to the soul as the principle of all its operations. The soul remains constantly lost in God's unity, where the Word flows incessantly and produces along with the Father and the Holy Spirit, consummating always the soul in God's unity of principle while continuing without ceasing the interior and exterior operations. This is the secret of creation and the redemption of human nature, which has been created so that the human may be re-cast in the original.

God sends these truths to the human being with the capacity to return and be re-made with God's principle. However, the person still has a very different nature from God. To be finally lost in God, she reenters the indivisible and indistinguishable unity, yet her being is separate and different from that of God. The human being is created and different from the uncreated. The Word has come to clothe human nature so that the human can participate in this good and to be united with the Word. But as this hypostatic union was only for the person of Jesus Christ, the Word Jesus Christ passes into all human beings in favor of this union. When the soul is re-made in its original, the Word takes total possession of her and becomes the only principle of all the operations of this soul, making in her and for her what pleases him. It is then that he makes within her *a new heaven and a new earth*. The soul then has no exterior or interior but has the same principle as Jesus Christ. All that is in the human being of Adam has been entirely destroyed and *passed away*. There is in the human being only what purely God is. This is what is left after the work that Jesus Christ does. All that was of Adam of sin and disobedience and what followed from that is entirely destroyed and annihilated.

Therefore, here is the *new heaven and the new earth*. This happens after all that is *old* has passed away.

For the *sea* which is not and does not appear, the storms and tempests are no more.

If in what I have said there are some things that are contrary to the beliefs of the church because of the frequent interruptions in writing, I submit all my heart to the church for the faith. I would give a thousand lives. I give this to the experience of your reverence, my Father, to whom I entrust all of this.

> And I saw the holy city, the new Jerusalem, coming down out of heaven from God, prepared as a bride adorned for her husband.
> (Rev 21:2)

After what has been said, we can hear the mystical meaning. John speaks clearly here of the renewal in the church, where the Spirit of the church will be renewed throughout the earth. This spirit is no other than the Spirit of the Word that possesses and makes the church infallible, while still being far away from its members. Therefore, the Spirit, will have a wonderful rejuvenation throughout the earth, according to the promise that has been made. It is then that the *New Jerusalem descends from heaven*.

To explain this, we must remember the three states of the church that are distinguished by three churches. The first is called the church militant. This is the one attributed to the one on earth. The second is attributed to the suffering souls in purgatory. The third, the triumphant is for the saints in heaven. I say that all three churches must be found in three different ages, in the church which is on the earth. The first age is found in the church militant which is the establishment in the age of combat and the martyrs. The second, the suffering church is now, having had since the first heresies more suffering than combat. This is an intimate suffering. All the holy confessors have been sanctified in this way. But in the third stage, the triumph of the church will come, and it is this *Jerusalem coming down out of heaven* giving to the church on the earth the quality of the church in heaven. She *comes* adorned and *as a bride adorned for her husband*. Because the marriage is consummated, she will remain ready to be on the earth the delights of *her husband*. But this only happens after an entire renewal, when the judgment of the evil has been made for the wars and carnage.

For the particular soul, these are the operations of the soul in favor of the church and neighbor, and all that may be made in and out of the soul *comes from heaven*. This is a state of communicated glory and triumph, so that what is made in heaven can be made on earth. After the renewal, all that is in her is no longer of her, because she *is no longer*. But God takes her out of external abjection by powerful and effective operations. These operations are made in a wonderful way, which does not prevent him from married and being in his unity. She comes *ornate* and *adorned*, God gives her through grace the entire light and brilliance of the majesty of God. She says, *If I met you outside, I would kiss you, and no one would despise me* (Song of Songs 8:1). Here is the last exterior clothing that the wife asks of her Spouse. She asks that she not be despised and that there be nothing unworthy in her for the salvation that God has given her. Until this time there were many external weaknesses that served to hide the interior grace.

> And I heard a loud voice from the throne saying, "See, the home of God is among mortals. He will dwell with them; they will be his peoples, and God himself will be with them." (Rev 21:3)

Who can doubt that the soul arrives here through detours and rude and strange ways? The soul arrives at a perfect transformation, which is the *tabernacle of God*, where she remains and reposes with an ineffable pleasure. She rests. God chooses her as an Ark of Alliance and takes pleasure in thousands and thousands of souls and *they will be his people*.

This renewed church extends throughout the world and will be the *home of God*. Then God takes his delights to enter and *dwell with them* where they *will* truly *be his people*. I know that he will invariably be in the holy sacrament on the altar as he was in the beginning. But as John says here, he will be in the souls of his spouses where they assemble in unity to make a single spouse. It is then that the same annihilation that re-makes the soul in God makes a union with God. This will be a consummation of unity between souls and God similar to rivers that flow to the sea become united with the sea, without separating from the others or the sea.

> "He will wipe every tear from their eyes. Death will be no more;
> mourning and crying and pain will be no more, for the first
> things have passed away." (Rev 21:4)

When a soul arrives here, there will be no more sorrow, *mourning*, and pain. Also, no more *tears*, afflictions, and displeasures because *death will be no more* and annihilation will be consummation. Until annihilation is perfectly consummated, there will always be some suffering. But here, there will be no more suffering but peace, joy, and contentment. O state, you are so grand, but you are rare! Jesus Christ may want to suffer within her. After Jesus Christ suffers in this way, he glorifies himself forever in the soul. It is in this state that Jesus Christ is glorified.

For the church, in this time there will be no more sorrow and sin. This will be the time of triumph of Jesus Christ and the church. The church after having carried the suffering Spouse will bring him glorious and triumphant. This is the time of the birth of Bridegroom who comes to his spouse and places her in a new state of childhood.

> And the one who was seated on the throne said, "See, I am mak-
> ing all things new." Also he said, "Write this, for these words are
> trustworthy and true." (Rev 21:5)

O this is true, O God, that *you make all things new* in your spouses and in your church! O new state, new life, new everything, you make all things new! This newness will be the admiration of human beings and angels. For *these words are trustworthy and true*, that you will accomplish this in the church of God.

> Then he said to me, "It is done! I am the Alpha and the Omega,
> the beginning and the end. To the thirsty I will give water as a
> gift from the spring of the water of life." (Rev 21:6)

After all the states are passed, *It is done!* The soul is in perfect consummation because Jesus Christ is the beginning and the *end* of all states. The soul begins through Jesus Christ and through him she ends and finds consummation.

All *begins* with the love and consideration of Jesus Christ. We give ourselves to him. Jesus Christ as the *Way* leads us on impenetrable paths. When he has led the soul through horrible and frightening deserts, he brings her to an end. All the long way, the soul does not perceive that it is Jesus Christ leading her but after having led her to the Father, she knows distinctly it is Jesus Christ who led her. He remained hidden so that she would lose herself and be reduced into unity. She discovers that in creatures is only error and lies, folly and blindness.

But when she is reduced into unity, he shows himself as *Truth*. He places her in the truth of God. The soul discovers that all is God and nothing of creature.

When in the truth, the soul discovers the perfect unity of the soul with God, suddenly Jesus Christ is given as *Life*. He is formed in her in a manner that has been explained. After having carried all of Jesus Christ's states in the soul and sacrificed herself, after having totally immolated herself, she enters into glory and joy. For all eternity the glorification of Jesus Christ will be in the soul and for the soul. After having been immolated and sacrificed with Jesus Christ, we will be glorified with Jesus Christ.

Jesus Christ said all this to his disciples, *I am in my Father, and you in me, and I in you* (John 14:20). And also, *So now, Father, glorify me in your own presence with the glory that I had in your presence before the world existed.* Also, *All mine are yours, and yours are mine; and I have been glorified in them* (John 17:10). Therefore, here is the state in which Jesus Christ is glorified in the soul. But before this state of the glorification of Jesus Christ, the soul must be placed in the truth, as he said, *My Father, Sanctify them in the truth* (John 17:17). We must be sanctified by the Father in truth before Jesus Christ is glorified in us. But again, before this time, what will happen? Jesus Christ says, *I sanctify myself, so that they also may be sanctified in truth* (John 17:19). This way we lose all propriety. And finally, Jesus says, *As you, Father, are in me and I am in you, may they also be in us* (John 19:21). This is the unity of principle after the reunion and the consummation of souls with the Father. Jesus describes the state of glorification, *The glory that you have given me I have given them, so that they may be one, as we are one* (John 17:22). Here is the consummation of all human beings in Jesus Christ. The Word of God who works entirely through him and without which nothing is done, reunites us in the unity of essence. He continues, *I in them and you in me, that they may become completely one* (John 17:23). Here the Word of the Father passes and produces continually and here the Word passes into souls and the flux and reflux of the Word passes into the soul and the soul passes into the Word of God. Jesus Christ adds, *Father, I desire that those also, whom you have given me, may be with me where I am* (John 17:24). This is the flow of the soul into its origin, where the Word is produced and where it flows into the soul. Jesus Christ says, *To see my glory, which you have given me because you loved me before the foundation of the world* (John 17:24). We are back to the principle. "Love has made you do everything through me, and nothing has been done without me, and the love I have for you makes me give you all things. For everything flows in me, just as everything has come out of me."

After having said this, Jesus Christ says he is the *beginning* and the end. *To the thirsty I will give water as a gift from the spring of the water of life.* Those who wait to buy this will never have it, because we have nothing to purchase this with. Jesus Christ *freely* gives this water. All we have to do is ask and tell him we are *thirsty*. He desires to give us this water and says, *To the thirsty I gave water.* Jesus Christ himself is the water. The goodness of God is inconceivable. After having seen that Jesus Christ is the beginning and the end, we see the ease with which we enter him. Jesus Christ removes all difficulties and assures us that he gives a drink of water from the source of life, which is himself, to all those who are thirsty. All those who are thirsty should go to him as he says in the Gospel, *Let anyone who is thirsty come to me* (John 7:37). So we understand that he prepares us with his singular merit to receive this water, and we have the courage to go to him. He says that he gives *freely*.

Will we not be condemned if we do not go to him? My God, the blindness of human beings is strange! To die of thirst so close to a fountain of water because they imagine that if they ask for water, he will not give it! However, the one who owns this water calls them and invites them with all his strength to come and take, he gives them this water freely. They do not want it. They cry and complain that they are thirsty. O folly and stupidity without equal! It is up to them to drink.

> "Those who conquer will inherit these things, and I will be their
> God and they will be my children." (Rev 21:7)

The *victory* that Jesus Christ asks of us is not one that we had to win by on our own. We are weak and would be defeated. Far from being *victorious*, we would be vanquished. Yet, he has promised victory a number of times in the apocalypse to those in the book of life. We do not see that those whom he calls victorious are not those who have fought. It is the Word of God who fights for us and wins the victory. What consists of this victory? It is to conquer the appalling monsters in us that would destroy us by taking us back to miserable Babylon. Those in whom he has won the victory are truly *his children*. According to Paul, we are his adopted children, to whom the freedom of children is given. *He is our God* because there is no more resistance in us.

> "But as for the cowardly, the faithless, the polluted, the murderers, the fornicators, the sorcerers, the idolaters, and all liars, their place will be in the lake that burns with fire and sulfur, which is the second death." (Rev 21:8)

Jesus Christ places the cowardly and the faithless in the ranks of the worst criminals that are excluded from his grace, at least as long as their crimes remain. The worst sinner can convert and become the greatest saint. But those with these vices are not in God's interior kingdom without leaving the vice. Our Lord puts the *cowardly* in this rank because they are always stopped by their fear. They never abandon themselves to God. Yet the greatest criminal may transfer his ardor from evil to good and work for the will of God. *The faithless* also become nothing because they need a great faith to believe, to hope against any hope, and a great courage to surmount all the obstacles and difficulties.

> Then one of the seven angels who had the seven bowls full of the seven last plagues came and said to me, "Come, I will show you the bride, the wife of the Lamb." ¹⁰ And in the spirit he carried me away to a great, high mountain and showed me the holy city Jerusalem coming down out of heaven from God. (Rev 21:9–10)

The *bride, the wife of the Lamb* who consummates the marriage, is the interior Spirit, the glorified church. She *comes down out of heaven* and comes from God. When the Lamb wishes to consummate the marriage with the soul, he comes and animates her with his life. The soul is lost, as we have seen, and made a new creature in Jesus Christ, as she is prepared for the spiritual marriage. This spouse is the soul returned into an essential union.

The church reanimated and revivified in all its members is the *wife of the Lamb*. Even though the church was the bride of Jesus Christ and the Holy Spirit at his birth, this marriage was not consummated. The marriage will only be on the earth when the church is in its triumph. This will be when the *spouse* descends from heaven because the church on the earth will participate in the advantage of those in heaven and will have consummation. Although the church is always one and indivisible, she has to stay until the consummation of the centuries and the doors of hell will not prevail against her. She will become a *New Jerusalem* and there will be a great renewal of the spirit within her. God will give an increased and renewed grace to her. In the nuptial kiss she will receive an abundant fertility so that there will be a great number of children with a total dependence on the Holy Spirit and the divine motion.

The Divine Mary, who is like the church as spouse of the Holy Spirit, has purity and integrity without stain. She is always full of grace according to her capacity which is always growing. She is very intimately united to God. However, when God would operate the mystery of the incarnation, he renewed her and in that moment her marriage to the Holy Spirit was consummated in an eminent manner and as an unparalleled favor. In the second coming of Jesus

Christ, who must come as King to inspire the new Spirit for all humanity, he consummates his marriage with the church. There will be an abundance of renewal and a most abundant plenitude that has never been. He sends pastors conformed to this dignity and eminence of graces.

> It has the glory of God and a radiance like a very rare jewel, like jasper, clear as crystal. (Rev 21:11)

The renewal of the pure and light-filled Spirit gives *glory* and radiance. The truths of the faith, however solid and true, have been enveloped in fog, but here, the truths appear with light and wonderful things that no one can ignore. Up to now it has been under a shadow and now it appears like full noon, like a clear and radiant light. This will be an eternal day because the truth has come on the earth in all its clarity. This truth is the New Jerusalem, which is the spouse descended from heaven but truth with light which will never be covered by the darkness. It is still sealed with several seals. But when the final seal is removed, O all human beings will see this with a brilliant and wonderful light. This truth is *radiant and surrounds the* New Jerusalem. It is brilliant like a *rare jewel* which is no other than pure charity. Its cleanliness, clarity, and purity are grand, transparent *like a crystal*. Because all is day and light, all the shadows are dissipated. Truth has been under a shadow but now this has changed into a beautiful dawn without darkness. We see all the objects that were hidden from view in the night.

> It has a great, high wall with twelve gates, and at the gates twelve angels, and on the gates are inscribed the names of the twelve tribes of the Israelites; [13] on the east three gates, on the north three gates, on the south three gates, and on the west three gates. [14] And the wall of the city has twelve foundations, and on them are the names of the twelve apostles of the Lamb. (Rev 21:12–14)

God did miracles for the Jewish people and sent them the holy patriarchs, prophets, and martyrs. No one could believe that the Jewish people would be rejected eternally by God. Jesus Christ and the twelve apostles were Jewish. God has shown this people a strange justice for seventeen centuries. But the time of God's mercy is very close, and the Jews will become the saints of God. We cannot penetrate God's ways because it is according to the grandeur of God. The righteousness of God has different and opposing ways to the ordinary manner of understanding.

It seems that justice for souls is like that for the Jews, selected from the cradle, to whom was given the grace of the ancient patriarchs full of visions, revelations, and prophecies. However, these souls, who dared for wonders, were rejected. And why? They were prideful in themselves and did not attribute these things to God so God rejected them as a pure effect of justice. He then takes other sinful souls, such as the Gentiles, who appear to be born in corruption and sin. It is these poor wretches whom he chooses for his thrones of mercy. However, the goodness of God is so great that, although he allows these falls and errors in souls, he does not allow them to perish suddenly but calls them at the end of their lives. Some are lost though through a loving but impenetrable divine justice.

This *city* so wonderful is the church, which after the renewal in this way, will have *gates* to receive *the twelve tribes of Israel* and all the nations of the earth. O holy church whom I revere, I am astonished when I speak of your renewal since it does not condemn your previous state. I say that the renewal is an increase and extension of grace, according to what is expressed in the Song of Songs 7:8, *I say I will climb the palm tree and lay hold of its branches.* I will climb, which means, will communicate to her abundantly, and take hold of her branches and fruit. I will make her at the same time more fertile. God takes pleasure in visiting his vineyard again and to bring forth fruit that she has never yet produced. O church entirely holy, you will be more holy in the extension of your holiness. You will be great throughout the earth. There will not be a bird hidden under your branches.

To return to the subject, the church has a *great, high wall.* This wall is Jesus Christ himself, who guards and surrounds all the parts. His height and grandeur is immense. His *twelve gates* show that he has points of entry on all sides of the world because he has children on all sides of the world. All countries have children who are received into his bosom, and Jews enter in who were dispersed throughout the world. After their dispersion, they will be reunited in a wonderful way.

Twelve angels guard the gates to show that God continually watches over all the cares of his church so there are no surprise attacks. The *angels* are like pastors who bring back the wandering sheep from among the Jews, who have been lost a long time in the desert and have become savages. They do not know anymore the Pastor of Israel, who leads all of them. But finally, the time will come when they will be brought back. O when they know the true Pastor of Israel, then Israel will become docile, they will return like his flock from the extremities of the earth. Their conversion will also be as good as their mistake was long

An admirable and holy edifice, *the wall,* is no other than Jesus Christ in his mystical body. Only *one* wall composed of many rocks shows the perfect unity of the church. These are *like living stones* (1 Peter 2:5). This shows us that is not so much the union of the bodies, or of exterior ceremonies, but the union of spirits and hearts that God asks of us. Christians should be with *one heart and soul* as in the time of the primitive church when they united in faith (Acts 4:32). But since then, they have been disunited in spirit and heart, in different sentiments and affections. Sin has made the members rebel. Moreover, most are only Christians in name and figure. They are members of the church externally but in the inside, they have no true spirit of religion, which is a spirit of adoration and sacrifice, an interior spirit. Because of this, they have no true harmony. What does Jesus Christ do in his renewal? He unites them with a wonderful harmony of spirit, heart, and faith. Then the body of the church becomes a united heart and soul, consummated in the unity of the Spirit. O church, abandoned to God! But where is there perfect conformity among the children in both the exterior and the interior? O Christian religion, full of grand things, but the greatest you ignore and little practice! Now the Christian religion is not unified. But when the Spirit unites them, they will all be consummated in Jesus Christ. Formed through simplicity, in the eternal marriage of the Lamb and the second coming will continue throughout eternity.

The *apostles* are the *foundation* and rocks of the church. The *twelve names of the twelve apostles of the Lamb* are on the wall to show the united spirit of heart and mind, the interior spirit which is the Spirit of the apostles. This edifice is spiritual with the twelve fruits of the Holy Spirit, which will serve as a crown. Jesus Christ communicates the Spirit of the apostles in newness to his church.

The soul, when it is the spouse of the Lamb, becomes a *strong wall.* Because of her firmness, she has a perfect unity without division. She has *twelve gates* to show that she has as much freedom and breadth as she was formerly constrained and constricted. Until then it seemed that the beauty of this soul was to have no entrance or exit like *a garden locked, a fountain sealed* (Song of Songs 4:12). But now God uses all the gates to communicate with her and through her to communicate with others. He also opens the gates to give full consummation, to help each soul according to their need and state.

Each of the four states has three degrees. The first, the *three gates of the East,* is the active purgation, which contains the beginning, the progress, and the end. Then the soul enters *three gates of the North,* a state of passive light and sensible love with a beginning, progress, and end in the state of faith. Next to them, the burning and ardent *gates of the South* consumes everything gradually by its heat and does not leave anything not consumed and devoured. This state is the longest of all because all will be consumed. The *three gates of the West* are the consummation of the soul in its lost in God and end. Like the others, it has a beginning, progress, and end. After this, the soul is like the church receiving a Spouse. God puts, as I have said, *twelve gates* in his spouse, to give her ease to help the souls in other states, and to receive him in her breast and in her heart which is inseparably united in God. These gates are for her to receive the *twelve tribes*, who are the interior souls in different states. The *foundation of this wall* are the twelve fruits of the Holy Spirit. The soul rests in perfect charity on the cornerstone Jesus Christ.

> The angel who talked to me had a measuring rod of gold to mea-
> sure the city and its gates and walls. [16] The city lies foursquare, its
> length the same as its width; and he measured the city with his
> rod, fifteen hundred miles; its length and width and height are
> equal. (Rev 21:15–16)

The interior *city* and exterior *wall* mark the perfect equality in the perfect accord of spirit. The soul must be one both exterior and interior.

The *foursquare* of the city shows how the soul is lost in the unity of God only. She participates in *its length and width and height* and depth which are four equals. However, the *measure* of each side *is fifteen hundred miles*. This shows at the same time the broad expanse because she is in the immensity of God. No more is the creature limited, but she rests eternally consummated in the immensity. My God, the great mysteries contained in this! They are inexplicable! God possesses his creature both interior and exterior!

The *four* show the equality and uniformity of the church in herself. The church and the world are contained in the immensity of God. O temple! O church very wonderful in itself, but too humiliated by her children's disorders and her pastor's lack of purity and holiness. What does a holy ministry require from them? The time will come when the priests and pastors will be saints. But now, O God, the priests and pastors are corrupt! Self-interest, self-love, vanity, and self-will have corrupted them. But the Lamb will be their priests, pastors, and saints.

> He also measured its wall, one hundred forty-four cubits by
> human measurement, which the angel was using. (Rev 21:17)

The wall's measure shows the renewed church with all the people and nations. The Spirit communicates dependence and docility in moving in the interior. The Spirit communicates faith to all the nations, showing the largesse, liberty, and grandeur of her exterior.

> The wall is built of jasper, while the city is pure gold, clear as
> glass. (Rev 21:18)

For the church, its exterior are the ceremonies, practices, and ordinances which are very beautiful, firm, solid and pure like a *wall built of jasper*. But the exterior that we admire is nothing compared to the goodness, purity, solidity, and simplicity of the Spirit. Scripture describes all these qualities. She receives its rays and the Spirit fills, moves, and leads the church. For her, she lets the Spirit lead, govern, and enlighten without resistance. But, O church, if you are such in yourself, how are your children raised to your Spirit? It is the renewal that they need, the spirit of their mother who is given to all her children. This *city of pure gold* shows sublime charity and purity, which is like pure gold without any mixture. This gold is clear and transparent *as glass* to receive the beauty of the clarity and flames of the Holy Spirit, which is like simplicity and cleanliness.

The soul arrives here in the same way in both her interior and exterior. She is all beautiful and solid outside because God establishes her in perfect immobility both exterior and interior, adorned externally with the virtues, and power to be consumed in God. God makes her admirably constant after all the annihilation that she has suffered. This is gold without mixture because it is pure charity without mixing in self-interest. This is a *very pure glass* because of its simplicity and candor that is no longer hidden. This is glass that receives pure and full impressions from the divine light. There is no more propriety but now the fire of reflection.

> The foundations of the wall of the city are adorned with every jewel; the first was jasper, the second sapphire, the third agate, the fourth emerald, [20] the fifth onyx, the sixth carnelian, the seventh chrysolite, the eighth beryl, the ninth topaz, the tenth chrysoprase, the eleventh jacinth, the twelfth amethyst. [21] And the twelve gates are twelve pearls, each of the gates is a single pearl, and the street of the city is pure gold, transparent as glass. (Rev 21:19–21)

The foundation of the wall are the principal points of the faith which rules all the exterior conduct the church and the soul. All are enriched by *jewels*, that is to say, the practical exterior with pure virtues. All the exterior is sustained by fruits of the Holy Spirit, to show that all the exterior comes from dependence on the Spirit in the interior that governs and leads.

John shows the principal virtues Christian in these *precious stones*. All the stones show the exterior and theological virtues that are the diamond, ruby, and the most precious significant stones. The virtues of which he speaks are the virtues which serve the neighbor: respect, simplicity, humility, patience, charity, support of the neighbor, the gift of teaching, instruction, correcting, fortifying, helping, and clothing in God.

The *pearls which are the twelve gates* show the purity of the interior voice that gives entry to all and receives the different persons. The exterior of the church has uniformity of faith and sentiments in *one wall*. Through the gates will come Jews, Turks, barbarians, infidels, heretics, schismatic, bad

Christians, false Catholics, impious, and atheists. All will come from different countries and laws and religions without the doors changing for their reception. They will be received not only in the wall, which is the exterior of the church, and therefore the same devotees of today. But they enter into the same city, that is to say, they participate in his Spirit, they become all *interiors*. All will be led by the Holy Spirit and all will be placed in the truth.

The beautiful city is *Truth*. The same Spirit has conceived them and given them movement. O Truth, Truth, you are the *New Jerusalem descended from heaven, spouse of the Lamb* without stain. Because the Lamb is immolated by an excess of mercy, the Lamb meets you, O Truth, by the same mercy. This is the truth that is sealed that was sealed in heaven and has been raised by the Lamb to come to the earth. This truth is a *grand and very high wall* that is like a rampart because nothing is as strong and high as the truth. This is only *one* wall because of its uniformity and equality. It is guarded by *twelve angels* who stop the spirit of lies from entering because lies will be banished forever and cast into the abyss. The *twelve tribes* of interior souls and nations are received into the knowledge of the truth and enter into the truth of the faith and interior with the spirit. God is worshipped in spirit and truth. *The names of the twelve apostles are written* because it is through them that Jesus Christ begins and communicates his truth. Also, they fill the spirit with truth. *This city is four* to show his perfect righteousness and on every side we see equality and righteousness. However, there is a depth, *an immense height, width, and length.* The outside of truth, *the wall* is strong and unbreakable. It is pure, clean, and right but the inside is spirit compared to *gold* because of its purity and the truth is united to pure charity and *light like crystal.* Its simplicity is like glass with a *pure and clean light.*

O Truth, you are beautiful but you are very little known! Truth is supported by the virtues that serve the *foundation.* It becomes easy to see the virtues formed in truth and sustained by truth. Before this time, there were shadows of virtues. Virtues are lost without truth. The soul is only found when placed in truth.

This truth has *twelve gates* to receive all those that enter it. These gates are made of pearls, yet it is only *one pearl.* This pearl is Jesus Christ, who is the way, and the gate leading the souls into truth. No one may enter the truth without him. He is the Truth. This truth is truly the legitimate *spouse of the Lamb.* O great Truth, you are now banished from all the earth but soon you will be known, loved, and followed on all the earth.

> I saw no temple in the city, for its temple is the Lord God the Almighty and the Lamb. (Rev 21:22)

This place can be applied to the church, because there is a temple here where the Lamb reposes. He himself is the *temple*, the sacrifice, and the victim.

O God, the individual soul feels the truth of these words! They have a temple within themselves, where they retire, where they pray and adore. This temple is a place of refuge, where they are assured and covered from the oppression of their enemies. But since the loss of the soul in God, they do not find the temple as a refuge and this astonishes them since she is pursued without mercy by her enemies. She cannot find the temple or a place to go for answers. Until she learns this secret, which is, that *the Lord God the Almighty and the Lamb* want *to be her temple*. In him is her refuge, prayer, solace, and sacrifice, all is in God and all will be found contained in him in a wonderful manner. All is made by God and in God. Jesus Christ is the great Priest. He is also the victim and the sacrifice. But there is no more temple in the soul because her temple is God in a way that must be experienced.

For Truth, she has no other *temple than God*. She is in God and God is in her.

> And the city has no need of sun or moon to shine on it, for the
> glory of God is its light, and its lamp is the Lamb. (Rev 21:23)

The church *has no need of created light*, because *God alone is its light* and *Jesus Christ its lamp*.

The soul *has no need* of this illustration because she had distinct and small lights that appeared grand. All these lights are useless, but *God is* her *Sun and her* true *Light*. His grace is *her lamp*. When the soul arrives here she no longer needs distinct light, she distinguishes nothing in these lights. To the contrary, she distinguishes all in God that pleases him to show her with his ineffable secrets.

All created lights are brilliant and some more than others. In the lights received in the creature, some shine brighter than others. I say all created lights are lights God send to the soul before the soul passes into God. But once the soul passes into God she has only his general light. This is the *light of God himself*. God himself is the light and the soul experiences a general light. The soul may want distinct lights from time to time, as the general light absorbs all. God is a general light which can only be distinguished by its unity and Trinity. The soul sees all things in God in a wonderful way that is blissful.

The truth is God himself because God is truth and the truth is all light and all brilliant from the light of God.

> The nations will walk by its light, and the kings of the earth
> will bring their glory into it. ²⁵ Its gates will never be shut by

day—and there will be no night there. ²⁶ People will bring into
it the glory and the honor of the nations. ²⁷ But nothing unclean
will enter it, nor anyone who practices abomination or false-
hood, but only those who are written in the Lamb's book of life.
(Rev 21:24–27)

The nations will walk by its light of the truth and the church when they will
all be united in her. The spirit and will of human beings will all be united
within God, there will be no more false lights which makes them lost. But
the divine light is all light.

A certain soul placed in the divine light may help an infinite number
of persons.

All the *kings* and sovereigns of *the earth* will cede their honor and
glory to God alone. *The gates* of the church and truth *will never be shut* to
anybody. Because *there will be no night there* nor darkness. The gates will be
closed to error and lies. *People will bring into it the glory and honor of the
nations* because all will give God homage.

Nothing unclean will enter the holy church because nothing unclean
will enter the truth. *But* those who are admitted in that time are *only those
who are written in the Lamb's book of life*. It is for these that God made a
great carnage to destroy their enemies. Nothing unclean will enter the pure
and clean church, from which he will banish and tear out all the bad grain
that has been planted there.

The soul that has arrived in God is destroyed of all uncleanness and all
radical impurity has been torn out because *nothing unclean will enter God*.

There are two types of impurity. One is that which God calls *abomination* and the other *lies*. The abomination is propriety, as we have seen
because nothing is an abomination before God except propriety and lies.
These are two vices absolutely opposed before God because of the sovereignty and truth of God.

Then the angel showed me the river of the water of life, as clear
as crystal, flowing from the throne of God and of the Lamb.
(Rev 22:1)

The *river* is the grace of God, which he pours constantly from himself to
souls whom he saves. This *clear* grace is pure from its source and cannot be
spoiled by the bad use of creatures. This river is the abyss where souls are
lost in God and united to God. It goes out *from the throne of God and of the
Lamb* because its source is God and merited for us by Jesus Christ.

Through the middle of the street of the city. On either side of the
river is the tree of life with its twelve kinds of fruit, producing its

> fruit each month; and the leaves of the tree are for the healing of
> the nations. (Rev 22:2)

The *tree of life* is pure and perfect love, which is found in truth, in the
church, and in the soul who arrives here. This love is always ardent and
pure and remains constantly in the soul that is placed in truth. This tree has
twelve fruits of the Holy Spirit which are given to the soul according to her
need. *The leaves* are the ways these fruits are communicated to humanity,
healing the nations. The leaves are the most common graces distributed to
all people for the healing of their ills, sins, and weaknesses. O church, this
tree is well-given to you, but the nations do not eat it and they do not heal.
But as soon as people come into you, they will be nourished, refreshed, and
healed. These fruits and this tree are always in the church.

They are also in annihilated souls, where pure love is felt and distinguished by its effects. These souls in which God has placed certain qualities
and unction heal a large number of people through interior grace.

> Nothing accursed will be found there any more. But the throne
> of God and of the Lamb will be in it, and his servants will wor-
> ship him; ⁴ they will see his face, and his name will be on their
> foreheads. (Rev 22:3–4)

O church, you will not have any more wars or curses because your children
will not be rebellious.

O Truth, there will be no more lies on earth and all will be light and
truth. We will discover *the face of God* and be given knowledge of God so
clear that the beatific vision cannot be greater.

This view of the face of God brings intimate union by seeing the face
of the Lamb. This causes a profound knowledge given through Jesus Christ,
who reveals his secrets. Paul talks about this, *And all of us, with unveiled
faces, seeing the glory of the Lord as though reflected in a mirror, are being
transformed into the same image from one degree of glory to another* (2 Corinthians 3:18). He speaks of the immediate union by which Jesus Christ is
fully revealed and manifested to the soul. Following this perfect transformation, God always reveals his secrets more clearly, going from light to light,
which is a confirmation of true grace. In this state, I say, *nothing accursed
will be found there* because there will be no sin. God does not condemn the
works that are done in his will. The soul here will have lost all propriety and
self-will, as we have seen by what is written. The source of sin is banished
from her, and there will be no other will than the will of God. How would
she find a will to sin? This is impossible.

The *name of the Lamb will be on their foreheads.* This means that finally we divinize their exterior and is a proof of what they experience in their interior. Their exterior even preaches and announces God.

> And there will be no more night; they need no light of lamp or sun, for the Lord God will be their light, and they will reign forever and ever. (Rev 22:5)

There will be no more night because the light of truth has no darkness. There will be no more night, because there will be no more sin.

This state is only discovered late to the soul that possesses it, always believing that the weaknesses of nature are sinful. But this is not so according to what the Lord declared to Paul for himself, *My grace is sufficient for you, for power is made perfect in weakness. So, I will boast all the more gladly of my weaknesses, so that the power of Christ may dwell in me* (2 Corinthians 12:9). When the state is advanced, the weaknesses cease. Then the light is given to help us see that the state glorifies God a lot. Because we see that the creature has in its nature only the quality of being a creature, which means it remains in always in its baseness. However, as I have said, towards the end, all ceases, as the sun advances the dark diminishes, like the day only comes little by little. It is God's way in eternal day with the light of truth.

It will also be this way in the church of God, where a measure of the darkness of error and lies will pass away and the truth will appear as it really is. The light overcomes the darkness and dissipates the darkness entirely. In the beginning, the darkness was stronger than the light. Following this, they seem intermingled one with another, and it is difficult to discover who has the upper hand until finally the day overwhelms the darkness and the darkness recedes before the light. This light is God who brings eternal day, but a day that is not subject to the darkness, a day that will never end.

> And he said to me, "These words are trustworthy and true, for the Lord, the God of the spirits of the prophets, has sent his angel to show his servants what must soon take place." 7 "See, I am coming soon! Blessed is the one who keeps the words of the prophecy of this book." (Rev 22:6–7)

O God, what joy you bring to the poor hearts who are entirely yours and hold nothing back from you, who know that your interior and exterior kingdom will arrive, and that *these words are trustworthy and true!* Whoever prevents your reign was in errors and lies. You reign by the *truth* and in the *truth.* You have willed, O God, to have this announced so clearly, that it is almost impossible, when these words are read by *your servants,* not to discover your truth, your external and interior reign, in all souls. O God, you are going to reign in all hearts, you reign already in millions of hearts, which is absolutely unknown to those who do not feel it but is known to God and to those souls to whom God is manifested. You have given, O Lord of Spirit, your interior Spirit to John to speak clearly of these interior things and the way you have for souls that you call to be your spouse, for the souls betrothed to you in faith, that you call to be espoused through eternity. You gave John the gift of *prophecy* to predict your exterior reign for all the earth, and also describe the interior reign so clearly that even those who do not live it cannot deny seeing it.

But, O holy prophet, you say that Jesus Christ *is coming* soon. Alas, there have already been seventeen centuries! It is true that what precedes this reign of Jesus began a long time ago, but the reign of Jesus has not come through all the earth, although it is in a great quantity of hearts, having more people in this age than ever before. You say, O Lord, that you *are coming* soon! Alas, that these moments are so long! But thousands of centuries for you are like a moment. O Desire of Nations, you have been desired for almost four thousand years. It seemed, as the prophets spoke, that your day was near. However, is he late? Your second coming is desired in all the souls who sigh for your reign, and you do not come! You come, O King. Pardon me, if I say this. You came to reign in a thousand hearts in an unknown manner. We will see in eternity how this interior spirit has been spreading in all the passing centuries and how this increases every passing day. But you have not come in the full extent of your reign to make known your strength in all the earth. It is your universal reign that I desire, O God, and about which I am passionate. If you delay coming, your servants will hear the reproaches that some made against the prophets. We always say, wait, wait. We waited and waited (Isaiah 28:10). O God, it is your way to increase the desire and test of patience of your servants. Such a good deserves that one finds it by a long and strong patience.

When God begins to come in a soul, God promises first to take her as a spouse. God desires her with ardor, as we read in the Song of Songs. It appears as an easy marriage that will consummate everything. But alas! He appears close, but he is far away. The soul sees the favors and the goodness of the Spouse and the soul believes that there is only one step needed to be united. The soul believes that she has attained the summit of perfection, but she has not yet started. Alas, she is wrong. She sees this well after a long and terrible experience, that such a great good is not yet close. It is then that she says to her God: "You had promised to come earlier, and you have not kept that promise, and now you seem farther away than ever." O these moments before God are long and painful years! O Love, you do not deceive us. It is the creature who deceives and thinks she can be admired at the wedding without stopping the habits of her captivity. O she is so wrong and has so much trouble allowing this! This makes her angered because she has so much trouble being seen and having to accommodate herself to the will of her Spouse. However, O Sacred Spouse, you *come soon* if we consider who you are and the baseness of the creature, to whom you deign to unite. You do not delay this beautiful gift.

Blessed is the one who keeps the words of the prophecy, that is to say, blessed are those in whom the words of the prophecy are fulfilled, though filled with misfortune in appearance.

> I, John, am the one who heard and saw these things. And when I heard and saw them, I fell down to worship at the feet of the angel who showed them to me; [9] but he said to me, "You must not do that! I am a fellow servant with you and your comrades the prophets, and with those who keep the words of this book. Worship God!" (Rev 22:8–9)

This is a repetition of what has been said above, so I will not say anything more. All I will add here is to show the happiness of interior souls in whom what is written here is happening, since even the angel admits to be no more than these interior souls. O truly angelic souls, you are contained in a body like a small and obscure prison. But God takes pleasure in hiding your treasures in these vases of earth, finally so the strength is not attributed to human beings but to God who knows and sees the beauty and nobility of this soul covered externally with dirt. God does his delights, when his servants are the subject of rejection and contempt. These souls are not known. To the contrary, they receive curses and insults from the world that makes them suffer. The world hates them and persecutes them and calls them infamous. Yet the world knows that they are unworthy of these people, so they keep them away from them. By doing this, the world renders justice by distancing themselves from the faithful.

Finally, these angelic souls are kept away from the eyes of people. God makes and conserves these souls in their purity and stops other people from having knowledge of them so that God alone receives all the glory. God's glory should not be poured upon a creature, and this is why this subject is written about in this book. John wanted to make too much of this angel as people usually do to those of extraordinary esteem. But it is necessary to look at them in God and not only to look at God within them.

> And he said to me, "Do not seal up the words of the prophecy of this book, for the time is near. [11] Let the evildoer still do evil, and the filthy still be filthy, and the righteous still do right, and the holy still be holy." (Rev 22:10–11)

O wonderful words! O words admirable and fearsome brought together, but *words* that you do not want to seal, because you want them to know and be known, *the time being close*! The time is so close, O God, that it is already come. You punish injustice with greater injustice.

Here he speaks of two kinds of people *who commit injustice* and sin and feel the misery of propriety. For the first, it is obvious that this is a sin and the punishment of a sin. For this one, God makes it possible to reach the person by the miseries suffered, God hides him in herself and this person grieves for her misery. She sees clearly that she cannot bring any remedy, and that God alone can heal, because all her efforts for healing only serve to increase the evil. She fears not being agreeable to God. But what does God say? That *whoever is in* this filth, I only allow this for my glory, *there is even more*, until what is left is nothingness.

And the one who is righteous still has a justice that the person is given by God. These righteous people still justify themselves to a certain degree, and then having exhausted all acquired justice, God makes them enter into another state. God communicates his infused justice, and the self-acquired righteousness must give its place to the infused justice. And as the acquired justice has swelled the person in herself, God uses filth and misery. Under this apparent cover, God takes away the propriety of their own justice in which they rested and gives them his own justice, at which the soul has no more of its own propriety. For *those who are holy* and who are lost in God, participate in the holiness of God, without delighting in anything of the self. Those who are holy in this way *are sanctified again*. She will be always transformed in the holiness of God, losing everything of propriety. Whoever loses propriety and is received in God is holy. But as her transformation may increase each day, she is sanctified every day more and more.

> "See, I am coming soon; my reward is with me, to repay according to everyone's work. ¹³ I am the Alpha and the Omega, the first and the last, the beginning and the end." (Rev 22:12–13)

O God, *you are coming soon* with mercy and justice. *You will repay according to everyone's works*. Only works done in your will are acceptable. All other works, even grand works, appear good in the day but they are born of the will of human beings and of the flesh. Those born of the will of flesh are criminal. Those born of the will of human beings are imperfect. Only those works born of the will of God are acceptable. Simple work done in God's will appears infinitely more precious than all the grand work done before human beings, which is done for the love of glory and self-interest, done for the will of human beings and not for the will of God. O yet we are so wrong! All the works that God condemns appear holy and simple yet are rejected! O God, O

God, you have none of the thoughts of human beings, and your ways are not the ways of human beings. You are God who scrutinize hearts. You do not look at the grandeur of the action but the intention that has made the action and the purity of love. You say again the beautiful words that you are *the Beginning and the End, the Alpha and the Omega*, that is to say, the premier principle of the interior and the consummation of the same interior. You are the principle from which we are derived, and you are the end in which we are finished. It is in you that we begin and we end.

The enlightened saints of the true light have said that we must put ourselves in the spirit. They believed that in order to be strong they must always meditate and think on Jesus Christ. They were wrong. We need not reason about Jesus Christ, but only let him guide us in all ways on his impenetrable routes and to let him really possess us and do all of his will. Reasoning does not give us these things, but abandon does. We would always reason on imaginary qualities of a soul and neglect the possession of the same soul. We would never acquire strength and knowledge that the soul would give about himself, to see ourselves in a different way.

Jesus Christ is a great book written inside and outside of us. It is impossible to read him if he does not manifest himself. What is interior is infinitely more than it appears, as it says in the Song of Songs. He alone manifests himself to the soul. This is not through reason, but the impression that he makes to the soul of himself and his states, as Paul expresses when he says, *For I carry the marks of Jesus branded on my body* (Galatians 6:17). He does not say that he reasons on Jesus Christ, but that he carries his states. Then he confesses, that he does not live anymore of his own life, but that *Jesus Christ lives in him* (Galatians 2:20). Paul abandoned himself into the hands of God, to let himself by annihilated and his life be destroyed, to give rise to the life of Jesus Christ.

> Blessed are those who wash their robes, so that they will have the right to the tree of life and may enter the city by the gates. [15] Outside are the dogs and sorcerers and fornicators and murderers and idolaters, and everyone who loves and practices falsehood. (Rev 22:14–15)

Blessed are those who wash their robes in the blood of the Lamb; these are the poor souls who by abandonment and complete trust throw themselves into the arms of God. They give themselves to him that he may purify them. It is of these that it is said, *Though your sins are like scarlet, they shall be as white as snow*. These are the souls, who persuaded of their extreme misery and helplessness, have thrown themselves without hesitation into the immense sea of the blood of Jesus Christ. O there they are promptly purified and saved from trouble and ennui! Instead of believing they can presume things and think they can save themselves by their own efforts, they know they are far from being able to purify themselves. O if they comprehend even a little of the happiness of abandonment and trust in God! I have written so much that it is useless to repeat it. All I will say is that these abandoned souls have *their robes washed clean in the blood of the Lamb* in a salvation bath that whitens and purifies in a moment all of their disorders. They have all love, and have experienced the uselessness of their efforts, they know that it is the *Lamb without stain* to whom they owe their purity, as Jesus Christ said in favor of Magdalene, *Her sins, which were many, have been forgiven* (Luke 7:47).

There are two types of souls. In the first, the purity is not lost. In the second, after dirtying themselves, the beautiful baptismal robes are purified in an instant in the love of the Lamb by love and trust. They have the same *right* as the first ones to the *tree of life* because it is the blood of the Lamb that gives them this right. *They may enter the city by the gate*, which means that our Lord gives them entry into their interior.

> "It is I, Jesus, who sent my angel to you with this testimony for the churches. I am the root and the descendant of David, the bright morning star." (Rev 22:16)

O Jesus, have you spared anything to make your will known to humanity, to manifest yourself to them to save them? O Jesus, the name that charms and raises, name of joy and salvation, you always *send your* angel before you *to give testimony* of you and your truth. This angel is, as we have seen in John, the penance that prepares the way for the Bridegroom. But once the angel gives his testimony, the Bridegroom himself comes to manifest himself.

Jesus Christ has already sent his angel to announce to human beings the true way that they must keep, the way of penitence. This angel has appeared, but it is not enough. We need Jesus Christ to appear. The church saw this angel and she will soon see her Bridegroom. As the star of the morning precedes the sunrise and the day, also Jesus comes first in the soul as a *star* luminous and *bright*, before placing her in the full day of his glory. Jesus Christ comes to the soul in a distinct light before placing her in the general and indistinct light.

Jesus Christ comes first in the soul as Way; this is the *star of the morning*, that leads the soul into the Truth of the full day, of Jesus Christ himself. Then Jesus Christ arrives in his second coming as Life to animate all things (John 14:6).

Jesus Christ takes pleasure in calling himself *the Son of David* like David who had a profound interior. Jesus Christ comes into souls to communicate to them an interior. We should understand that as he is the son of David, and was chosen by his Father, he wants to communicate his spirit in all those to whom he comes. Furthermore, it is David who had washed his clothes in the blood of the Lamb, even before he had spread it, by an anticipated faith and by an unequaled trust. Jesus Christ was also *rejected*. A stem that is cut off is rejected. Jesus Christ is like a stem cut off from the earth, but the rejection of this root in the sepulcher of death becomes a tree of life.

Jesus Christ is the same in the soul. The soul has lost all sight of and thoughts of Jesus Christ, being lost in the immensity of God. It is then that Jesus Christ comes out as a new rejection, and he communicates to the soul in a manner so admirable that the soul in this rejection believes and become fruitful in a surprising way.

> The Spirit and the bride say, "Come." And let everyone who hears say, "Come." And let everyone who is thirsty come. Let anyone who wishes take the water of life as a gift. (Rev 22:17)

The Spirit and the bride say to Jesus: *Come.* The Spirit and the bride are the Spirit and the church, the Truth and the pure soul. The *church* that is united to the Spirit, says animated by the Spirit that Jesus Christ come so that he reigns and reign promptly. He comes in his second coming to fully consummate his marriage.

The *Truth*, who is one with the Spirit, invites the Bridegroom to come, since the truth on the earth comes to make Jesus seen in his second coming, as it has been described.

The Spirit and the bride say, Come. We must know that when the soul arrives in God, animated by the Spirit of God, she no longer has any prayer of propriety, but the *very Spirit intercedes with sighs too deep for words.* Now there is only one thing left for the consummation of this wife, which is, that Jesus Christ makes his mystical incarnation within her, which is the second coming. Jesus Christ comes first by his grace, and he leads the soul in this way to God. Then he comes by incarnation, to animate and vivify her, to be in her a seed of immortality, to live in her in all his states. As Jesus Christ only will consummate his wife, the Spirit and the bride of one accord, having only one voice and one prayer, invite him to come.

But if this bride and Spirit invite him to come to her, they invite him so much more to come to his church, to be known in all the earth, to enter into possession of his reign, to manifest his truth. *The Spirit and the bride say, Come!* Come, O Desire of Nations, come, you who are the joy and contentment of people, come and finish their misfortune and begin their happiness: but, without regarding their interest, come take possession of your kingdom; come reign as Sovereign; come consummate your marriage. Come, O Jesus! O Jesus! Come be King!

After the desire of the Spirit and the bride has been expressed, Jesus, the Bridegroom of souls, invites all the transformed souls to come and fall down before him, to those calm and tranquil waters, to this water which nourishes, makes fruitful, and refreshes the person who drinks it. But, O blindness of human beings! It only depends on them to have life and to let themselves die! He wants to give them freely the water that gives life, and they only have to receive this. They only need to *wish* to have this, and they do not want this! Everyone complains of being changed, and no one wants to drink! All the world hates death. Everyone fears it and flees, and no one wants to go to the source of life to prevent death! O Christians, my brothers and sisters, it is easier for you to have life than you think. You only have to *come to* Jesus with simplicity and trust, and he will give you life with abundance. In John 7:37–38 he says that *If anyone is thirsty and comes to him, there will be inside of him a river of living water which will flow back to eternal life.* This is the soul who has given herself to Jesus Christ, and who lives in him, and after drunk from the divine source, she is returned by the Bridegroom to be a source of living waters for others. But again, O Love, all the good that you give, you give *freely*! Interior souls have the knowledge and the experience all together that ravishes them. Because they see all that Jesus Christ has given them; he gives to them freely. They see in themselves no merit or virtue. To the contrary, it seems that any way to try to merit this is tedious, when instead they owe everything to the One who gives them freely. Also, their only ambition is to love freely and without self-interest.

> I warn everyone who hears the words of the prophecy of this book: if anyone adds to them, God will add to that person the plagues described in this book; [19] if anyone takes away from the words of the book of this prophecy, God will take away that person's share in the tree of life and in the holy city, which are described in this book. (Rev 22:18–19)

The truth has this of its own, so that we can neither increase nor diminish it, without altering or corrupting it. Virtues can be increased but truth suffers if we add or subtract from it. Truth is always the same. It is always naked because we cannot cover it without changing it and making it fall asleep. God loves his truth. He is jealous and wants everyone to walk in his truth.

John writes in his Gospel all the states that God makes souls pass through. He omits nothing. Some would like to form and create states other than these and depart from the truth. Whoever wishes to assure others that John's states are not real, would be lying, and that person would not deserve to know states so divine and real. There are some who condemn these states and want to measure his goodness by their reason. God gave his only Son, who delivered himself to death for us. Those who doubt it because they have not experienced it should listen to these words of John. They will see that the goodness of God in souls surpasses all that can be said.

> The one who testifies to these things says, "Surely I am coming soon." Amen. Come, Lord Jesus! [21] The grace of the Lord Jesus be with all the saints. Amen. (Rev 22:20–21)

O Jesus! You promise and assure us! However, even though your word is true, you wait so long. O this delay is long for a heart that loves you! We want your glory and want you to reign in all the hearts and all the earth! So come, O my King, come begin your reign, and do not wait any longer. Overthrow everything that opposes your kingdom. Reign as Sovereign. If we have even a little love for God, we would think of nothing else but this reign of Jesus Christ. All self-interest would be banished. We would be interested in God alone and the reign of the Lamb, even if it costs us all that we are. *So come*, Lord Jesus! Let *the grace of the Lord Jesus* prepare us all for the second coming. Amen!

Conclusion

If there is anything in this whole work that does not conform to the faith of the church, I retract it with all my heart.

Bibliography

Anonymous. "Supplement to the Life of Madame Guyon." Translated by Nancy Carol James. In *The Pure Love of Madame Guyon*, 85–104. New York: University Press of America, 2014.

Bedoyere, Michael de la. *The Archbishop and the Lady*. New York: Pantheon, 1956.

Bossuet, Jacques Benigne. *Quakerism a-la-mode, or A History of Quietism: Particularly That of the Lord Archbishop of Cambray and Madam Guyone*. London: Printed for J. Harris and A. Bell, 1698.

Bremond, Henri. *Apologie pour Fenelon*. Paris: Perrin, 1910.

Caussade, Jean Pierre de. *Abandonment to Divine Providence*. New York: Image, 1975.

———. *On Prayer: Spiritual Instructions on the Various States of Prayer according to the Doctrine of Bossuet, Bishop of Meaux*. Translated by Algar Thorold. London: Burns, Oates & Washbourne, 1931.

Conzemius, Viktor. "Quietism" In *Sacramentum Mundi*, Vol. 5, 169–72. New York: Herder & Herder, 1970.

Fénelon, Francois de Salignac de La Mothe. *The Archbishop of Cambray's Dissertation on Pure Love, with an Account of the Life and Writings of the Lady, for Whose Sake the Archbishop was Banished from Court*. London: Thomson, 1750.

———. *The Complete Fénelon*. Brewster, MA: Paraclete, 2008.

———. *The Maxims of the Saints Explained, concerning the Interior Life*. Bordeaux: n.p., 1913.

Gondal, Marie-Louise. *Madame Guyon: un noveau visage*. Paris: Beauchesne 1989.

Gough, James. "Comparative View of the Lives of St. Teresa and M. Guion." In *Life of Lady Guion*, 237–39, Bristol, UK: Farley, 1772.

———. "Life of Michael de Molinos and Progress of Quietism." In *The Life of Lady Guion*, 308–24. Bristol, UK: Farley, 1772.

Green, Joel B. *Conversion in Luke-Acts: Divine Action, Human Cognition, and the People of God*. Grand Rapids: Baker Academic, 2015.

Guyon, Jeanne de la Mothe. *Autobiography of Madame Guyon*. Vols. 1 and 2. Translated by Thomas Taylor Allen. London: Kegan Paul, Trench, Trubner, 1897.

———. *Jeanne Guyon's Christian Worldview: Her Biblical Commentaries on Galatians, Ephesians, and Colossians with Explanations and Reflections on the Interior Life*. Translated by Nancy Carol James. Eugene, OR: Pickwick, 2018.

———. *Jeanne Guyon's Interior Faith: Her Biblical Commentary on the Gospel of Luke with Reflections on the Interior Life*. Translated by Nancy Carol James. Eugene, OR: Pickwick, 2019.

———. *Les justifications de Mme J.-M.B. de La Mothe-Guyon, ecrites par elle-meme, avec un examen de la IXe et Xe conferences de Cassien touchant l'etat fixe d'oraison continuelle, par M. De Fénelon*. 3 parites. Cologne: Poiret, 1720.

———. *Les livres de l'Ancien Testament de Notre-Seigneur Jésus-Christ avec des explications et réflexions qui regardent la vie intérieure.* 12 vols. Cologne: Poiret, 1714–15.

———. *Les livres du Nouveau Testament avec des explications et reflexions qui regardent la vie interieure.* Cologne: Poiret, 1713.

———. *Le Nouveau Testament de Notre-Seigneur Jésus-Christ avec des explications et réflexions qui regardent la vie intérieure.* 12 vols. Cologne: Poiret, 1714–15.

———. *The Soul, Lover of God.* Translated by Nancy Carol James. New York: University Press of America, 2014.

———. *The Way of the Child Jesus: Our Model of Perfection.* Translated by Nancy Carol James. Arlington, VA: European Emblems, 2015.

Holcombe, William H. *Aphorisms of the New Life: With Illustrations and Confirmations from the New Testament, Fénelon, Madame Guyon, and Swedenborg.* Philadelphia: Claxton, 1883.

James, Nancy C. *The Apophatic Mysticism of Madame Guyon.* Ann Arbor, MI: UMI Dissertation Services, 1998.

———. *The Complete Madame Guyon.* Brewster, MA: Paraclete, 2011.

———. *I, Jeanne Guyon.* Jacksonville, FL: Christian Books, 2014.

———. *The Pure Love of Madame Guyon.* New York: University Press of America, 2007.

———. *Standing in the Whirlwind.* Cleveland, OH: Pilgrim, 2005.

James, Nancy C., and Sharon D. Voros. *Bastille Witness: The Prison Autobiography of Madame Guyon.* New York: University Press of America, 2012.

James, William. *Varieties of Religious Experience.* New York: Collier, 1961.

Johnson, Luke Timothy. *The Gospel of Luke.* Collegeville, MN: Liturgical, 1991,

La Combe, Francois. *A Short Letter of Instruction, Shewing the Surest Way to Christian Perfection.* Translated by J. Gough. In *Life of Lady Guion*, 295–307. Bristol, UK: Farley, 1772.

Mudge, James. *Fénelon the Mystic.* Cincinnati: Jennings and Graham, 1906.

Poiret, Pierre. "The Theology of Emblems: Preface to the Emblems of Father Hugo and Madame Guyon." Translated by Nancy Carol James. In *The Soul, Lover of God*, xxxiii–xl. New York: University Press of America, 2014.

Ramsay, Chevalier. "Life of Francis de Salignac de la Mothe Fénelon, Archbishop and Duke of Cambray." In *Life of Lady Guion*, Vol. 2, 325–72. Bristol, UK: S. Farley, 1772.

Saint-Simon, Duc de. *Historical Memoirs of the Duc de Saint-Simon.* Vols 1 and 2. Edited and translated by Lucy Norton. New York: McGraw-Hill, 1967.

Underhill, Evelyn. *Mysticism: A Study in the Nature and Development of Man's Spiritual Consciousness*, 12th ed. Cleveland, OH: World, 1965.

Upham, Thomas C. *Life and Religions Opinions and Experience of Madame de la Mothe Guyon.* 2 vols. New York: Harper & Brothers, 1847.

Wesley, John. *An Extract of the Life of Madame Guion.* London: Hawes, 1776.

Made in the USA
Monee, IL
21 October 2023

44950337R00115